MANAGEMENT, WORK
AND ORGANISATIONS

Series editors: **Gibson Burrell**, The Management Centre, University of Leicester
Mick Marchington, Manchester School of Management UMIST
Paul Thompson, Department of Human Resource Management,
University of Strathclyde

This series of new textbooks covers the areas of human resource management, employee relations, organisational behaviour and related business and management fields. Each text has been specially commissioned to be written by leading experts in a clear and accessible way. The books contain serious and challenging material, take an analytical rather than prescriptive approach and are particularly suitable for use by students with no prior specialist knowledge.

The series is relevant for many business and management courses, including MBA and post-experience courses, specialist masters and postgraduate diplomas, professional courses and final-year undergraduate courses. These texts have become essential reading at business and management schools worldwide.

Published

Paul Blyton and Peter Turnbull **The Dynamics of Employee Relations** (3rd edn)
Sharon C. Bolton **Emotion Management in the Workplace**
Peter Boxall and John Purcell **Strategy and Human Resource Management**
J. Martin Corbett **Critical Cases in Organisational Behaviour**
Keith Grint **Leadership**
Marek Korczynski **Human Resource Management in Service Work**
Karen Legge **Human Resource Management:** anniversary edition
Stephen Procter and Frank Mueller (eds) **Teamworking**
Helen Rainbird (ed.) **Training in the Workplace**
Jill Rubery and Damian Grimshaw **The Organisation of Employment**
Harry Scarbrough (ed.) **The Management of Expertise**
Hugh Scullion and Margaret Linehan **International Human Resource Management**
Adrian Wilkinson, Mick Marchington, Tom Redman and Ed Snape **Managing with Total
    Quality Management**
Diana Winstanley and Jean Woodall (eds) **Ethical Issues in Contemporary Human
    Resource Management**

For more information on titles in Series please go to www.palgrave.com/busines/mwo

Invitation to authors

The Series Editors welcome proposals for new books within the Management, Work and Organisations series. These should be sent to Paul Thompson (p.thompson@strath.ac.uk) at the Dept of HRM, Strathclyde Business School, University of Strathclyde, 50 Richmond St Glasgow G1 1XT

Leadership
Limits
and Possibilities

Keith Grint

First published 2005 by
PALGRAVE MACMILLAN
Houndmills, Basingstoke, Hampshire RG21 6XS and
175 Fifth Avenue, New York, N.Y. 10010
Companies and representatives throughout the world.

PALGRAVE MACMILLAN is the global academic imprint of the Palgrave Macmillan division of St. Martin's Press, LLC and of Palgrave Macmillan Ltd. Macmillan® is a registered trademark in the United States, United Kingdom and other countries. Palgrave is a registered trademark in the European Union and other countries.

ISBN 10: 0–333–96387–3
ISBN 13: 978–0–333–96387–6

This book is printed on paper suitable for recycling and made from fully managed and sustained forest sources.

A catalogue record for this book is available from the British Library.

Library of Congress Cataloging-in-Publication Data

Grint, Keith.
 Leadership / Keith Grint.
  p. cm—(Management, work and organisations)
 Includes bibliographical references and index.
 ISBN 0–333–96387–3
  1. Leadership. 2. Executive ability. 3. Organizational effectiveness. I. Series.

HD57.7G757 2005
658.4′092—dc22   2004051151

10 9 8 7 6 5 4 3 2 1
14 13 12 11 10 09 08 07 06 05

Printed and bound in China

Contents

List of Figures

Acknowledgements

Some of this material has its origins in an ESRC Senior Research Fellowship # H52427500197.

A section of Chapter 2 was originally published as '21st Century Leadership' in Cooper, C.L. (ed.) (2004) *The 21st Century Manager: Changing Management in Tomorrow's Company* (Oxford: Oxford University Press). A section of Chapter 5 was originally published as 'Overcoming the Hydra: Leaderless Groups and Terrorism' (2004) in Gabriel, Y. (ed.) *Premodern Stories for Late Modernity: Narrative Tradition and Organization* (Oxford: Oxford University Press).

Preface

Like all books this one is the product of many people but the responsibility remains mine alone. I would like to thank the Saïd Business School and Templeton College, Oxford for facilitating a sabbatical term during which the first draft of this book was completed; the second was completed at Lancaster Management School. I would also like to thank the RAF for taking me under their proverbial 'wing' and allowing me to follow two of their Intermediate Management and Leadership courses during the Autumn of 2003. In particular, the following RAF members gave unselfishly of their time and thoughts: Flight Sergeants: Geoff Hancocks, Chris Bragan, Paul Phillips and Andy Richardson; Warrant Officer Geoff Steen; Squadron Leader Andy Williams; and Wing Commander Dan Archer. I'd also like to thank the two syndicates of sergeants that I followed who must remain anonymous but will know who they are. Many students suffered various versions of these chapters over the last few years so thanks to all the management undergraduates and postgraduates at Oxford and all the executives who have had the misfortune to be sat in one of my sessions. Many of my academic colleagues also played a role in some of these chapters and I would especially like to thank David Collinson, Mike Harper and Yiannis Gabriel for their unstinting support and helpful criticism. Beyond academia a special word to all my various karate coaches – Paul Bayliss, Rob King, Ian Cuthbert and most especially Paul Wood, who at different times taught me karate and equally importantly facilitated my philosophical education. Finally, a word for my primary charges: Kris, Beki, Katy – and their respective charges: Nicky, Simon and Richie; and for Sandra – without whom none of this is worth doing.

Introduction

Although leadership research seems to be increasing exponentially we have yet to establish what it is, never mind whether we can teach it or predict its importance. In this context I consider leadership as limited in two senses: first, our understanding is limited even if our information is apparently unlimited; second, despite all the claims for leaders as the solution to all kinds of problems, I will suggest that the role of individual *leaders* is very limited, even if the significance of leader*ship* should not be underestimated.

This book is designed to explore the theoretical definitions and practical accomplishments of leadership. It is not intended as a complete review of the extant literature – which would takes years to read never mind assimilate and review – nor is its primary focus on retreading the traditional approaches; I have attempted this in several other publications and interested readers are referred to these (Grint, 1998, 2000; Bratton *et al.*, 2004).

The first chapter takes Gallie's notion of an Essentially Contested Concept as the principle explanation for our limited advances in defining leadership and suggests that a consensus on a definition of leadership is unlikely, even in the long run. It then establishes a four-fold typology that embodies some of the most important varieties of leadership definition and illustrates why the quest for a consensus is both forlorn and unnecessary. Instead there are (at least) four quite different ways of understanding what leadership is:

- **Person**: is it WHO 'leaders' are that makes them leaders?
- **Result**: is it WHAT 'leaders' achieve that makes them leaders?
- **Position**: is it WHERE 'leaders' operate that makes them leaders?
- **Process**: is it HOW 'leaders' get things done that makes them leaders?

This may explain why we have so much trouble explaining leadership, trying to understand it and trying to teach or reward it. Of course, some of these definitions overlap and it may be that leadership oftentimes involves all four elements, but sometimes they mean radically different things to different people. In each section I first consider some of the leadership theory in the field and then proceed to explore the field through a related case of leadership practice that highlights the different ways of understanding leadership, often by picking an extreme case to illustrate the viability of the argument.

Chapter 2, for example, takes the last definition – Leadership as Person – and explores two aspects of the identity of the 'leader' that might not normally be considered but can be summarised as 'putting the "ship" back into leadership'. Leadership as Person implies that there is something remarkable about the character of the leader that makes him or her a leader, and this is often related to assumptions concerning leaders having been 'born' rather than made, though as has been recounted many times – all of us are born. However, the problems of taking this approach are established in two different dimensions, both concerned with leader'ship'.

The first 'ship' concerns the traditional assumptions about leaders as 'individuals' and suggests that this assumption is extremely tenuous: leadership is necessarily a relational not a possessive phenomenon for the individual 'leader' without followers is demonstrably not a leader at all. This issue is evaluated through that most conventional and ostensibly 'possessive' characteristic of individual leaders: charisma. Through an analysis of several individuals held to be charismatic I suggest that the identity of the leader is essentially relational not individual: thus leadership is a function of a community not a result derived from an individual deemed to be objectively superhuman.

The second element of the identity of leader'ship' is the extent to which this identity is necessarily limited to human embodiment. I argue that in all but a very few cases leadership is essentially hybrid in nature – it comprises humans, clothes, adornments, technologies, cultures, rules and so on and so forth. There are, in effect, almost no cases of successful human leaders bereft of any 'non-human' supplement – that is, naked. This argument is then used to establish the nature of hybrid leadership on D-Day, 6 June 1944 and in particular with regards to the primary means for the first assault troops to land and cross the beaches: small boats. In the event many of these hybrids had significant weaknesses but they were primarily a consequence of political and cultural arguments rather than scientific or technical limitations. In short, these troops were led, and sometimes misled, in and through hybrid leaders.

Chapter 3 configures leadership through its results. In the last decade there have been many examples of Leadership-by-Results – and many examples where the results expose the consequences of this apparently Machiavellian embodiment: Enron and Worldcom to name just two business cases, though the conflict over Iraq would be another. In the first part of this chapter we consider the extent to which results are caused by leaders and the ethical aspects of this assumption. We then proceed to take two forms of leadership that appear to be radically different in their results to test the viability of defining leadership by its apparent results: the 'successful' leadership of Mahatma Gandhi and Mother Theresa and the 'unsuccessful' leadership of slave rebellions in Roman and Nazi times. The conclusion, uncomfortable though it may be for some, is that the linkage of results to 'successful' leaders is usually tenuous and even nominal 'failures' can be configured as successful leadership. These very same lessons have important ramifications for contemporary and future leadership: it is extraordinarily difficult to quantify the result of leadership, and yet the results of leadership seem extraordinarily important. To analyse either of these we need to be very clear about what we mean by leadership but that does not mean we need to agree on its 'true' or 'objective' nature. On the contrary this is neither necessary nor helpful, though we do need to be clear about what *we* mean by leadership.

Chapter 4 takes the third of the four approaches – leadership as a process – and investigates the extent to which the method by which leadership is executed enables us to differentiate leadership from any other organizing category, such as 'management' or 'administration'. In this case I take the process of leadership literally and consider the process through which leaders 'learn to lead'. Learning to lead is a complex phenomenon and one that remains controversial. This discussion starts with some of the learning literature and suggests that a parallel can be drawn between learning to be a parent and learning to be a leader: in both cases, and counter-intuitively, it is the junior that teaches the senior how to do the senior's job: children teach adults how to be parents and subordinates teach their superordinates how to lead. This is not just because power is a relationship and not a possession but because much of both parenting and leading seems to be acquired through experiential – and reflective – trial and error. Moreover, the engagement in a learning process is performative in two senses: first the engagement is rooted in discursive practices that constitute rather than merely reflect 'reality'; second, it is a performance that needs to be continually reproduced for it to be effective. But there is more to this parallel than an interesting argument: children can be extraordinarily effective in teaching parenting skills because of their open and honest feedback. A number of historical cases then explore this argument and provides the basis for the claim that Calchas, the mythical Trojan who helped the Greeks defeat the Trojans, provides an interesting case for modelling the way leaders might recruit and retain people willing to replicate this open and honest feedback that alone may stop them from failing in the long term.

The second part of the process chapter moves us from the theoretical class room to the practical experience of learning to lead by way of a study of an RAF leadership training course. We explore the process of leadership here because the RAF provides a classic case where formal authority is tightly embedded in, and executed through, the military hierarchy: the process is tightly demarcated, transparent and well tried. However, the learning literature suggests that such an organizational setting is ill-equipped to provide the best environment for learning, so how do the RAF manage to teach leadership? The case suggests that it embodies much that resonates with the Community of Practice ideas originally formulated by Wenger (1998) and that these notions also generate some important limits to the assumption that the process of leadership is inherently embodied in the acts of individuals.

The final chapter moves from learning the process of leadership to evaluating the importance of leadership as a position. This most traditional way of understanding leadership is explored through a brief review of the contemporary debates on complexity, networks, hierarchies and heterarchies. It has been argued for some time that organizations of all forms are changing their architecture to divest themselves of unnecessary management layers and to become flatter, slimmer and more agile. As such the formal leaders of these organizations have to respond by leading in a different way, by distributing authority and responsibility downwards so that they 'facilitate' rather than control their followers. By recent convention Distributed Leadership has been invested with all kinds of positive values and considered as a way of transcending the current 'crisis in leadership' that allegedly prevails. However, taking two case studies I suggest that this may not be so, either in temporal terms or in moral evaluation. In the first case – that proclaims the arrival of a new leadership model – I consider the role of Distributed Leadership in the (re)acquisition of civil rights for African-Americans in the 1960s through the alternative narratives of the charismatic leader, Martin Luther King, and the mass movement of Distributed leaders. In the second case – that attributes an essentially moral compass to Distributed Leadership – I consider how the model informs an analysis of the leadership of terrorist groups, in particular al-Qaida. Distributive Leadership can, then, provide both a constructive and a destructive approach to organizations and it can explain not just why democratic organizations are more successful but also the resilience of terrorist groups in the face of conventional democratic authorities.

This brings us back to the beginning, because how we define leadership determines how we deal with such groups: if leadership is concerned with results or with individual charismatics who lead from the top we can (literally) undermine the organization by beheading the leadership – as the US-led coalition forces tried to do in the second Iraq war; but if leadership is more concerned with the community and with the process of leadership then such a strategy is unlikely to succeed. Leadership, then, is not just a theoretical arena but one with critical practical implications for us all and the limits of leadership – what leaders can do and what followers should allow them to do – are foundational aspects of this arena. Leadership, in effect, is too important to be left to leaders.

1

What is leadership: person, result, position or process?

Introduction

This chapter begins by setting out the context for answering the question – what is leadership? The first section considers whether this question needs to be contextualized in space and time and proceeds to investigate the links between ethics and leadership. It then confronts the issue of leadership definitions and explains why these definitions may be contested and why no consensus is either likely or necessary – because leadership is 'an essentially contested concept'. Taking each of the primary definitions in turn, the chapter explores the foundational assumptions of the different answers to the question by structuring the debate around four different answers: Person, Result, Position or Process. That leadership often draws upon on all four modes is self-evident but it is also the case that different people and organizations approach the answer to the definitional question quite differently and this may have profound effects upon how we perceive, recruit, reward and apportion responsibility to 'leadership'.

Time for leadership?

Leadership, or the lack of it, seems to be responsible for just about everything these days. On the day this was written – 22 April 2004 – the front page of the *Guardian* newspaper has four stories, three of which relate to leadership: global warming – and the lack of leadership in attending to the problem; a series of suicide bombings in Basra, related to the leadership of Blair, Bush, Saddam Hussein and al-Qaeda; and Blair's leadership over the British government's U-turn on holding a referendum over the new European constitution. The back page has three further stories, two of them about leadership: the 'lead' taken by Stuart MacGill, an Australian cricketer who announced he would not tour Zimbabwe on moral grounds; and a threat by the

Portuguese football team, Porto, to take Chelsea to the ruling body Fifa for trying to 'mislead' Porto's coach, Jose Mourinho, towards a new job in England. These notions of leadership are distinctly different but all have some commonality: they imply change, relationships and morality – though the writers and the actors involved also seem to disagree about all of these aspects. But has leadership changed since the beginning of the twenty-first century or even the beginning of the twentieth century? Do we need to reconstruct leadership because the situation has changed irrevocably and that is why five of the seven lead stories in today's newspaper relate to leadership?

If the assumption is that space and time are irrelevant to modelling leadership, then it does not matter what the twenty-first century organization or business will look like because the leadership format will remain stable: leadership requirements are eternal. Thus the question is not what leadership model is most suitable for the future but what kind of leadership model is best, period. This kind of model has been associated with a wide number of leadership theories, including Carlyle's 'Heroic Man' and some trait theories that suggest certain traits are both essential to leadership and essentially unchanging across space and time. Some form of charisma, the ability to envision a radically different solution to an aged problem, the ability to mobilize followers and so on are, in this approach, just a few of these universal requirements because the future is merely a reflection of the past.

The most radical version of this approach relates to the 'hard-wiring' model of evolutionary psychology. In this perspective leadership is something that we have always had and something that some of us are born with. This genetic make up tends to propel 'alpha-males' – those with high levels of testosterone – into positions of leadership where – if successful – they then generate high levels of serotonin, a hormone associated with happiness. The subsequent forms of natural selection eliminate all but the fittest, or rather all but the most appropriate for leadership positions (Nicholson, 2000: 97–125). In effect, the requirements of leadership are hard-wired into humans and remain relatively stable across space and time. Or as Nicholson (2000: 1) puts it: 'We may have taken ourselves out of the Stone Age but we haven't taken the Stone Age out of ourselves.'

Under these circumstances we might, perhaps, follow Plato in concentrating on the question: 'Who should rule us?', even if his answer – the wisest rather than the most popular – runs contrary to our current democratic trend. But if leadership is hard-wired then simply facilitating the process of natural selection should be sufficient to resolve the problem because the kind of leadership is unlikely to change in the near or distant future. The persistence of this selection model is evident in the large number of TV programmes that operate on precisely this philosophical basis, such as Big Brother, Popstars, Fame Academy and so on. We might then ask whether all the concern for different leadership styles is mere propaganda, a shifting debate about morality generated by the chattering classes or by those who believe history is on their side but ultimately deployed by those with what Nietzsche called 'the will to power'. In other words, the ideological justification for domination may vary but the cause remains the same.

Often this approach relates the apparent universality and timelessness of human leadership to our animal nature because leadership in animals appears unchanging and tends to be amongst the most hierarchical and brutal. Lion leadership, for example, is primarily undertaken by lionesses in terms of hunts and tending the young but the alpha male dominates in terms of eating privileges and chasing away rival males. Wolf packs tend to be family units of between 2 and 12 individuals led by the alpha pair who alone breed. A strict hierarchy exists within wolf packs in which the alpha male leads hunts and territorial defence while the alpha female leads the pups.[1]

But if human leadership is a mirror of the animal world then we should most closely resemble the world of chimpanzees, our closest genetic cousin. De Waal's (2000: 77–135) account of Chimpanzees suggests that leadership is not determined by size or necessarily by hard-wiring but by coalition building. Hence during the observation period three different males (First Yeroen, then Luit and finally Nikkie) took control over the group but this was only possible by alliances built up over time both with one of the two other adult males and with the larger group of females. Moreover, no leadership was permanent or self-stabilizing – each of the three leaders had to create and recreate the network of support and undermine the counter-alliances on a regular basis to maintain control. What is also intriguing is that the final male leader, Nikkie, who was rather young to be the group leader, had great difficulty maintaining control over the female adults and only succeeded by sharing his authority, collective leadership, with the oldest male, Yeroen, who undertook the 'policing' activities in the group on Nikkie's behalf. De Waal (2000: 118), in a reformulation of Thomas Hobbes's precondition for submission to a leader, suggests that this may be a consequence of the perception amongst the females that Nikkie was unable to protect them from attack. Whatever the cause it does seem that chimpanzee leadership is essentially rooted in the ability to create and maintain a network of support – and to undermine any rivals attempting to build competitive alliances.

A related biological argument suggests that human altruism is not an ethical philosophy rooted in helping others, possibly by leading them, but a gene-based determinant. In other words, what might appear to be altruistic behaviour is in effect the consequence of genes maximizing the chance of their survival. Hence although laying down one's life for one's brother or sister might appear to be altruistic, the supporters of Socio-biology (E.O. Wilson, 1975) or the Selfish Gene (Dawkins, 1989) would probably relate this action to the propensity of related genes in kin groups to protect each other. Of course this raises enormous problems for anything other than Transactional Theories of leadership because only self-interest can determine follower- and leader-behaviour. There will certainly be no likelihood of Transformational Leadership succeeding because this suggests followers should subordinate their personal interests to those of a group that are unlikely to be restricted to kin groups. However, experiments by Falk et al. (2003) suggest that self-oriented behaviour has significant limits. In the first experiment two people are required to share £100, but one (A) will decide who gets what. It is then up to the other (B) to accept their 'share' or reject the entire package, and if the latter course is chosen then A is deprived of his or her share too. Since even £1 is better than nothing, it would be logical for B to accept whatever A offers but the experiment suggests that when B's share drops below £25, B usually punishes A by refusing to participate at all. Related experiments in public good confirm the suspicion that there is a lot more to behaviour than gene-based selfishness and people are willing to punish selfish behaviour, even if it causes them harm too.[2]

Moreover, if the assumption is that space and time are critical to changing organizational forms rather than genes or traits, because the organizational form determines the appropriate kind of leadership, and that organizational form changes, then we need to be very clear about the future and equally clear about the connection between the context and the leadership kind required. Precisely what context requires what kind of leadership remains subject to dispute but there are several variants rooted in different models of time, of which four will detain us here.[3]

The linear model perceives time as both a straight line and (usually) an ever-improving line such that our notions of, and expertise about, leadership improves across time, irrespective of space. Thus historically we might consider how the prior authoritarian and absolutist models of political and business leadership have gradually changed from tyrannies to participative democracies. In this 'whig' model of historical change, Genghis Kahn, Louis XIV, Hitler and Stalin are replaced by democratic leaders; authoritarian business bosses, such as Henry Ford and Robert Maxwell, are replaced by liberals such as Richard Branson; and authoritarian military models, for instance, the Prussian Army of Frederick the Great, are replaced by decentralized military models, for instance, the Strategic Corporal model currently under development by the US Marine Corps (Krulak, 1999) or the Distributive Leadership approach that we will consider in Chapter 5. If this model were adopted we would expect the future leaders to be ever more liberal and participative, in line with Western democratic philosophies drawn from the enlightenment. Such a model is certainly popular – as witnessed by the popularity of Fukuyama's (1993) claim about the end of history: democratic capitalism had both undermined all ideological opposition and marked the zenith of political systems. However, the events since 9/11 indicate that, to paraphrase Mark Twain, the reports of the death of all opposition are premature. Furthermore, such a model has yet to account for the rich diversity of leadership forms that have existed in both time and space: in short, there have been more casualties to authoritarian leadership in the twentieth century than in any other, there are many examples of decentralized leadership in previous centuries, and the growth of fundamentalist religious governments – of all kinds and including Christian, Hindu and Muslim – in the last two decades does not bode well for a continuously enlightening leadership style.

Indeed, the metaphorical straight line that connects the problems of the past to the solutions of the future resonates with the popularity of the quest for the 'answer' to the leadership 'question'. Many harassed executives attend many 'leadership course' ostensibly in the hope that the solution to their leadership problem will mysteriously emerge from participating in the course in a manner akin to the smoke from the Vatican chimney that marks the election of a Pope – and thus the 'solution' to the leadership 'problem'. But the quest for an answer, like the search for the Holy Grail, is unlikely to be successful because the leadership problem is inherently intractable – that is impossible or difficult to manage. Rittel and Webber (1973) observed problems could be divided between 'Wicked' and 'Tame'. The latter could be complex issues but each 'Tame' problem was theoretically capable of resolution through the application of established techniques and processes; that is to say, 'tame problems' can be solved by management. However, if the problems are essentially novel, indeed unique, if they embody no obvious resolution point or assessment mechanism, if the cause, explanation and apparent resolution of the problem depends upon the viewpoint of the stakeholder, and if the problem is embedded in another similar problem, then the problem is Wicked. Wicked Problems are potentially open to better or worse developments but not 'right' or 'wrong' solutions and are thus only amenable to leadership – defined as dealing with something novel – rather than management – defined as dealing with something which is both known and which has a pre-existing resolution. A Tame problem, however complex, is teaching your children to pass their driving test; a Wicked problem is remaining a successful parent to them. A Tame problem is 'winning' the war in Iraq; a Wicked problem is securing a just and lasting peace in Iraq. A Tame problem is heart surgery; a Wicked problem is providing unlimited health services to all who need them on the basis of limited resources.[4] Management might be focused on solving complex but essentially Tame problems in a unilinear fashion: applying what worked last time; but leadership is essentially about facing Wicked problems that are literally 'unmanageable'.

Perhaps, then, if space and time are important in generating radically different organizations and unique problems that demand significantly variable leadership forms then a contingency-based approach (Fiedler, 1997) would be better than a linear model. This suggests that once we have established the context and format of such organizations then, and only then, can we begin to decipher the 'needs' for leadership. This form of reasoning, often nestling within a functionalist philosophy, usually implies some form of materialist determinism; in effect the future material world will determine the cultural context that supports leadership. So, for example, if our future world is very dynamic, competitive and unstable, then we 'need' to provide flexible and decentralized leadership systems. On the other hand, if the future returns to the more stable global system that we allegedly experienced just after the Second World War, or if the future that we were allegedly about to enter resembles 'the end of history' that was almost upon us after the collapse of communism, then we can return to the stable hierarchies and centralized administrative leadership that dominated the 1950s and 1960s. For instance, it may be that 'crisis' situations require authoritarian or at least decisive leadership, while more stable periods facilitate the development of more liberal models. However, precisely what the context is – and how we come to agree on this – never seems clear. Moreover, as the scissor, paper, stone game analogy suggests, the context is constantly changing anyway as competing groups respond to each other; an idea that resonates closely to the 'fitness landscapes' of complexity theory where strategy is closer to walking on a water-bed than on dry land: everything moves as multiple actors enter and thus change the context (Battram, 1998: 209–23).

A third take on time is in a circular format. Here the fashions of leadership revolve across time and space so that authoritarian and liberal leaders displace each other in sequences that may last some time. There is no essential 'end point' in this model, just a sequence of revolutions but these changes can be related to the differing contexts within which they occur. In Barley and Kunda's (2000) version of this the endless cycle of management styles relates directly to a period within the Kondratiev economic 'long wave'. Hence, expansionary periods are associated with 'rational' or scientific forms of management, such as Scientific Management or Systems Theory approaches, while contracting economic periods are associated with more 'normative' management styles, such as Industrial Betterment, Human Relations and Organizational Cultures and so on. Here the future leadership style will depend upon the point of the next cycle so the trick is to predict the cycle and then derive the appropriate leadership style. Elitist models of leadership, such as Pareto's (1997), also tend to adopt the cyclical approach but lock them into the oscillating forms of elites rather than cycles of the economy. However, like Kondratiev's Long Wave theory, what appears an interesting argument has yet to establish itself as the accepted truth.

The final variant on temporal change is that there is no pattern here, just a sequence of changes that have no 'destination' and thus no prediction is possible: the future may be an extrapolation of past trends or it may reveal a cyclical return to 'old fashioned virtues' or it may simply be completely novel, something beyond our current comprehension. If the latter is true then the chances of anyone predicting entirely novel developments are remote and we shall simply have to wait and see. Of course, this then returns us to the possibility of an eternal leadership style: it doesn't matter what the future holds, 'traditional' leaders will still lead. But there is a different 'take' on the requirements of leadership that needs further exploration here: the very idea of 'requirements' legitimizes rather than simply explains the role of leaders.

It could be argued that the causal direction of the question should be reversed – thus the question should not be what kind of leader will the future organization need but what kind of future organizations will the current crop of leaders construct? This 'construction' can itself be of two variants.

First, leaders 'build' the future context – in the sense that Hitler laid the foundations for the Nazi State, or Roosevelt laid the foundations for the USA to enter the Second World War or Mao Tse-tung constructed the ideological basis for Communist China and so on. Of course, this leader-focused approach assumes that individuals rather than collectives are responsible for the construction of the future – in much the same way that Carlyle suggested, or in one of Napoleon's favourite examples 'The Gauls were not conquered by the Roman legions but by Caesar' (quoted in Goldsworthy, 2003: 377). Tolstoy believed the opposite – that leaders were merely propelled by their organizations as a bow-wave is propelled by a boat, but it can still be argued that the future is constructed by contemporary leadership even if that leadership has a collective form (Ackerman and Duvall, 2000).

Second, we need to consider whether we can ever secure a transparent rendition of the context without reference to the relationship between leaders and organizations. In other words, are leaders neutral in the interpretations of contexts and organizations or are they deeply implicated in those renditions – to the point where no 'objective' analysis is available? This goes beyond the popular idea that 'spin-doctors' are responsible for distorting the 'truth' because this kind of approach assumes there is an objective 'truth' out there somewhere, waiting for our language to describe it. Instead I would suggest that what counts as the 'truth' is always contested so the point is not what the spin-doctors are doing to the 'truth' but why we believe some versions of what we take to be reality but not others. Hence language does not so much describe reality as construct it. Or as Rorty (1999: xxvi) puts it, 'languages are not attempts to copy what is out there, but rather tools for dealing with what is out there'. Magritte's marvellous painting 'This is not a pipe' demonstrates this well – it is indeed not a pipe, it is a *representation* of a pipe in the same way that photos of missile sites or mobile biological laboratories are not objective evidence of missiles or mobile biological laboratories but photographic *representations* of these. The most recent case of a leader using this mode of persuasion might be Colin Powell, then the US Secretary of State, trying to persuade the UN on 6 February 2003 of the existence of Iraqi weapons of mass destruction by reference to photographic 'evidence'[5] (an echo of the famous 'Adlai Stevenson Moment' on 25 October 1962 when the then US Ambassador to the UN showed photographs of Soviet Missiles in Cuba to the UN Security Council).[6]

So who says what the context is (it's usually a crisis)? And who says that – as a consequence of the context – we therefore need leaders of a particular kind (it's usually 'decisive')? Usually the answer is: the existing leaders. If, for instance, we are to believe Prime Minister Blair and President Bush, the situation just prior to the second Gulf War was perilous – Saddam Hussein's weapons of mass destruction were on the verge of being mobilized and could be deployed within 45 minutes. This 'objective situation' clearly required leadership that was decisive and effective – hence the war against Iraq. But it is no longer clear precisely what this military threat actually was: it may be that there was no threat, so the situation did not require military conflict because the policy of containment was working and had done so since the end of the first Gulf war. Now the point is not whether there ever were weapons of mass destruction but that the situation is *constructed* by those with control over the information. Thus the anti-war campaigns tried and failed to construct an account of the situation that downplayed the threat. What remains, therefore is not a true and a false account of the situation because we will probably never know what that actually was. Instead we have contending accounts, some of which are perceived as more powerful than others and which are therefore able to mobilize support for particular actions. It is often very difficult, then, to establish what the context actually is and what the requirements of the situation are, and quite different forms of leadership have succeeded in markedly similar circumstances to bedevil our attempts to link the situation to the 'required' leadership (Grint, 2001).

Time for moral leadership?

If we cannot agree on whether the requirements for leadership have changed radically recently, can we at least agree that the time for moral leadership has arrived? If only we could agree on the definition of terms, and then agree on a process for peacefully resolving disputes, perhaps we could avoid the suffering of those at the 'wrong' end of leadership. Perhaps, but as we shall shortly see the calamitous consequences of leadership failures are seldom mechanically attributable to the moral treachery of our leaders. Adel Safty (2003), in contrast, argues that management and governance are neutral terms while 'Leadership is or at least ought to be normatively apprehended as a set of values with connotations evocative of the higher achievements of the human spirit.' Leadership is not only tied to these norms but the norms themselves are explained as 'the promotion of human development for the common good of people in a democratic environment'. In effect, leadership, which is necessarily moral, is also necessarily tied to democracy. Clearly this would place almost all of human history and society beyond the limits of ethical leadership.

However, there are many who would argue against the democratic essence of leadership: Plato certainly despised it as a system for encouraging leadership by demagogue rather than leadership by the wise, and the democratic element of leadership has certainly not been adequate in restraining several of the 'lapses' that Safty himself rails against: Lebanon, Grenada, Panama and the Persian Gulf wars to name a few. He rightly laments the havoc caused by leaders such as Mussolini, Hitler and Saddam Hussein but suggests that their catastrophic impact relates primarily to the absence of higher moral purposes and defines such people as Rulers rather than Leaders, in much the same way that MacGregor Burns (1978) distinguishes between Transformational Leaders and Power-Wielders, Zaleznik (1974) differentiates between psychologically 'healthy' and 'unhealthy' leaders, Howell (1988) contrasts Socialized and Personalized Leaders, and Bass (1985) distinguishes them between Authentic and Inauthentic/ Pseudotransformational Leaders.[7]

But there is a problem here: who decides on which side of the divide they sit? This is not just a question of applying twenty-first century Western standards as universally good, but suggesting that all the leaders defined as sitting on the 'wrong' side of the fence probably perceived themselves to have a 'moral' purpose. Of course, most of us would regard such claims as extraordinarily dubious – but we are not the ones who followed these people. Thus Hitler probably believed he was acting morally and in the best interests of the German population in his simultaneous assaults upon Jews, Communists, the disabled, Gypsies, homosexuals and anyone else who got in his way.

That most people disputed this assumption vigorously matters not one jot because to imply that these Rulers were simply evil is to simply miss the point – how did they mobilize so many followers if it was self-evident to all their followers that no good would come from their leadership? In other words, for all that I side with Safty in his assault upon immorality, what counts as immoral is neither easy to define nor does it explain the success of such leaders.

For instance, in May 2004 two American soldiers faced courts martial for actions that remain morally controversial: Specialist Jeremy Sivits was on trial in Baghdad for taking photographs of abused Iraqi prisoners inside Abu Ghraib prison, while Sergeant Camilo Mejia was on trial in Fort Stewart army base for abandoning his unit after six months in Iraq on the grounds that to remain would have been to follow orders that he believed were immoral or illegal. As Ramsey Clark (former US attorney general during the Vietnam campaign) suggested, 'The irony is that they are being court martialed over there [Iraq] for the very things that he is being court martialed for over here [USA] for not going back to do' (quoted in Goldenberg, 2004: 4).

Another example would be the dropping by the Bush administration of the word 'Crusade' in the war against terrorism. Did not the original Crusaders believe they were acting morally, doing their God's work? Did not Saladin's followers believe exactly the same thing – but from the opposite direction? And do not many contemporary terrorists proclaim their acts to be moral, as defined by their own religious perspective? Indeed, it does not actually matter what we think of the (im)morality of contemporary terrorist organizations and their leaders – it's what their followers think that matters and most of them seem to believe they are acting morally in their quest to free their communities from oppression, drive out the non-believers, return the earth to its rightful owners, or push humanity to oblivion as quickly as possible.

In this respect it is more than likely that the followers of bin Laden believe him to be acting 'morally' even if the rest of the world does not. The same logic must apply in Serbia where, in December 2003, the ultra nationalist Serbian Radical Party secured the single largest proportion of the Serbian Parliamentary votes (28 per cent of the votes and 33 per cent of the seats) whilst its two most (in)famous members, the formal leader Vojislav Seselj, and the former Yugoslav President Slobodan Milosevic, were on, or awaiting, trial at the UN tribunal in The Hague for alleged war crimes.

The solution for Safty is 'People-Driven Moral Leadership', though most of the examples used derive from the overthrow of old Soviet bloc or eastern dictatorships rather than contemporary democratic societies. And there's the rub: for Safty it seems that democracy, morality and authentic leadership go hand in hand; they reflect and reinforce each other. But don't all the democratic leaders claim this – even when, for many of their citizens, they are manifestly not acting democratically, morally or authentically? Indeed, People-Power may be in line with the wishes of the majority but this does not make it moral, does it? If the majority of a population decide to enforce a religious law that requires the stoning of 'fallen' women is that essentially and objectively moral because it is democratically decided?

A related problem concerns the importance of emotion to leadership. It is self-evident that leadership is not a wholly rational process any more than people are emotionless. And it is, therefore, equally obvious that emotions, or emotional intelligence, or whatever label is in vogue, is an important element of leadership. But this does not directly translate into the approach which suggests that people with high emotional intelligence (EQ) are morally superior to those without high EQ. Hitler, for example, was extraordinarily effective in manipulating people's emotions but this does not make him objectively moral. Moreover, it is because emotions are such a powerful motivator that we ought to limit their significance – that, after all, is the reason for living according to a system of laws rather that at the whim of a tyrant whose EQ is a liability for all who disagree with the tyrant.

The limits to the effectiveness of a call for 'morality' to be reinserted into political leadership are also self-evident in the inability of the UN to control its own members or to engage in effective peacekeeping duties. Those failures cannot be resolved by further appeals to moral behaviour any more than pacifism has proved effective in preventing wars (Cf. Ackerman and Duval, 2000; Schell, 2003). Indeed, as long as the UN remains dependent upon the military power of a few nations to do its global policing, it will remain a morally upright 'paper tiger'. An alternative solution to the problematic call for moral leadership is to demand a global parliament – a United Nations without the distorting influences of the Permanent Members of the Security Council and with the necessary powers to enforce the democratic decisions of the majority. Though again, a democratic UN does not guarantee moral behaviour, even if it is preferable to the status quo.

Perhaps we should look again at Karl Popper: he always claimed that democracy was not a good in and of itself but the best system available for inhibiting a greater evil: tyranny. Is this the unpalatable truth: that all claims to the moral high ground should be treated with suspicion? Moral leadership is not the way to secure democracy, morality and justice because morality, like power and leadership is an essentially contested concept; hence we might be better off seeking a more pragmatic alternative to the calls for 'moral leadership': a functioning global democracy – while no guarantee of global morality – might be the best opportunity we have for inhibiting their opposites.

Popper's suggestion that science should advance through the quest for fallibility rather than infallibility, accepting error rather than asserting perfection, might also be a useful analogy for our review of leadership. After all, if we could construct a science of leadership then the more we knew about what leadership was the closer we would be to perfecting and predicting it, wouldn't we? But has this happened?

What is leadership?

Despite over half a century of research into leadership, we appear to be no nearer a consensus as to its basic meaning, let alone whether it can be taught or its moral effects measured and predicted. This cannot be because of a dearth of interest or material: on 29 October 2003 there were 14,139 items relating to 'Leadership' on Amazon.co.uk for sale. Assuming you could read these at the rate of one per day it would take almost 39 years just to read the material, never mind write anything about leadership or practice it. Just two months later that number had increased by 3 per cent (471 items) to 14,610. Assuming this increase was annualized to 18 per cent we can look forward to just under 20,000 items by the beginning of 2005, 45,000 by 2010, 100,000 by 2015 and a little later we should have more items than people! Put another way, since there were just three books on followership available in 2003 we will soon get to the interesting position where there are more books on leaders than physical followers. It should be self-evident that we do not need more 'lists' of leadership competences or skills because leadership research appears to be anything but incremental in its approach to 'the truth' about leadership: the longer we spend looking at leadership the more complex the picture becomes.

Traditionally, leadership is defined by its alleged opposite: management. Management is concerned with executing routines and maintaining organizational stability – it is essentially concerned with control; leadership is concerned with direction setting, with novelty and is essentially linked to change, movement and persuasion. Another way to put this is that management is the equivalent of *déjà vu* (seen this before), whereas leadership is the equivalent of *vu jàdé* (never seen this before). Management implies that managers have seen it all before and simply need to respond correctly to the situation by categorizing it and executing the appropriate process; leadership implies that leaders have never seen anything like it before and must therefore construct a novel strategy. But this division is often taken to mean that different people are necessary to fill the different roles – hence anyone relegated to the role of 'mere' manager, cannot be considered as bringing anything unique to the party – after all, their task is limited to the mechanical task of recognizing situations and applying pre-existing processes. The consequence of the role subordination implied by this should be obvious: get out of management and into leadership! And if the organization is under-managed and over-led well it isn't your fault, is it? That most roles actually require both recognition and invention should also be clear.

Another way of approaching the problem might be to consider what the most popular textbooks have to say on the issue. Probably the top four selling general review texts on leadership in 2003 were Hughes *et al.* (1999), Northouse (1997), Wright (1996) and Yukl (1998). On the very first page of their book, Hughes *et al.* (1999) suggest that 'if any single idea is central to this book, it is that leadership is a process, not a position'. They then illustrate the gap between leadership research and personalized accounts of leadership by exploring three short case studies: Colin Powell, Madeleine Albright and Konosuke Matsushita. Now by any stretch of the imagination these three are leaders in a positional sense, irrespective of the processes that they employ, so already we have at best a contested concept and at worst a contradiction. They go on (1999: 8) to list the various definitional forms that include: inducing subordinates to behave in a desired manner; an influencing relationship, directing and coordinating group work; a volitional, as opposed to a coerced, interpersonal relationship; a transformative relationship; actions that focus resources to create desirable opportunities; creating the conditions for teams to be effective; and finally the one that they adopt, that leadership is the influencing of an organized group towards accomplishing its goals (Roach and Behling, 1984). Thus for Hughes *et al.*, 1999, and despite their examples the conclusion is that leadership, above everything else, is not a position but a process.

Northouse (1997: 2) begins by noting Stogdill's (1974: 7) famous quip that there are almost as many definitions of leadership as there are people who have tried to define it, and accepts that leadership has different meanings for different people. He then proceeds to relate Bass's (1990: 11–20) typology that distinguished between leadership as the focus of group process, the embodiment of the collective will, leadership as a personality issue, a complex phenomena that induces others to accomplish tasks, and finally leadership as an act or behaviour – the things leaders do to bring about change in a group. Noting the importance of power, processes, goal achievement and groups, Northouse (1997: 3) settles on a definition that suggests leadership 'is a process whereby an individual influences a group of individuals to achieve a common goal'. This is clearly very close to that adopted by Hughes *et al.* on the basis of Roach and Behling's definition.

In contrast, Yukl (1998: 2), who does accept that there is no 'correct definition', does not distinguish between leadership, management and 'the boss', also considers Katz and Kahn's (1978: 528) suggestion that leadership is 'the influential increment over and above mechanical compliance with the routine directives of the organization'. Leadership might also be demonstrated by 'those who consistently make effective contributions to social order and who are expected and perceived to do so' (Hosking, 1988: 153), or it may be 'a process of giving purpose to collective effort' (Jacobs and Jaques, 1990: 281), or 'the ability to step outside the culture … to start evolutionary change processes that are more adaptive' (Schein, 1992: 2), or even 'the process of making sense of what people are doing together so that people will understand and be committed' (Drath and Palus, 1994: 4). It could be the activity involved in 'articulating visions, embodying values, and creating the environment within which things can be accomplished' (Richards and Engle, 1986: 206). This is a much more differentiated collection of terms and Yukl (1998: 5) concludes that 'It is neither feasible nor desirable *at this point* in the development of the discipline to attempt to resolve the controversies over the appropriate definition of leadership' [my italics]. However, 'over time it will be possible to compare the utility of different conceptions and arrive at some consensus on the matter' (1998: 5). In other words, for Yukl at least, the problem is not inherent to the topic but a consequence of its novelty.

Finally, Wright (1996: 1) also begins by acknowledging the complexity and ambiguity of the concept, especially concerning the role of personality, the existence of leadership positions, the role of coercion, the determination of effects, and the evaluation of performance, nevertheless, he concludes that common to most approaches are the notions of influence and the role of followers.

Apart from noting the variegated properties of these definitions we are left more rather than less confused by them. Leadership does seem to be defined differently and even if there are some similarities the complexities undermine most attempts to explain why the differences exist. That is to say, that we know differences exist but we remain unable to construct a consensus about the concept. However, the dissensus seems to hang around four areas of dispute, leadership defined as: *person, result, position and process.*

There are several potential resolutions to this problem of leadership definition:

1. Stop the research now: since the research is making things worse not better we should stop while we are not totally confused.
2. Keep going in the hope that someone will eventually discover the truth about leadership and save us all 39 years of wasted reading time.
3. Reconstruct why we are unable to generate a consensus on what leadership is and consider what this might mean for leadership *practice* as well as theory.

The rest of this chapter focuses upon the last of these and I want to suggest one explanation for the problem and a way of constraining its effects. I hesitate to use the word 'resolution' because the explanation actively inhibits any resolution, but it does enable us to establish some parameters that we might use to understand why the differences exist in the first place. In other words, this does not provide a first step towards a consensus but a first step towards understanding why a consensus might be unachievable. Moreover, the point is not simply to redescribe the varieties of interpretation but to consider how this affects the way leadership is perceived, enacted, recruited and supported. For example, if organizations promote individuals on the basis of one particular interpretation of leadership then that approach will be encouraged and others discouraged – but it may well be that other interpretations of leadership are critical to the organization's success. Hence the importance of the definition is not simply to delineate a space in a language game and it is not merely a game of sophistry; on the contrary, how we define leadership has vital implications for how organizations work – or don't work.

Leadership: an essentially contested concept?

50 years ago W.B. Gallie (1955/56) called power an Essentially Contested Concept (ECC). Gallie suggested that many concepts – such as power – involved 'endless disputes about their proper uses on the part of the users' to the point where debates appeared irresolvable. For example, a discussion about whether Bush or Blair are 'good' leaders is likely to generate more heat than light and precious little hope of a consensus amongst people who bring different definitions of 'good leadership' to the

debate. For Gallie (1964: 187–8), 'Recognition of a given concept as essentially contested implies recognition of rival uses of it (such as oneself repudiates) as not only logically possible and humanly "likely", but as of permanent potential critical value to one's own use or interpretation of the concept in question.' Examples of ECCs are multiple, as are the attempts to resolve the contestation: Strine *et al.* (1990), consider Performance as an ECC; Kellow (2002) applies it to Sustainable Development; Bajpai (1999) uses it to analyse Security; Cohen (2000) takes Civil Society as an ECC; and finally Terrorism is the subject of Smelser and Mitchell's (2002) application of an ECC.

The problem of evaluating leadership is exemplified by Jack Welch: was he 'the best' business leader of the 1990s because GE under his 'leadership' made more money than any other company or would GE have been this successful anyway and did his methods unnecessarily destroy hundreds of careers? We could equally argue that Sir Peter Bonfield, ex-CEO of BT, was 'the best' because despite losing over £30 billion it could be argued that he saved BT from bankruptcy. In other words, it is always possible to devise a way of measuring 'successful leadership' but the measures may not generate a consensus because they are neither objective nor do we all agree on the way to measure success because our definitions and interpretations of leadership are ECCs. Furthermore, and on a more practical note, if we select, criticize and reward people for their 'leadership' we should not be surprised if they fail to come to our standards – it may well be that their conception of 'leadership' is radically different from ours; thus we should then be in a position to add a clarifying statement – 'and by leadership we mean X not Y'.

Let us first generate the taxonomy of leadership. This must include the Process issues that most of the texts highlight, but also the Positional issues that they tend to use as illustrations of leaders. However, a huge amount of research has focused upon the Person of the leader as well, and it would be strange indeed if leadership research bore no interest in the result of leadership activity – though note that this takes as given that leadership makes a difference to the product, the results. This fourfold typology does not claim universal coverage but it should encompass a significant proportion of our definitions of leadership. Moreover, the typology is not hierarchical: it does not claim that one definition is more important than another and, contrary to the consensual approach, it is constructed upon foundations that *may* be mutually exclusive. In effect, we may have to choose which form of leadership we are talking about rather than attempt to elide the differences. It is however, quite possible that empirical examples of leadership embody elements of all four forms. Thus we are left with four major alternatives:

- Leadership as Person: is it WHO 'leaders' are that makes them leaders?
- Leadership as Result: is it WHAT 'leaders' achieve that makes them leaders?
- Leadership as Position: is it WHERE 'leaders' operate that makes them leaders?
- Leadership as Process: is it HOW 'leaders' get things done that makes them leaders?

All these aspects are 'ideal types', following Weber's assertion that no such 'real' empirical case probably exists in any pure form, but this does enable us to understand the phenomenon of leadership better, and its attendant confusions and complexities, because leadership means different things to different people. This is therefore a heuristic model not an attempt to carve up the world into 'objective' segments that mirror what we take to be reality. I will suggest, having examined these four different approaches to leadership, that the differences both explain why so little agreement has been reached on the definition of leadership and why this is important to the execution and analysis of leadership.

Defining leadership

Person-based leadership

Is it who you are that determines whether you are a leader or not? This, of course resonates with the traditional traits approach: a leader's character or personality. We might consider the best example of this as the charismatic, to whom followers are attracted because of the charismatic's personal 'magnetism'. Ironically, while a huge effort has been made to reduce the ideal leader to his or her essence – the quintessential characteristics or competencies or behaviours of the leader – the effort of reduction has simultaneously reduced its value. It is rather as if a leadership scientist had turned chef and was engaged in reducing a renowned leader to his or her elements by placing them in a saucepan and applying heat. Eventually the residue left from the cooking could be analysed and the material substances divided into their various chemical compounds. Take, for instance, Wofford's (1999: 525) claim that laboratory research on charisma would develop a 'purer' construct 'free from the influences of such nuisance variables as performance, organizational culture and other styles of leadership'. What a culture-free leader would like is anyone's guess and this attempted purification is literally *reductio ad absurdum*: a pile of chemical residues might have considerable difficulty persuading other people to follow it. Yet clearly some authorities remain wedded to such an approach and, to be fair, it may be that some chemical residues do, paradoxically, have exactly this ability: heroin, for example, is often blamed for 'leading' people astray. Moreover, this kind of approach might also suggest that the search for the answer to the question 'What is leadership?' is untenable because it implies an essential element, an essence that simply does not exist in such a form. At its most basic the 'essence' of leadership, *qua* an individual leader, leaves out the followers and without followers you cannot be a leader. Indeed, this might be the simplest definition of leadership: 'having followers'.

A complementary or contradictory case can also be made for defining leadership generally as a collective, rather than an individual, phenomenon. In this case the focus usually moves from an individual formal leader to multiple informal leaders.

We might, for example, consider how organizations actually achieve anything, rather than being over-concerned with what the CEO has said should be achieved. Thus we could trace the role of informal opinion-leaders in persuading their colleagues to work differently, or to work harder, or not to work at all and so on. This 'negotiated' or 'distributed' or 'deep' leadership is often overlooked precisely because it remains informal and distributed amongst the collective rather than emanating from a formal and individual leader. This does not necessarily imply that everyone is a leader – though it might do – but rather that a relatively small number of people are crucial for ensuring organizations survive and succeed – and this minority or critical mass, may or may not coincide with those in formal leadership positions (Gronn, 2003; Ridderstrale, 2002: 11). There are, for instance several hunter-gatherer societies, or rather 'bands', such as the Hadza of Tanzania, who are formally leaderless. Individuals do 'lead' in specific tasks at particular times but the identity of the task leader tends to change across time. Here, as in most such bands, decisions are made in a democratic forum by a consensus of adult members with dissenters free to leave if they wish. Similarly, Josephy (1993: 268–9) argues that conflict between Native American Indians and the US government over opening up the Oregon Trail in 1851 was, in part, rooted in the false assumption made by the latter that the Sioux nation could be bound by the word of a single leader – chosen by the Superintendent of Indian Affairs – when the Sioux themselves insisted that no single person could take such a decision.

Either way, leadership along this criterion is primarily defined by *who* the leader is or who the leaders are (formal and informal), and it may be that such an approach is associated with an emotional relationship between leader and followers or between leaders. At its most extreme, as in Le Bon (2002), this emotional relationship renders the followers in 'the crowd' incapable of discriminating between good and bad actions – as indeed does the leader of the crowd. Freud (Surprenant, 2002) however, retains the notion of the leader embodying the ego-ideal of the followers who project onto their leader all their aspirational characteristics.

Despite the Western fetish for heroic individuals as leadership icons it is not at all clear that such examples exist in social isolation. For instance, Newton may claim to have 'led' the discovery of gravity but it was, in effect, the result of collective work by Robert Hooke and Edmund Halley as well as Newton. Take the discovery of penicillin as a further example of this. In September 1928 Alexander Fleming was cleaning some Petri dishes in St Mary's Hospital, London, when he 'discovered' that bacteria had been impeded by a mould. On the conventional account, under his leadership the momentous discovery that *Penicillium* had antibacterial effects was followed by years of painstaking research and by 1942 penicillin was launched as a life-saving antibiotic. His leadership was subsequently recognized by 25 honorary degrees: providence may have played a hand but it was Fleming's research leadership that recognized its significance and developed the drug.

Yet the antibacterial properties of penicillin had been known since Lister's work in 1872 and Duchesne's doctoral thesis in 1897, though the strain that Fleming fortunately worked with – *Penicillium notatum* – was far more effective. Indeed, far from Fleming continuing to lead a dedicated research team to transform the mould into a miraculous cure for septic wounds in the Second World War, he actually abandoned research on it, regarding it at best as a 'local antiseptic', and made only one minor reference to it in 1931; the rest of his work focused upon the value of mercury-based compounds for treating wounds. Other researchers took up the project at various periods but without Fleming's help and it was not until the team of Howard Florey, Ernst Chain and Norman Heatley began working on the issue from 1938 to 1941 at Oxford University that any radical advance was made.

Without any assistance from Fleming (one of the team thought he was already dead) Florey *et al.* developed penicillin to the point where its therapeutic properties were self-evident and mass production was possible. The team then published their results in the *Lancet*, and the *British Medical Journal* published an editorial which, while noting Fleming's modest involvement at the beginning, lavished praise on the 'real' authors of the new 'wonder-drug'. Instantly Fleming mobilized Almroth Wright, head of Fleming's department at St Mary's Hospital, and Lord Moran, head of the hospital and confidant of Winston Churchill and Lord Beaverbrooke, to write to the *Times* proclaiming Fleming as the discoverer and thus a major press and political campaign was initiated that sidelined Florey *et al.* and promoted Fleming to 'leader' (Waller, 2002: 247–67).

Nevertheless, whoever is the 'real' leader, conventional leadership, it would seem, is naked. Search as one may for a definition of leadership that encompasses anything beyond the human, the most likely trail leads back to the comforting figure of a homo sapien. Few would disagree with Northouse's (1997: 3) view that leadership 'is a process whereby an individual influences a group of individuals to achieve a common goal' but my particular concern here is whether the identity of the leader is necessarily human, and if so is it sufficient just to be a human, in reality to be a naked leader?

In some ways the 'transparent' appearance of a human leader can be effective. For instance, in July 2002, the Chevron-Texaco Escravos oil terminal in Nigeria (then producing around 1/2 million barrels of oil per day) was closed by 150 women demanding schools, health clinics, pollution clean up, water supplies and jobs. After a 10-day occupation and no concessions from the company the women threatened to remove all their clothes – a symbol of enormous cultural shame – that eventually forced the company to agree to their demands.[8] Nevertheless, naked humans are often the weakest link in any hybrid and that generates a search for stronger resources. Edwards (1979) reinforces this with his argument that the development of what he called Technical Control – assembly lines and the like – was a form of non-human persuasion that developed in response to the problems of Personal Control in factories. Once bullying supervisors and factory bosses became counter-productive – because of the resistance they generated amongst the labour force – Technical Control replaced Personal Control because subordinates were less resistant to being 'led' by things than to being led by people. This, of course, begs the question: what does it mean to be 'led'? If 'to lead' implies 'to set goals and alter behaviour to achieve those goals' then we could still argue that assembly lines 'lead' people. That is, the machinery sets the required output of widgets and then persuades its human operatives to exert effort in specific ways to achieve this output. Of course, there is a human 'behind' the machinery but Edwards' claim is that machines embody superior persuasive techniques to humans in these circumstances.

We might want to differentiate here between leadership as means and ends. For instance, the assembly line is the *means* by which workers are 'led' to act. But the *ends* do not originate in the machinery; instead the 'ends' are constructed by the present but invisible human leader. So does this analytic separation solve the problem: non-humans can be the means to lead but not the ends? Well, self-evidently human leaders cannot dissociate themselves from technical supports completely, for even at a mundane level leaders usually act in a 'dressed' manner, surrounded by all kinds of technologies and non-human supports, so, in effect, there are no 'pure' leaders, though the issues of purity and contamination remain crucial (Douglas, 2002), hence all the concern for dressing in a culturally appropriate manner for a leader, whether that is a pinstriped suit, a sports jersey, a twin-set, a sari or whatever. Latour (1988), for example, makes a robust case for Actor-Network theory with his suggestion that a naked Napoleon would have been markedly less effective than a clothed Napoleon, surrounded by clothed soldiers with weapons.

Actor-Network Theory has a history and origin that need not detain us here (see Callon, 1986; Latour, 1993; Law and Hassard, 1999) but it suggests both that wholly social relations are inconceivable – because all humans rely upon and work through non-human forms, through hybrids – and that humans distinguish themselves from animals, amongst other things, on the basis of the durability or obduracy of their relations. That is, they encase their social relations into material forms. This does not mean that material forms determine things but that these material forms are an effect of the relations.

Does this imply anything about the link between hybridity and agency? We do not need to enter the debate about whether the future is destined to be dominated by robots or Cyborgs here (see Brooks, 2002; Geary, 2002; Haraway, 1991) to note the increasing degree of hybridity amongst 'people'. In Actor-Network terms agency sits in the hybrids, rather than located within either the humans or the non-humans whose relationship forms the hybrid actant (Latour, 1993). And an actant – that is something that acts or to which activity is granted by others – implies no special motivation of human individual actors, or of humans in general. An actant can literally be anything provided it is legitimated as the source of an action (Latour, 1993: 4). Hence, for example, when the regular 'Human versus Machine' chess competitions appear, are we to assume that the 'Machine' side has no human input or that the 'Human' side has had nothing to do with technology?

Yet it could still be argued that non-human leadership fails because the non-human element of the network does not instigate the changes and does not act as a *mobilizer* of networks: human leaders are not naked but naked technologies cannot lead because they do not instigate the vision or mobilization. Thus it is the pivotal *creative* role played by humans in these collaborative hybrids that distinguishes them as *primus inter pares*. But this is a little like saying the driver is the most important part of a car; in some sense that might be true but without a car you cannot drive (Michael, 2001). And precisely what the creative forces of the network are is debatable: God, alcohol, human emotion, destiny, culture and genes are all potential culprits here. Moreover, since invented futures have to be inscribed and communicated, and since humans are never without technological supports, we might still argue that human–non-human networks are critical for leadership. In essence, we might conclude that the search for an essence is irrelevant because the important element is the hybrid not the elements that comprise the hybrid, nor any alleged network essence. If this is valid then 'human' leaders should be reconsidering how they can strengthen the links in the hybrid networks not because non-humans do not embody volition but because non-human leadership is as mythically pure as human leadership. And there lies the (essentially contested) rub – it isn't the consciousness of leaders that makes them leaders or makes them effective, it's their hybridity; not how they think but how they are linked. We will pursue this particular creature in Chapter 2.

Result-based leadership

It might be more appropriate to take the result-based approach because without results there is little support for leadership. There may be thousands of individuals who are 'potentially' great leaders but if that potential is never realized, if no products of that leadership are forthcoming, then it would be logically difficult to speak of these people as 'leaders' – except in the sense of 'failed' or 'theoretical' leaders': people who actually achieve little or nothing. On the other hand, there is a tendency (e.g., Ulrich *et al.*, 1999) to focus on products as the primary criteria for leadership: since X achieved a 200 per cent increase in profits, or 'led' the team to victory, or successfully 'led' the defence of the nation, they must be successful leaders. Of course, there is then an issue about *which* products should be pursued by leaders and Elkington (1999) has argued vigorously that unless the 'Triple Bottom Line' – environmental quality and social justice as well as economic prosperity – are included then product or results-based approaches are ultimately doomed. But there are two other issues that need further examination here: first, how do we attribute the collective products of an organization to the actions of the individual leader? Second, assuming that we can causally link the two, do the methods by which the products are achieved play any role in determining the presence of leadership?

The first issue – that we can trace effects back to the actions of individual leaders – is deeply controversial. On the one hand there are several studies from a psychological approach that suggest it is possible to measure the effect of leaders (e.g., Gerstner and Day, 1997) but more sociologically inclined authors often deny the validity of such measures (e.g., Alvesson and Sveningsson, 2003). A related controversy suggests that this dispute is itself deeply encased within most traditional approaches to leadership and implies that leaders embody agency. Lee and Brown (1994) suggest that to be human is to possess agency but this, of course, begs the question of agency itself. Volition is the exercise of freewill or conscious choice, as opposed to determinism, hence, if human action is determined (by coercion, biological genes or technology or whatever) then the intentional element of leadership is removed and we may have a problem in determining individual responsibility. In effect, we may have products but no responsibility and therefore no leadership: thus the legal defence enacted by those who regard themselves as acting under duress. In fact, taking this approach to its logical conclusion in the case of biologically inherited characteristics would be to suggest that those leaders with 'criminal genes' are not responsible for their leadership of criminal gangs, even if the results are significant in terms of people killed or money stolen and so on. And if we insist that action is determined by biological requirements over which individuals have no volitional control then we might even consider looking for the leadership gene that is making them act.

Yet we still regard people as leaders even if they are not 'responsible'. For example, we do not hold young children or the insane as responsible for their actions but they can still lead others on. Indeed, it may be that some cult leaders are schizophrenic – and thus not capable of volitional control as we ordinarily understand it – but they are still leaders. In other words, even individuals who are irrational, unreasonable, insane or under the influence of drugs, can still act as leaders provided we assess their leadership through the results of their action rather than their intention, volition or responsibility.

One could also argue that leadership can be linked to fatalism amongst followers or subordinates. For example, Nelson, Churchill, Hitler, Martin Luther King, Joan of Arc and General Patton, to name but a few, are all associated with significant achievements – for better or for worse – but all believed themselves to have been chosen by fate for a particular and very significant mission on earth. This fatalism induces enormous self-confidence and facilitates what others would regard as dangerous risk-taking. Yet this stymies our account of leadership – for now leadership is divorced from volition. In effect, if leaders believe themselves to have no choice and no freedom of action, because of a particular belief structure or threat, or religion or whatever, then no matter what we, the observers, might decide, these leaders experience their leadership as non-volitional, as determined by forces beyond their control.

The most extreme case against results-based leadership – especially the results of 'Great Men' – is made by Tolstoy in *War and Peace* in which he likens leaders to bow-waves of moving boats – always in front and theoretically leading, but, in practice, not leading but merely being pushed along by the boat itself. In the same context-determined approach, Peter Sellers in the movie *Being There* plays Chancy Gardner, a simple-minded gardener who is mistaken for a very successful business executive. Because of the assumptions made by those around him Chancy's homilies on gardening are interpreted as Zen-like statements of wisdom about the economy and as a consequence Chancy becomes the 'leading' economic forecaster to the US President.

In such approaches the role of the leader is not necessarily to cause things to happen but to act as 'hero' when events work out advantageously and to act as 'scapegoat' when things go wrong; after all, it is usually very difficult, for example, to establish precisely what contribution a professional sports' coach makes to a team's performance – but it is usually far easier (and cheaper) to replace the coach than to replace the entire team. So while Gemmill and Oakley (1997) conclude that leadership is probably just an 'alienating social myth' – an essentially contested concept if ever there was one – it might also be a convenient social myth. Whether it is a myth or not depends upon causally relating the results to the leader and, as such, the practical achievements rather than the personal characteristics of the leader are manifestations of this shifting in attention from leadership as a noun to leadership as a verb (Hosking, 1988). Even when we may be assured that individuals are responsible for remarkable results the failure of such 'stars' to perform elsewhere suggests that results are as much to do with a supportive culture and system as anything individuals can do. For example, the analysis of 1000 'star' US stock analysts in the 1990s by Groysberg et al. (2004) suggests that it is very difficult for them to replicate their success elsewhere because they are so dependent on their prior support system and because the staff of their new organizations often resent the new 'transplants' and overall performance often deteriorates.

This brings us to the second issue at the heart of result-based leadership – does the process by which the results are achieved actually matter? Most certainly, the office or school bully who successfully 'encourages' followers to comply under threat of punishment becomes a leader under the results-based criteria – providing they are successful in their coercion and its effects. But such a results-based approach to leadership immediately sets it at odds with some perspectives that differentiate leaders according to some putative distinction between leadership – which is allegedly non-coercive – and all other forms of activity that we might regard as the actions of a 'bully' or a 'tyrant' and so on. Northouse (1997: 7–8), for instance, examines 'leaders who use coercion [such as] … Adolf Hitler … Jim Jones'. But he then suggests that we should distinguish between coercion and leadership and thus writes a large proportion of human 'leadership' out of view by implying that 'Leaders who use coercion are interested in their own goals and seldom interested in the wants and needs of subordinates.' A recent review by Doh (2003) of six leading leadership scholars reflects this line and suggests that the use of 'unethical' methods negates the claim to 'leadership'. Since what counts as 'ethical' behaviour is not discussed this leaves us stuck in the contestable ethical treacle: it could be argued that Hitler was unethical and therefore was not a leader or it could be argued, as suggested above, that since Hitler managed to align his followers' 'ethics' in line with his own the issue is not the pursuit of some indefinable ethical position but the mutual alignment of what counts as 'ethics'.

The confusion between coercion and leadership, and the conflation of coercion and self-interest, are dubious logical steps at best and at worst remain essentially contested concepts. It should be apparent that many coercive leaders believe themselves to be working for the benefit of the group not themselves and, furthermore, it is difficult to think of any leader who is not, to some extent, coercive. Indeed, most aspects of leadership use motivational strategies that can be regarded by some people – especially those subject to them – as coercive. Thus a religious charismatic might regard his or her actions as simply based on revealing the truth to their followers – who are then free to choose to follow or not as they wish. But if the followers believe that failure to adhere to religious principles will lead to eternal damnation and a slow roast in hell, then they might consider that as coercive. Equally, an employer may not regard an employment contract as coercive since both parties freely enter into it, but if the employee feels that failing to work at the requisite level will lead to 'the sack' – with all its attendant embarrassment, discrimination and penury – then he or she may believe the contract to be coercive. Nevertheless, for those who perceive leadership to be primarily focused on results, the process by which these results were obtained, or even whether the leader was responsible for them, may be insignificant.

Of course results-based leadership need not be restricted to authoritarian or unethical leaders; on the contrary, it can also be exemplified by eminently practical people who may be distinctly uncharismatic but very effective in getting things done. Much of their work may often go unnoticed but it may also be critical in keeping the organization moving, and this form of leadership may be associated with an appeal to the interests of followers, rather than their emotional relationships.

One particularly well-supported case of this is Benjamin Franklin whose approach seems not to have been one of articulating a compelling vision and rousing the emotion of followers to transcend their personal interests in favour of the greater good. On the contrary, Franklin's pragmatic leadership was rooted in finding practical solutions to outstanding problems that engaged the interests, rather than the emotions, of others. Yet those mobilized by Franklin were not simply involved in an exchange process with him, as understood in transactional theories of leadership, because, for example, in instigating the development in Philadelphia of a police force, a hospital, a paper currency, paving, lighting and volunteer fire departments and so on, Franklin's skill lay in persuading his colleagues to help solve their own practical problems (Mumford and Van Doorn, 2001). An important point here is the visibility of Franklin's leadership, for although the results are clear, the hand that secures the results is not. In effect, if Franklin had died early in his career it may well be that much of this backroom networking may not have become apparent and that he would not have been considered a great leader. Thus results-based leadership can embody both highly visible charismatic individuals and almost completely invisible 'social engineers' but, as I suggested above, not everyone accepts that the most important issue is the results rather the methods, so does focusing upon the processes by which leadership is recognized offer a radically different perspective?

Process-based leadership

There is an assumption that people that we attribute the term leadership to, act differently from non-leaders – that some people 'act like leaders' – but what does this mean? It could mean that the context is critical, or that leaders must be exemplary or that the attribution of difference starts early in the life of individuals such that 'natural' leaders can be perceived in the school play grounds or on the sports field etc. But what is this 'process' differential? We might drag on stage a whole host of leadership types to flesh out this typology. The errant sergeant major would be a good start with the archetypal call: 'Do as I say not as I do', which can, of course, be linked to its opposite 'Walk the Talk.' So are leaders those that allegedly embody the exemplary performance we require to avoid any hint of hypocrisy? And when sacrifice is required or new forms of behaviour demanded from followers is it exemplary leaders that are the most successful?

Perhaps, but think of two counter-examples that contradict this ideal type: first, sergeant majors tend to secure followers whether they embody exemplary action or not. We might argue, following Northouse, that coercive sergeant majors who scream at recruits on the parade ground are not 'really' leaders, but if their leadership processes do indeed produce trained soldiers are we to deduce that the military, because it is rooted in coercive mechanisms, cannot demonstrate leadership? Or is it that what counts as legitimate leadership processes depends upon the local culture? That is, soldiers expect to be coerced and would probably not recognize attempts by their sergeants or officers to reach a consensus by egalitarian debate as 'leadership'? And since military cultures differ radically in space and time we cannot even suggest that the processes of leadership can be recognized by their occupational context because that also remains contested. If it did not then we would have difficulty explaining the outbreak of mutinies or even the Xmas Truce in December 1914 (Weintraub, 2002).

The second counter-example is Admiral Nelson, an individual whose military successes were almost always grounded in a paradoxical situation wherein he demanded absolute obedience from his subordinates to naval regulations but who personally broke just about every rule in that same rule book (Grabsky, 1993). Yet Nelson's success was not simply a consequence of rule-breaking actions but also a result of his engagement with, and motivation of, his followers, most importantly his fellow officers in his battle fleet, his 'Band of Brothers' (Kennedy, 2001). Hence, at one level this process approach may encompass the specific skills and resources that motivate followers: rhetoric, coercion, bribery, exemplary behaviour, bravery and so on. Leadership under this guise is necessarily a relational concept, not a possessional one. In other words, it does not matter whether you think you have great process skills if your followers disagree with you. Thus it may be that we can recognize leadership by the behavioural processes that differentiate leaders from followers, but this does not mean we can simply list the processes as universally valid across space and time.

After all, we would not expect a second century Roman leader to act in the same way as a twenty-first century Italian politician, but neither would we expect an American Indian leader to act in a fashion indistinguishable from an American President (Warner, 2003). Yet it remains the case that most of our assumptions about leadership relate to our own cultural context rather than someone else's.

Indeed, while many accounts of the leadership process might focus upon the acts of 'Great Men' it has long been a point of great controversy as to whether men and women lead in the same way or in ways that are genetically or culturally influenced by their genders. And while Carlyle's heroic 'men' *solve* the problems of their followers Heifetz and Linsky (2002) suggest that leadership is really related to what they call 'Adaptive' rather than 'Technical' work. Here Adaptive work requires novel responses by those facing the problem and thus leadership means making followers face up to their own responsibilities. Technical work, on the other hand, can be resolved by managers who have the authority to execute pre-existing routines and procedures. In sum, if there is an essential process of leadership for Heifetz and Linsky it is as much to do with making followers responsible as with anything the leader does – an interpretation directly at odds with that of Carlyle. Gemmill and Oakley (1997: 281) take a similar line to suggest that 'Leadership as a social process can be defined as a process of dynamic collaboration, where individuals and organizational members authorize themselves and others to interact in ways that experiment with new forms of intellectual and emotional meaning.'

In effect, the process approach to leadership is more concerned with how leadership works – the practices through which they lead – their rhetorical skill that entrances the followers, or their inducing of obedience through coercion or whatever happens to work. But whatever the dispute about the processes, none of these seem important without some element of positioning. What, for instance, is the use of great rhetorical skill or having a big stick when you are in solitary confinement or on a desert island?

Position-based leadership

Perhaps the most traditional way of configuring leadership is to suggest that it is really concerned with a spatial position in an organization of some kind – formal or informal. Thus we can define leadership as the activity undertaken by someone whose position on a vertical, and usually formal, hierarchy provides them with the resources to lead. These are 'above us', 'at the top of the tree', 'superordinates' and so on. In effect, they exhibit what we might call 'Leadership-in-Charge'. This is how we normally perceive the heads of vertical hierarchies, whether CEOs or military generals or Head Teachers or their equivalents. These people lead from their positional control over large networks of subordinates and tend to drive any such required change from the top. That 'drive' also hints at the coercion that is available to those in-charge: a general can order executions, a judge can imprison people and a CEO can discipline or sack employees and so on. But note that Hughes *et al.* (1999) remain adamant that position is not related to leadership so, yet again, we have an ECC at the heart of the issue.

A related aspect of this vertical structuring is what appears to be the parallel structuring of power and responsibility. Since the leader is 'in charge', then presumably he or she can ensure the enactment of his or her will. But we should be wary of this parallel universe that irreversibly links a hierarchy of labels to a hierarchy of power because there are good grounds for linking them both in obverse and in reverse. That is to say, that the hierarchy of power simultaneously inverts the hierarchy of labels. While a formal leader may *demand* obedience from his or her subordinates – and normally acquire it because, *inter alia*, of the resource imbalance – that obedience is never guaranteed. In fact, following Lukes (1979), one could suggest that power encompasses a counterfactual possibility, a subjunctivist verb tense rather than just a verb – it could have been otherwise. Indeed, one could well argue that power is not just a cause of subordinate action but also a consequence of it: if subordinates do as leaders demand then, and only then, are leaders powerful.

The limitations of restricting leadership to a position within a vertical hierarchy are also exposed when we move to consider Leadership-in-Front, a horizontal approach, in which leadership is largely unrelated to vertical hierarchies and is usually informally constituted through a network or a heterarchy (a flexible and fluid hierarchy). Leadership-in-Front might be manifest in several forms, and where it merges into Leadership-in-Charge might be at the penultimate rank at the bottom of a hierarchy. For instance, within an army such leadership might be manifest in corporals who have some degree of formal authority but may secure their position with the private soldiers – their followers – through leading from the front. Indeed, the leadership abilities of low-level leaders may be critical in differentiating the success of armies, both in prior conflicts and in the current focus on 'strategic corporals' in the US Marine Corps (Krulak, 1999).

More commonly, though, we might conceive of Leadership-in-Front from a fashion leader – someone who is 'in front' of his or her followers, whether that is trends in clothing, music, business models or whatever. These leaders provide guides to the mass of fashion-followers without any formal authority over them. But leading from the front also encompasses those who guide others, either a professional guide showing the way or simply whoever knows the best way to an agreed destination amongst a group of friends on a Sunday stroll; both guides exhibit leadership through their role in front but neither is necessarily formally instituted into an official hierarchy. Indeed, often these informal guides – such as Native American Indian guides in the US Army in the nineteenth century – are situated beyond the boundaries of the formal organization. And again these horizontal leaders are commonly related to a temporal dimension: they are 'the first' to signify, recognize or embody new fashions and they are also the first to shed 'yesterday's' approach and maintain their leadership by being 'ahead of their time'.

Often such informal horizontal leaders position themselves in conscious opposition to vertical leaders: for instance, Michael Moore's career as film maker embodies little of the conventional authority rooted in organizational hierarchies but his films against President George W. Bush and the Iraq War – *Fahrenheit 9/11* – and against the American gun-culture – *Bowling for Columbine* – demonstrate a very powerful form of leadership against the establishment. We might even retrace the origins of the English words for leadership to shed light on this aspect. The etymological roots of 'Leadership' derive from the Old German '*Lidan*' to go, the Old English '*Lithan*' to travel, and the Old Norse '*Leid*' to find the way at sea. Thus the origins tend to support both vertical and horizontal positional approach.

The horizontal perspective generates a rather more positive role for the followers of leaders. The English word 'Follower' is derived from the Old English word *Folgian* and the Old Norse *Fylgja*, meaning to accompany, help or lead. The etymological roots are relatively positive and are reproduced in the following current definitions:

1. An ordinary person who accepts the leadership of another
2. Someone who travels behind or pursues another
3. One who follows; a pursuer, an attendant, a disciple, a dependent associate, a retainer

However, the negative images of 'follower' are more clearly visible in these definitions:

4. A person or algorithm that compensates for lack of sophistication or native stupidity by efficiently following some simple procedure shown to have been effective in the past
5. A sweetheart, a Trollope
6. (Steam Engine) The removable flange of a piston
7. The part of a machine that receives motion from another; Gaelic, for instance, surname ending in 'agh' or 'augh' means 'follower of' – Cavanagh stands for 'Follower of Kevin'

Those readers familiar with Harry Enfield's character 'Kevin' – a teenage nightmare of sullenness and irresponsibility – will note that the diminution of the role of follower in the light of the superordinate 'leader' is much closer to the vertical notion of leadership than its horizontal equivalent.

Leadership-in-Front might also be provided in the sense of legitimizing otherwise prohibited behaviour. For instance, we might consider how Hitler's overt and public anti-Semitism legitimated the articulation of anti-Semitism by his followers. And again it has been suggested that acts such as suicide provide 'permission' by 'leaders-in-front' for others to follow, hence there are often spates of similar acts in quick succession almost as if the social behaviour operates as a biological epidemic (Gladwell, 2002).

Leadership along this positional dimension, then, differs according to the extent to which it is formally or informally structured, and vertically or horizontally constituted. Leadership-in-Charge implies some degree of centralizing resources and authority, while Leadership-in-Front implies the opposite.

Conclusion

I began by suggesting that although it has become fashionable to comment on the importance of leadership, in its positive and negative impacts, it is by no means clear that the twenty-first century poses unique problems for leaders, let alone that some people's definitions of 'moral' leadership is the solution to the world's contemporary problems. Indeed, there appears to be little consensus on what defines leadership and hence considerable conflict over what counts as demonstrations of leadership, whether leadership can be taught and what its effects might be. Following a brief review of four leading leadership texts I then reduced the multiplicity of accounts to four approaches to leadership that embody significantly different approaches. Although all four approaches are adopted by different organizations at different times the lack of clarity as to which definition of leadership is being used can inhibit organizational success.

If organizational leaders assume that leadership is primarily *positional* so that, for example, only those people in formal positions of power are recognized as leaders, then those without formal positions may well be discouraged from taking actions that are vital for organizational success but deemed by the formal leaders to be irrelevant. Hence it may be that risk-taking, showing initiative, taking responsibility and so on are not actions that non-formal leaders will take. The result may well be an extremely bureaucratic and torpid organization.

On the other hand, for some interpretations leadership is essentially related to *results*, though whether we can causally relate the results to an individual leader, and, if we can, whether we can ignore the processes by which these results were achieved, or what the results were, is very debateable. Nevertheless, if organizations consider leadership to be manifest only or primarily through results and nothing else then we should not be surprised to find hospitals and schools manipulating their activities to generate the requisite results even if the overall performance as a health or education provider plummets. Nor should we be surprised by the Enrons of this world: if shareholders only recognize result-based leadership then ethical and process issues tend to be sidelined.

Those *processes* of leadership imply that we can distinguish leaders from non-leaders on the basis of examining what it is that leaders do but, irrespective of the issue of coercion, it is still not clear that successful leaders are necessarily exemplary nor that such processes are generic across space and time. Again, if the form by which leaders are judged is the extent to which they embody the required formal processes then we may end up with leaders who are excellent 'actors', whose behaviours are tightly tied to the monitoring requirements but who are actually rather ineffective in generating results.

Finally, I suggested that even when we revert to the *person* of leaders we are still no nearer a consensus, not simply because so much lies in the eyes of the beholder but also because leaders appear to be essentially hybrids of human and non-humans. Yet, even here the traditional analytic approaches to understanding and predicting leadership proved inadequate because hybrid leadership is a performance to be achieved not a script to be rolled out. In short, hybrid leadership is more appropriately configured not simply as a verb rather than a noun but as a specific tense of verb: subjunctivist – something that *might* occur, rather than something that has occurred or will occur. And if it does occur then leadership is an effect as much as a cause of this. Leadership remains then, like power, an ECC. And because it remains contested exactly how we recognize, train, teach, exert and limit leadership depends fundamentally on that first definitional step.

Notes

1. See: Mech, D.L. 'Leadership in Wolf, *Canis lupus*, Packs' at http://www.npwrc.usgs.gov/resource/2001/leader/results.htm and http://home.globalcrossing.net/~brendel/wolf.html
2. For related papers see: http://ideas.repec.org/e/pfe29.html
3. See Hassard, 1996 for a review of the importance of Time in organizations.
4. Thanks to David Knowles of the Kings Fund for this example.
5. See http://www.cnn.com/2003/US/02/05/sprj.irq.powell.transcript/
6. See http://www.cs.umb.edu/jfklibrary/cmc_exhibit_2002.html This episode is also captured in the 2002 movie *Thirteen Days*.
7. See Chapter 9 of Bratton, J., Grint, K. and Nelson, D. (January 2004), *Organizational Leadership* (Mason OH: Thomson-Southwestern).
8. http://www.corpwatch.org/news/PND.jsp?articleid=3128 accessed 20 November 2003.

Leadership as person: putting the 'ship' back into 'leader-ship'

Introduction

This chapter takes its starting point from the approach to leadership that perceives it to be a consequence of a person – an individual human who embodies and demonstrates personal characteristics traditionally associated with leaders. However, the first part suggests that this reduction of leadership to the individual human constitutes an analytically inadequate explanatory foundation and this is illustrated by reference to the importance of followers and especially their commitment to 'sense-making', to their community and to independence from their leader. Hence the subtitle: putting the 'ship' back into leadership. I go on to suggest that leadership might be better configured as a function of the community – 'the god of small things' – rather than the result of superhuman individuals. However, this expansion of the term 'person' is still unable to explain how leadership actually occurs and for this I then explore the viability of approaching leadership beyond its individual human embodiment and beyond a collective human form towards a notion of hybridity. That notion is then tested against a second account of putting the ship back into leadership – this time moving beyond the 'ship' conceived as the crew to the literal ships that were used to 'lead' troops on D-Day to the Normandy beaches.

Leadership, followership, commitment and independence

When listing the traits required by formal leaders it is usual for a class to come up with any number of characteristics: charisma, energy, vision, confidence, tolerance, communication skills, 'presence', the ability to multitask, listening skills, decisiveness, team building, 'distance', strategic skills and so on and so forth. No two lists constructed by leadership students or leaders ever seem to be the same and no consensus exists as to which traits or characteristics or competences are essential or optional. Indeed, the most interesting aspect of list-making is that by the time the list is complete the only plausible description of the owner of such a skill base is 'god'. Irrespective of whether the traits are contradictory it is usually impossible for anyone to name leaders who have all these traits, at least to any significant degree; yet it seems clear that all these traits are necessary to a successful organization. Thus we are left with a paradox: the leaders who have all of these – the omniscient leaders – do not exist but we seem to need them. Indeed, complaints about leaders and calls for more or better leadership occur on such a regular basis that one would be forgiven for assuming that there was a time when good leaders were ubiquitous. Sadly a trawl through the leadership archives reveals no golden past but nevertheless a pervasive yearning for such an era. An urban myth like this 'Romance of Leadership' – the era when heroic leaders were allegedly plentiful and solved all our problems – is not only misconceived but positively counter-productive because it sets up a model of leadership that few, if any of us, can ever match and thus it inhibits the development of leadership, warts and all. It should be no surprise, then, to see, for example, the continuous re-advertising of vacancies for head teachers when the possibilities of success are either beyond the control of individuals or so clearly defined by comparative reference to Superman and Wonderwoman that only those who can walk on water need apply: not for these leaders the Latin warning: *nemo sine vitio est* (no one is without fault).

The traditional solution to this kind of recruitment problem, or the perceived weakness of contemporary business chief executives or directors of public services or not-for-profit organizations, is to demand better recruitment criteria so that the 'weak' are selected out, leaving the 'strong' to save the day. But this is to reproduce the problem not to solve it. An alternative approach might be to start from where we are, not where we would like to be: with all leaders, because they are human, as flawed individuals, not all leaders as the embodiments of all that we merely mortal and imperfect followers would like them to be: perfect. The former approach resembles a White Elephant – in both dictionary definitions: as a mythical beast that is itself a deity, and as an expensive and foolhardy endeavour. Indeed, in Thai history the King would give a White Elephant to an unfavoured noble because the special dietary and religious requirements would ruin the noble.

The White Elephant is also a manifestation of Plato's approach to leadership, for to him the most important question was 'Who should lead us?'. The answer, of course, was the wisest amongst us: the individual with the greatest knowledge, skill, power and resources of all kinds. This kind of approach echoes our current search criteria for omniscient leaders and leads us unerringly to select charismatics, larger than life characters and personalities whose magnetic charm, astute vision and personal forcefulness will displace all the bland and miserable failures that we have previously recruited to that position – though strangely enough using precisely the same selection criteria. Unless the new leaders are indeed Platonic Philosopher-Kings, endowed with extraordinary wisdom, they will surely fail sooner or later and then the whole circus will start again, probably with the same result.

Of course for Plato it was more than likely that the leaders would be men, after all Greek women were not even citizens of their own city states, though he did admit that it was theoretically possible that a woman might have all the natural requirements of leadership. Since Plato's time, assumptions about the role of gender in leadership have varied enormously, even if the presence of women as leaders has proved remarkably limited and remarkably stable. It is well known that the proportion of women declines rapidly as they rise through the organizational hierarchies (see Bratton *et al.*, 2004: 180–99) but the explanation for this often reproduces the person-based criteria for defining leadership. For example, Goldberg (1993) and Browne (2002) insist that the chemical hormones, especially testosterone, generate behavioural patterns that leave men 'naturally' more suited to positions of dominance and leadership than women who are 'naturally' less aggressive. Whether aggression is necessarily and essentially linked to leadership is, of course, a moot point; aggressive men may bully their subordinates into compliance but this does not necessarily equate with effective leadership, especially in the long run. Thus even if we could select for aggression we cannot determine whether this particular 'trait' is advantageous for leadership.

An alternative approach is to start from the inherent weakness of leaders and work to inhibit and restrain this, rather than to assume it will not occur. Karl Popper provides a firmer foundation for this in his assumption that just as we can only disprove rather than prove scientific theories, so we should adopt mechanisms that inhibit leaders rather than surrender ourselves to them. For Popper, democracy was an institutional mechanism for deselecting leaders, rather than a benefit in and of itself, and, even though there are precious few democratic systems operating within non-political organizations, similar processes ought to be replicable elsewhere. Otherwise, although omniscient leaders are a figment of irresponsible followers' minds and utopian recruiters' fervid imagination, when subordinates question their leader's direction or skill these (in)subordinates are usually replaced by those 'more aligned with the current strategic thinking' – otherwise known as Yes People. In turn, such subordinates become transformed into Irresponsible Followers whose advice to their leader is often limited to Destructive Consent: they may know that their leader is wrong but there are all kinds of reasons not to say as much, hence they consent to the destruction of their own leader and possibly their own organization too.

Popper's warnings about leaders, however, suggest that it is the responsibility of followers to inhibit leaders' errors and to remain as Constructive Dissenters, helping the organization achieve its goals but not allowing any leaders to undermine this. Thus Constructive Dissenters attribute the assumptions of Socratic Ignorance rather than Platonic Knowledge to their leaders: they know that nobody is omniscient and act accordingly.

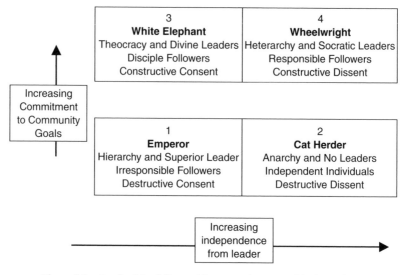

Figure 2.1 Leadership, followership, commitment and independence

Of course, for this to work subordinates need to remain committed to the goals of the community or organization while simultaneously retaining their spirit of independence from the whims of their leaders, and it is this paradoxical combination of commitment and independence that provides the most fertile ground for Responsible Followers. Figure 2.1 above outlines the possible combinations of this mix of commitment and independence. Again this is for illustrative purposes and generates a series of Weberian 'ideal types' that are neither 'ideal' in any normative sense nor 'typical' in any universal sense. On the contrary, these types are for heuristic purposes, designed to flag up and magnify the extreme consequences of theoretically polar positions.

Despite these reservations, Box 1 – the hierarchy – probably contains the most typical form of relationship between leaders and followers wherein a conventional hierarchy functions under a leader deemed to be superior to his or her followers by dint of superior *personal* qualities of intelligence, vision, charisma and so on and so forth, and thus to be responsible for solving all the problems of the organization. Such imperial ambitions resonate with the label for this form of leader: the emperor. In turn, that generates followers who are only marginally committed to the organization's goals – often because these are reduced to the personal goals of the leader – and hence the followers remain literally 'irresponsible' through the Destructive Consent that is associated with the absence of responsibility.

Box 2 is rooted in a similar level of disinterest in the community but, combined with an increase in the level of independence from the leader, the consequence is a formal 'anarchy' – without leadership – and without the community that supporters of anarchism suggest would automatically flow from the absence of individual leaders. The result is a leader that resembles a Herder of Cats – an impossible task.

Box 3 – the theocracy – generates that community spirit in buckets but only because the leader is deemed to be a deity, a divine leader whose disciples are compelled to obey through religious requirement: the White Elephant described above. That consent remains constructive if, and only if, the leader is indeed divine, a god in whom omniscience and omnipotence are unquestionably present. However, it is clear that although many charismatics generate cults that would ostensibly sit within this category the consent is destructive because the leader is in fact a false god, misleading rather than leading his or her disciples.

The final category, Box 4 – the heterarchy – denotes an organization where the leaders recognize their own limitations, in the fashion of Socrates, and thus leadership is distributed according to the perceived requirements of space and time (a rowing squad is a good example of a heterarchy in which the leadership switches between the cox, the captain, the stroke and the coach depending on the situation; the English rugby team that won the World Cup in 2003 operated on the same basis with a formal captain (Martin Johnson), plus 'captains' of the forwards, the backs, the line out and the scrum (Catt, 2004). That recognition of the limits of any individual leader generates a requirement for Responsible Followers to compensate for these limits which is best served through Constructive Dissent, in which followers are willing to dissent from their leader if the latter is deemed to be acting against the interests of the community.

Perhaps an ancient Chinese story, retold by Phil Jackson (1995: 149–51), coach of the phenomenally successful Chicago Bulls basketball team, makes this point rather more emphatically. In the third century BC the Chinese Emperor Liu Bang celebrated his consolidation of China with a banquet where he sat surrounded by his nobles and military and political experts. Since Liu Bang was neither a noble by birth nor an expert in military or political affairs some of the guests asked one of the military experts, Chen Cen, why Liu Bang was the Emperor. In a contemporary setting the question would probably have been: 'what added value does Liu Bang bring to the party?' Chen Cen's response was to ask the questioner a question in return: 'What determines the strength of a wheel?' One guest suggested the strength of the spokes but Chen Cen countered that two sets of spokes of identical strength did not necessarily make wheels of identical strength. On the contrary, the strength was also affected by the spaces between the spokes, and determining the spaces was the true art of the wheelwright. Thus while the spokes represent the collective resources necessary to an organization's success – and the resources that the leader lacks – the spaces represent the autonomy for followers to grow into leaders themselves.

In sum, holding together the diversity of talents necessary for organizational success is what distinguishes a successful from an unsuccessful leader: leaders don't need to be perfect but, on the contrary, they do have to recognize that the limits of their knowledge and power will ultimately doom them to failure unless they rely upon their subordinate leaders and followers to compensate for their own ignorance and impotence. Real White Elephants, albinos, do exist, but they are so rare as to be irrelevant for those who are looking for them to drag us out of the organizational mud; far better to find a good wheelwright and start the organizational wheel moving. In effect, leadership is the property and consequence of a community rather than the property and consequence of an individual leader.

Moreover, whereas White Elephants are born, wheelwrights are made. In fact the analogy is useful in distinguishing between the learning pedagogies of both, for while those who believe themselves born to rule need no teachers or advisers, but merely supplicant followers, those who are wheelwrights have to serve an apprenticeship in which they are taught how to make the wheel and in which trial and error play a significant role.

The attribution of god-like qualities by irresponsible followers to allegedly omniscient leaders also generates an equivalent assumption about the power of leaders. While Plato's leaders rest like mythical Greek gods in mount Olympus manipulating the lives of mortals at will and with irresistible power, Popper's leaders should be resisted for precisely this reason. Yet it should also be self-evident that an individual can have virtually no control over anything or anybody – as an *individual*. Indeed, we have known for a long time that leaders spend most of their time talking – not actually 'doing' anything else. In effect, leaders might pretend to be omnipotent, to have the future of their organizations and its members in their hands, but this can only ever be a symbolic or metaphorical control because leaders only get things done through others. In short, the power of leaders is a consequence of the actions of followers rather than a cause of it. If this were not so then no parents would ever be resisted by their children, no CEO would ever face a defeat by the board of directors, no general would suffer a mutiny, and no strikes would ever occur. That they do should lead us to conclude that no leader is omnipotent and that the kind of leadership is a consequence of the kind of followership, rather than a cause of it. Thus while Plato's leaders might construct formal hierarchies for subordinates to execute their perfect orders, Popper's leaders work through networks and relationships because that's where power is actually generated: it is essentially distributed like a wheel not concentrated in what is actually a White Elephant.

None of this is new: Helmuth von Motlke, Chief of the Prussian General Staff from 1857–88, understood Clausewitz's dictum that the local concentration of force was critical for military success and recognized that the nascent system of decentralized leadership already present in the Prussian army was crucial to achieving this. After all, a central commander in Berlin, or even 5 miles behind the battle had no way of understanding, let alone controlling, what was happening in each and every sector of the battle. The result was a system of leadership rooted in Mission Command – *Auftragstaktiker* or general directives, not specific orders, strategic aims not operational requirements, thereby enabling decentralized control that facilitated distributed leadership and the ability of local ground commanders to seize the initiative rather than await orders.[1]

Leadership as the god of small things

Another resolution of this paradox is that the focus should be shifted from the leader to leader*ship* – such that as a social phenomenon the leadership characteristics may well be present within the leadership team or the followers even if no individual possesses them all. Thus it is the crew of the metaphorical 'ship' not the literal ship's 'captain' that has the requirements to construct and maintain an organization; hence the need to put the 'ship' back into 'the leadership'. In other words, rather than leadership being restricted to the Gods it might instead be associated with the opposite. As Arundhati Roy remarks about her own novel, 'To me the god of small things is the inversion of God. God's a big thing and God's in control. The god of small things …'[2] Here I want to suggest that leadership is better configured as *The God of Small Things*.

The Big Idea, then, is that there isn't one; there are only lots of small actions taken by followers that combine to make a difference. This is not the same as saying that small actions operate as 'Tipping Points' (Gladwell, 2002), though they might, but rather that big things are the consequence of an accumulation of small things. An organization is not an oil tanker which goes where the captain steers it but a living and disparate organism, a network of individuals – its direction and speed is thus a consequence of many small decisions and acts (Barabási, 2003; Kilduff and Tsai, 2003). Or, as William Lowndes (1652–1724) [Auditor of the Land Revenue under Queen Anne] suggested, 'Take care of the pence and the pounds will take care of themselves.' This has been liberally translated as 'Take care of the small things and the big things will take care of themselves,' but the important thing here is to note the shift from individual heroes to multiple heroics. This doesn't mean that CEOs, Head Teachers, Chief Constables, Generals etc are irrelevant; their role is critical but limited and dependent upon the actions of subordinates, and indeed their own preparation for the 'big' decision that may derive from the accumulation of many small acts and decisions. In the words of Lord Naoshige (1538–1618) (a samurai war lord), 'Matters of great concern should be treated lightly' (Tsunemoto, 2000: 27).

Another way of putting this is that the traditional focus of many leadership studies – the decision-making actions of individual leaders – is better configured as the consequence of 'sense-making' activities by organizational members. As Weick (1995) suggests, what counts as 'reality' is a collective and ongoing accomplishment as people try to make sense of the 'mess of potage' that surrounds them, rather than the consequence of rational decision-making by individual leaders. That is not to say that sense-making is a democratic activity because there are always some people more involved in sense-making than others and these 'leaders' are those 'bricoleurs' – people who make sense from variegated materials that they are faced with, and manage to construct a novel solution to a specific problem from this assembly of materials.

Because of this, success and failure are often dependent upon small decisions and small acts – both by leaders and 'followers' who also 'lead'. This implies that we should abandon Plato's question: 'Who should rule us?' and focus instead on Popper's question: 'How can we stop our rulers ruining us?'.[3] In effect, we cannot secure omniscient leaders but because we concentrate on the selection mechanism those that become formal leaders often assume they are omniscient and are therefore very likely to make mistakes that may affect all of us mere followers and undermine our organizations.

Take, for example, Sir Clowdisley Shovell (1650–1707) a British Admiral who, returning home from an attack on Toulon in 1707, in his flagship 'Association', allegedly hanged a sailor who had the temerity to insist that the fleet was heading for the rocks off the Isles of Scilly. The fleet was subsequently lost on the aforementioned non-existent rocks with between 800 and 2,000 dead from all 4 ships.[4] Or the equally infamous Vice-Admiral Sir George Tryon whose actions on 22 June 1893 caused the loss of his own flagship, the *Victoria*, after he insisted that the fleet, then split into two columns, turn towards each other in insufficient space. Despite being warned by several subordinates that the operation was impossible Tryon insisted on its execution and 358 sailors were drowned – including Tryon. At the subsequent courts martial of Rear Admiral Markham on the *Camperdown* that rammed the *Victoria*, he was asked, if he knew it was wrong why did he comply? 'I thought' responded Markham, 'Admiral Tryon must have some trick up his sleeve.' The court found Tryon to blame but accepted that it 'would be fatal for the Navy to encourage subordinates to question superordinates'.[5] Thus, to misquote Burke, it only takes the good follower to do nothing for leadership to fail.[6]

Nor are attributions of omniscience limited to national military or political leaders alone. For example, when the Air Florida 90 ('Palm 90'), flight crashed on 13 January 1982 in poor weather conditions it is apparent from the conversation between Captain Larry Wheaton and the first Officer Roger Pettit that the latter was unconvinced that the plane was ready for lift off, yet his failure to stop Wheaton from going ahead inadvertently led to the crash.[7] Precisely the same thing occurred in the Tenerife air crash where the co-pilot thought that there was a problem but failed to prevent the pilot from taking off in a dangerous situation because his warnings were too 'mitigated' (another plane was taking off directly in front of them and, unbeknown to the co-pilot, his own pilot did not have permission to take off) (O'Hare and Roscoe, 1990: 219).

A similar level of 'inappropriate subordination' or 'irresponsible followers' seems to have occurred in Marks and Spencer. According to Judy Bevan, Richard Greenbury, having achieved significant successes, became more and more isolated from his subordinate board members to the point where they only engaged in Destructive Consent and not Constructive Dissent. As she remarks about one of the final board meetings through the words of a board member:

> The thing about Rick is that he never understood the impact he had on people – people were just too scared to say what they thought. I remember one meeting we had to discuss a new policy and two or three directors got me on one side beforehand and said they were really unhappy about it. Then Rick made his presentation and asked for views. There was total silence until one said, 'Chairman we are all 100% behind you on this one.' And that was the end of the meeting. (Bevan, 2002: 3)

Alfred Sloan, according to Drucker (2001: 254) faced a similar problem with his board but was able to recognize the manifestations of Destructive Consent, 'Gentlemen, I take it we are all in complete agreement on the decision here?' [Consensus of nodding heads.] 'Then I propose we postpone further discussion of this matter until our next meeting to give ourselves time to develop disagreement and perhaps gain some understanding of what the decision is all about.'

Three hundred years earlier Yamamoto Tsunetomo (2000: 37) recalled a similar problem in Japan:

> Last year at a great conference there was a certain man who explained his dissenting opinion and said that he was resolved to kill the conference leader if it was not accepted. This motion was passed. After the procedures were over the man said, 'Their assent came quickly. I think that they are too weak and unreliable to be counsellors to the master.'

This problem persists across all areas; take the case of Wayne Jowett who was erroneously injected with Vincristine, by the intrathecal (spinal) route on 4 January 2001, under the supervision of the Specialist Registrar Dr Mulhem, by Dr Morton, a Senior House Officer at the Queen's Medical Centre Nottingham (QMC).[8] Such a procedure almost always results in death but the issue here is not that a mistake was made. According to the BBC version of events:

> Dr Mulhem read out the name and dose of the drug, but he did not say how it should be administered and said that when he saw the Vincristine that he was thinking of another drug which is administered spinally. Dr Morton asked whether the Vincristine should be given spinally and said Dr Mulhem had told him yes. *He said he was surprised by this, but had not felt he could challenge a superior* (my emphasis).[9]

Note here how that the subordinate is, once again, concerned about the veracity of the decision made by the superordinate but feels unable or unwilling to challenge that decision.

If Paul O'Neill (former Treasury Secretary to George W Bush) is to be believed, then the American President operates along similar lines: he simply does not listen to his advisers prior to making decisions which are almost always rooted in political advantage – to the point where cabinet meetings were 'like a blind man in a roomful of deaf people' (quoted in Teather, 2004: 17). Unfortunately, not only are all leaders flawed – and thus incompetent to some degree or other – but most people are actually unable to recognize their own levels and areas of incompetence: to put it another way we don't know what we don't know (Kruger and Dunning, 1999).

Nor are the problems of knowledge and competence limited to individuals. In September 1998 Long Term Capital Management (LTCM), a Hedge Fund, was in debt to the tune of $4.6 billion and was only bailed out by the intervention of the US Federal Reserve organized by Greenspan.[10] LTCM included 2 Nobel Economics Prize winners and an ex-VC of the American Federal Reserve. It used complex math formulas to spread risk across a range of stocks, bonds etc and its sophistication encouraged Robert Merton (one of the Nobel Prize winners) to claim that the model 'would provide the perfect hedge'; it obviously did not (Stein, 2003: 56:5).

What can be done about this problem? Clearly the provision of honest and timely advice to leaders – Constructive Dissent – provides an appropriate solution but it is equally clear, first that leaders tend to discourage this by recruiting and appointing subordinates that are 'more aligned with the official line' – that usually means syco-phants and 'Yes People' who provide Destructive Consent. Moreover, leaders' unwill-ingness to admit to mistakes reinforces followers' attribution of omniscience. Historically only the royal 'Fool' or court jester could provide Constructive Dissent and survive, primarily because the advice was wrapped up in humour and therefore could be publicly dismissed by the monarch, even if privately he or she could then reconsider it rather more carefully. There is, perhaps, no better example of the diffi-culty and importance of this role than the Fool in Shakespeare's *King Lear*.

Lear, having given away his kingdom to his daughters in a show of bravado and omnipotence, is warned first by his loyal follower, Kent, that the action is foolhardy but Kent is exiled for his honesty. Then the Fool attempts the same advice but does so through a series of riddles that, unfortunately, Lear only begins to understand when it is too late:

> *Fool:* That lord that counsell'd thee
> To give away they land,
> Come place him here by me,
> Do thou for him stand:
> The sweet and bitter fool
> Will presently appear;
> The one in motley here,
> The other out there
>
> *Lear:* Dost thou call me fool, boy?
>
> *Fool:* All thy other titles thou hast given away; that thou wast born with.
>
> *King Lear*, Act 1 Scene 1, 154–65

It is possible to recreate the role of honest advisor played by Shakespeare's Fool with-out the 'motley' clothes and perhaps with more success, either by leaders relying on one or more individuals whose position cannot be threatened by the advice proffered, and it may also be possible to institutionalize the role by requiring all members of a decision-making body to enact the role of Devil's Advocate in turn. In this way the advice is required by the role and not derived from the individual and hence should provide some degree of protection from leaders annoyed by the 'helpful' but perhaps embarrassing advice of their subordinates.

Alternatively, in some cases the consequences of decisions by leaders are so critical that procedures may be developed to inhibit individual error of the kind exemplified in *Dr Strangelove* subtitled '*Or how I learned to stop worrying and love the bomb*'. In Stanley Kubrick's 1964 movie, an impotent US Air Force Commander single-handedly initiates the Third World War, aided and abetted by equally incompetent political and military leaders (several played by Peter Sellers). The notoriously dark humour of the film however, underlines the dangers of allowing individuals with limited knowledge to take critical decisions.

Ironically, and probably unknown to the film makers, two years before the film's release such a situation was almost enacted during the Cuban Missile Crisis in 1962. On Saturday 27 October that year, as the US and the USSR brought the world ever-closer to a nuclear stand-off over the deployment of Soviet nuclear missiles in Cuba, an American U-2 spy plane was shot down over Cuba at 13.41 hrs. At 16.00 hrs the American Joint Chiefs of Staff recommended an invasion of the island by Monday 29 October at the latest. Half an hour after this recommendation was made the American Navy destroyer, the USS Beale (DD 471), made sonar contact with an unknown submarine. At 16.59 hrs the Beale dropped five signalling depth charges on what turned out to be the Soviet submarine B-59. These depth charges are very small explosives designed to force the submarine to identify itself, rather than designed to destroy the submarine. Half an hour later, with no response from the submarine, the USS Cony dropped five more signalling depth charges on the B-59 which then tried to evade its American pursuers for four hours. However, technical problems on the submarine led to increased temperatures on the submarine (100°F), an oxygen problem and the beginnings of health problems amongst the soviet crew. According to the Soviet captain's (Valentin Savitsky) account, at this point the B-59 was then rocked by 'something bigger than a signalling depth charge'. Savitsky then ordered the crew to prepare for firing a nuclear torpedo at their 'attackers'. As he apparently stated: 'Maybe the war has already started up there, while we were doing somersaults here. We're going to blast them now! We will die but we will sink them all – we will not disgrace our navy.' Fortunately, the Soviet Navy's Rules of Engagement at the time required the agreement of three officers: the Captain plus the two deputy commanders. The first deputy commander agreed, but the second – Vasili Arkhipov – refused and the Captain was unable to fire the torpedo; instead the B-59 surfaced at 20.50 hrs. Understandably, Vasili Arkhipov was later lauded as 'the man who saved the world' but it is also important to note that the fail-safe procedures were critical to inhibit the intention of the captain (Blanton, 2002).

Perhaps the thing to note from these examples is that attributing god-like qualities to leaders does not result in god-like qualities – but it might encourage us to think of leaders as gods and take 'appropriate action'. For example, during the 2002 Football World Cup I asked my MBA class what kind of leader the English coach, Sven Goran Eriksson, was? The immediate answer from one English student was that since England had just beaten Argentina 'Sven must be a God!' But when I then asked what would happen if England lost their next game against Brazil the same student responded, 'We will crucify him!' Here is an intriguing dialogue for it exposes the attributions of saint and sinner, saviour and scapegoat, that hoists leaders onto pedestals that cannot support them and then ensures those same leaders are hoist by their own petard. What this also reveals is the consequence of attributing omnipotence to leaders – we, the followers, are rendered irresponsible by our own action, for when the gods of leadership fail their impossible task – as fail they must eventually – we followers have a scapegoat to take all the blame for what is, in reality, our own failure to accept responsibility.[11]

Alternatively, the Leadership as Person approach might be configured not so much as a self-imposed cover to distract us from our own frailty but a functional necessity for different groups at different times. Abraham Lincoln is an interesting illustration of this phenomenon: either a 'charismatic' leader who single-handedly saved the American union, revoked slavery and in Wills' (1992) terms, 'rewrote American history', or an ordinary and non-charismatic mortal who was not a champion of civil rights but a champion of the union, and was not a champion of freedom but wanted to free the slaves only to deport them, whose memory has been variously reconstructed and paraded to suit the perceived needs of later generations. Thus, his image only developed after his death, it waxed and waned over time and only really became identified with ideas of charisma at the beginning of the twentieth century (Schwartz, 2000). In effect, the image was both contested and changed as Americans faced a different world and required a different leadership icon through which the new world could be reinterpreted.

Similarly, our notions of Hitler as a charismatic leader need to be addressed very carefully. Lloyd George described him as 'a born leader, a magnetic dynamic personality with a single minded purpose' and this is supported by William Shirer, an American journalist watching the crowd at the 1934 Nürnberg rally – 'They looked up at him as if he were a Messiah, their faces transformed into something positively inhuman' (quoted in Lewis, 2003: 5–7). But contrast this with Fritz Wiedemann, Regimental Adjutant to the sixteenth Bavarian Reserve Infantry Regiment, who was singularly unimpressed by Corporal Hitler in the First World War:

> Hitler did not cut a particularly impressive figure. … (he) was an excellent soldier. A brave man, he was reliable, quiet and modest. But we could find no reason to promote him because he lacked the necessary qualities required to be a leader. … When I first knew him Hitler possessed no leadership qualities at all. (Quoted in Lewis, 2003: 4)

Quite how Hitler is transformed from a modest corporal into an egotistical tyrant is the subject of much dispute but suffice it to say that, like many historical leaders of significance (good and bad), Hitler came to believe himself destined to lead, in this case Germany to world domination. Lewis suggests that Hitler's treatment in 1918 for 'gas-induced blindness' by Edmund Forster, a psychiatrist specializing in military 'hysteria' was pivotal in this transformation. Forster recognized that Hitler was unlike any other 'hysterical' patient because he had no medical reason for the apparent blindness (normally diagnosed as lack of will) – but contrary to the norm – was desperate to return to the front. Forster's experimental solution was to suggest to Hitler that he was in fact permanently blind – unless Hitler was in fact the one person destined to lead Germany out of the abyss it had fallen into, in which case he would be able to heal himself through the domination of the will; he ostensibly did just this and the rest is (controversial) history. Whether an accurate explanation for Hitler's transformation or not, the point here is that self-belief, the submission to fate and destiny, both propels individuals to take enormous risks and generates a level of self-confidence that few conventional leaders display.

Nevertheless, the contested nature of charisma, both in terms of its origins and existence, leaves unresolved the yearning for perfection in leaders that perhaps also reflects our collective dissatisfaction with the lives of unacknowledged followers – the gods of small things. As Albert Schweitzer in his autobiography *Out of My Life and Thought* remarked,

> Of all the will toward the ideal in mankind only a small part can manifest itself in public action. All the rest of this force must be content with small and obscure deeds. The sum of these, however, is a thousand times stronger than the acts of those who receive wide public recognition. The latter, compared to the former, are like the foam on the waves of a deep ocean.

This is a critical assault upon the idea that leadership can be reduced to the personality and behaviour of the individual leader and implies that we should recognize that organizational achievements are just that – achievements of the entire organization rather than merely the consequence of a single heroic leader. Yet although it is collective leaders and collective followers that move the wheel of history along it is often their formal or more Machiavellian individual leaders who claim the responsibility, leaving most people to sink unacknowledged by history, nameless but not pointless. George Eliot (1965: 896) makes this poignantly clear at the end of her novel *Middlemarch* in her description of Dorothea:

> Her full nature, like that river of which Cyrus broke the strength, spent itself in channels which had no great name on the earth. But the effect of her being on those around her was incalculably diffusive: for the growing good of the world is partly dependent on unhistoric acts; and that things are not so ill with you and me as they might have been, is half owing to the number who lived faithfully a hidden life, and rest in unvisited tombs.

This does not mean that individual leaders play no role, but it does suggest that their role is often quite limited. For instance, although we still tend to reconstruct the competition between democratic political parties as if it could be reduced to a personality contest between the various leaders, the empirical research (see, e.g., King (ed.), 2002) suggests that party leaders often have little or no effect upon elections. Figure 2.2 summarizes the data for six democratic countries between 1996 and 2000 and although there are national differences, what is surprising is how little difference the personality of the leader actually makes.

In reviewing the evidence for American Presidential elections between 1980 and 2000 Bartels (2002: 65) suggests that the percentage difference to the vote made by the personality traits of the candidate never generates more than a 3.5 per cent advantage and seldom provides a sufficient swing to make a difference to the final figures

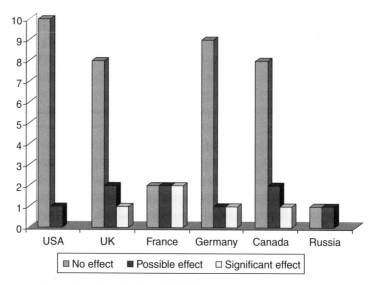

Source: Reconstructed from King (ed.), 2002: 213

Figure 2.2 Leaders' personalities and elections, 1960–2000

(for example, Bartels claims that Reagan's personality added 1 per cent to the Republican vote in the 1980 election but since the Republicans won the vote with 55.3 per cent of the total votes that personality bias was irrelevant. On the other hand, the only time it has made a difference was in 2000 when George W. Bush's personality traits (allegedly) added 0.4 per cent to the total republican vote – and since the Republicans 'won' with 49.7 per cent of the vote that 0.4 may have been critical.

Leaders may be important but there are whole rafts of other elements that are also important and it is often these that make the difference between success and failure. Perhaps the least understood or evaluated of these other elements is the role of the followers, without whom leaders cannot exist. A useful way to consider the all too easily overlooked role of followers in the construction of a leader's power is to envisage the difference between a domino-run and a Mexican wave. In the former all the power resides in the first movement that stimulates the dominoes to fall in sequence, generating a 'run'. Thus power lies with the pusher, the leader. But a Mexican wave that runs around a sports stadium does not depend on an individual leader to make it work; it works without apparent leadership and it 'dies' when the collective decide not to engage in further 'waves'.

In effect, power is a consequence as much as a cause of followership: if – and only if – followers follow leaders become powerful, but that act remains contingent not determined, and certainly not determined by any future imaginings because acts are quintessentially indeterminate: followers always have the choice not to act, and though they may pay the consequences of not acting the point is that no leader or situation can guarantee followership – leaders are neither omnipotent nor omniscient – but irresponsible followers can make them appear both. Worse, irresponsible followers allow irresponsible leaders to take us to their private and unachievable utopias via three-easy-steps that usually include (1) blaming someone else for everything; (2) leaving all decisions in the hands of the leader and ceasing to take personal responsibility for actions taken in their name; and (3) taking on trust the leader's version of the 'truth'. Responsible followers may not be able to lead us to utopia but they can prevent us from ending up in the dystopia that irresponsible leaders usually end up in, and perhaps that pragmatic foundation is the best way forward.

There is another criticism of leadership as Person that needs addressing at this point; thus far the discussion has been limited to leaders as People – assuming that the Person is a human. But all the examples used illustrate that leadership is never simply human because no human leader operates independently of non-humans. Thus we need to go beyond the criticism that leadership is essentially related to followership to the point where leadership is analysed in the contexts within which it operates – where hybrids rule not humans.

Leadership and hybridity

Let us return to the definitions of leadership to assess whether the substitution of a hybrid leader for a human leader can be achieved without violating some overriding principle of coherence in the term 'leadership'. If we can establish that viewing the identity of leadership as essentially hybrid rather than person-based is a legitimate approach then the conceptual space that 'leadership' inhabits becomes significantly more open to debate. On the one hand this may make the debate even more complex and confused, but on the other hand it might also explain why that debate is so contested – because what counts as leadership cannot be shaped into a consensual form.

We can stray back into the prior definitions here to demonstrate the issues. Perhaps the easiest case to deal with would be Positional Leadership. Recall that this definition of leadership can relate to informal leadership, a horizontally based position within a heterarchy. If a human can lead others by being a guide, by showing the way, then it seems hybrids can too. A dog, for example, can lead us home – providing the dog knows where home is – and is therefore part of a home–human–dog hybrid; a lighthouse can do the same, as can a satellite navigation system.

But can an 'ideal' also proffer leadership? This seems a reasonable extrapolation, for instance, many of the Marxist guerrillas of the 1960s and 1970s were 'led' or 'misled' by the ideal of equality: a non-human that had little formal authority over them. Similarly, many members of the German SS were 'led' by the racist ideals of National Socialism or by their 'oaths of obedience' to Adolf Hitler. Here the oath, the verbal utterance, led them – even if most of us would insist that it led them 'astray'.[12] That ideal might also be materialized as a flag or symbol – the Hammer and Sickle, the

Swastika, the Stars and Stripes or the Union Jack, hence their perceived 'desecration' by burning. Indeed, the Regimental Colours, the military unit flag, is often regarded as 'leading' soldiers, as were the Roman Legions' standards, for they symbolized in dramatic and intense form all that the soldiers stood for. We can go further than this to suggest that it is the leadership symbol itself that is critical and not just what it symbolizes. If this were not the case then when the Romans lost their legionary standards they would simply replace them with new ones – rather than disband the legion, as they tended to do (Warry, 1980: 136–7).

But is the volitional element an insurmountable problem here after all? That is, is the inability of the flag to invent a future and to act in a volitional manner the issue that marks the boundary between leadership and symbolism? Certainly the flag can represent a future but it cannot invent one. Thus if leadership is defined as the invention of a future and the mobilization of followers to achieve that future, then surely the flag can only lead in the second sense? Well a flag might embody the future, as Figes and Kolonitskii (1999: 1–2) suggest, at the beginning of the Russian revolution:

> Language was used to define identities and create new meanings in the politics of 1917 ... songs and texts, symbolic flags and emblems, pictures and monuments, banners and slogans, common speech and rumour, dress and body language, ritualized demonstrations by the crowd, parades and other ceremonies [were used] to represent and show allegiance to the idea of 'the revolution'. ... Each faction fought to control the symbolic system of the revolutionary underground ... Whoever mastered the red flag, or monopolized the meaning of its lexicon, was in pole position to become the master of the revolution too. ... Flexibility was a cardinal advantage in this symbolic battle: the party whose political language was able to accommodate the greatest number of different idioms and dialects, and yet unite them all in a common understanding which had real significance for people's daily lives, was likely to attract the most support and dominate the revolutionary discourse.

Of course, *what* particular future is embodied in the flag is still up for debate, so it is not that the flag leads because of *what* is symbolizes but that its followers attribute to the flag a future that they find attractive – even if that attribution is not consensual amongst the followers. As a particular case in point, when two mutinies broke out in the British Navy in 1797 the mutineers ran up the red flag, but the Admiralty interpreted the flag of the first mutineers at Shiphead as representing an industrial dispute, while the second, at Nore, was interpreted as the red flag of political rebellion; the first mutiny was settled as an industrial dispute and the second resulted in mass executions (Grint, 2001).

The contradictory interpretations of what appear to be the same thing also relates to the ability of things to lead – or even follow – us. For example, we might distinguish between cars that lead us and cars that follow us. The latter are rooted in market research and focus groups that apparently reveal what *we want*, while the former are designed by people who allegedly 'know' what *we need*. Thus cars that lead us have to persuade us that the status quo is inadequate and that they embody the future. Of these perhaps the 2002 Renault Mégane II was a useful case with its distinctly 'novel/ugly/retro' back. Patrick le Quement, Renault's chief designer, appeared adamant that designers should predict the future and not merely pander to customers' contemporary wants. As he said of the Mégane II, 'These cars have a strong character. Some people may not like them at first but I have a feeling that their hesitation won't last' (quoted at www.brasileuro.com/design.html). Here, the car users are being 'configured' by the car designer (see Grint and Woolgar, 1997).

We might even consider how we can be led to do things by as yet unseen technologies. How, for example, many German soldiers were persuaded to fight on to the bitter end in the Second World War on the promise of German 'wonder-weapons' which would, they were informed, turn the tide against the Allies. Such weapons had no formal authority over the soldiers but they promised a utopian future for all those that 'followed' them. Take, for example, Helmut Altner, a 17-year-old German recruited at the end of the war to defend Berlin. On 12 April 1945, just three weeks before the end of hostilities, a second Lieutenant explained to him that the new wonder-weapons which would save Germany were on their way to the front and included rifles that shot round corners (Altner, 2002: 44).[13] So in this sense a hybrid (for these weapons were not autonomous of humans) can exhibit Positional Leadership in exactly the same way that Joan of Arc led the French against the English: she was not an 'isolated peasant girl on foot' but a woman in the uniform and armour of a man, mounted on a horse and carrying her mythical banner and sword in front of a French army. In short, she led through a complex ensemble of symbols and practices which her followers and to some extent her English opponents recognized.

But what about apparently human-less technologies – can they lead us? Take, for example, traffic lights which have formal authority embedded in their legal significance; if you were to ignore the 'lead' provided by a red light, you could be prosecuted, and for most of the time at least, the results of traffic light leadership is that most drivers follow their 'lead'. The same occurs for speed cameras, roadblocks and doors that mark the boundaries of property and so on. In short, traffic lights and technologies can be 'in charge' of us – they can demonstrate leadership by persuading us to follow their lead. But note again that their 'leadership' – their ability to get followers to follow their 'lead' – is not autonomous but hybrid. A traffic light system without the legal support and police enforcement cannot lead us.

Another example might be the cropping machines that the Luddites tried to destroy in late eighteenth and early-nineteenth-century England. Here the machines were given legal authority and rights that deterred their assailants and punished those that refused to be deterred. Such machines personified the future, where machines displaced workers, and were steeped in the new logic of the 'rational economy' – the market – that undermined the logic of the 'moral economy' (see Grint and Woolgar, 1997).

Leadership might also be manifest in something like a plan. The landing plan for D-Day, for instance, encompassed legal military authority over the subordinate human elements on 6 June 1944, as the plan for Omaha Beach in Figure 2.3 suggests.

Time in minutes from H Hour	Easy Green	Dog Red	Dog White	Dog Green
H - 5			16 DD Tks Co. C 743 Tk Bn	16 DD Tks Co. B 743 Tk Bn
H	4 LCTs (8)Co A 743 Tk Bn	4 LCTs (8)Co A 743 Tk Bn		
H+01	6 LCVPs (200) Co E 116th	6 LCVPs (200) Co F 116th	6 LCVPs (200) Co G 116th	6 LCVPs (200) Co A 116th
H+03	3 LCMs 146th Eng.	3 LCMs 146th Eng. +Ctl boat	3 LCMs 146th Eng. 5 LCVPs HQ G,H AA Btry	3 LCMs 146, 2 LCAs Co.C 24Rng
H+30	5 LCVPs Co H 116th. HQ	8 LCVPs HQ Co H&F AA Bt	1 LCVP 149 Eng. Beach Bn 1 LCM 121 Eng Bn	8 LCVPs HQ Co A&B AA Btry
H+40	1 LCM 112th Eng Bn	1 LCM 149 EngBeach Bn 4 LCVPs		4 LCAs HQ 1 Bn, 6 LCVPs Co D 116th 1 LCM 121 Eng.
H+50	7 LCVPs Co L 116th	7 LCVPs Co I 116th	7 LCVPs Co K 116th	7 LCVPs Co C 116 lcm 121EnBn
H+57		8 LCVPs HQ Co 3 Bn Co M 116th		4 LCVPs Co B 81 Wpns Bn
H+60	1 LCT 121 Eng Bn	4 LCTs 121 Eng Bn 1 LCVP	1 LCVP HQ Co 116th	3 LCTs 121 Eng Bn 5 LCAs Cos A&B 5th Rangers
H+65				7 LCAs 5th Ranger Bn
H+70	1 LCI 149 Eng Beach Bn	1 LCI 112 Eng Bn	1 LCI Alt HQ Co 116th	8 LCAs 5th Rangers Bn 2 LCTs 1 LCM 121 Eng Bn
H+90			5 LCTs 58 FA Bn Armd	
H+100			1 LCI 6th Eng Sp Brig	
H+110	13 DUKWs 111 FA Bn	7 DUKWs AT plats 2, 3 Bns	2 LCTs 467 AAAW Bn	10 DUKWs AT plat 1 Bn
H+120	3 LCTs 467 AAAW Bn, AT Co 116	5 LCTs 467 AAAW, AT Co, 149 Eng Beach Bn	1 LCI HQ Co 104 Med Bn	2 LCTs 467 AAAW Bn
H+150		3 LCTs DD Tk, 12 DUKWs 461 Amphib Truck Co	3 LCTs, 3 LCMs Navy salvage	5 LCTs

Key:
DD Tks: Dual Drive Tanks (Amphibious Shermans)
DUKW: Amphibious trucks
Eng Bn: Engineering Battalion
LCA: Landing Craft (Assault)
LCI: Landing Craft (Infantry)
LCM: Landing Craft (Medium)
LCT: Landing Craft (Tank)
AAAW: Anti Aircraft Artillery Weapon
LCVP: Landing Craft (Vehicle,Personnel)

Figure 2.3   Landing diagram, Omaha beach, 116th RCT

In fact, this plan led the Americans astray in the sense that it implied a control over events on Omaha beach that proved impossible to achieve, and the assumptions built into the plan effectively inhibited the attempts of others to lead the troops off this beach. Nevertheless, on Utah (US), Sword (UK), Gold (UK) and Juno (Canada) beaches the plans led the way by imposing a temporal sequence and spatial deployment on those landing.

But can non-humans that do not embody formal authority lead us? Ironically this is probably the easiest case to make. Take, for example, the case of a derailed train heading in your direction. It has no formal right to the space you are occupying in the waiting room but you might be well advised to submit to its 'lead' and get out of the way as fast as possible. The same can be said for those facing a guided missile, or a tank heading towards them. That missile or tank may be illegitimate in the eyes of the law, it may even be heading your way by accident, but it does have an uncanny ability to persuade most people to follow its lead and move. That does not mean it will *determine* your actions. Altner (2002: 135) recalls learning that a bridge in Berlin was about to be blown up before the advancing Soviet army in April 1945, and watched,

> as people went and stood on it, women with babies in their arms, mothers holding crying children by the hand, old men and youngsters of both sexes, even soldiers, and they would not let themselves be driven away by threats or by force. They stood there quietly, not listening, just looking at the water and staying silent until the bridge was blown as the first tank appeared on the bank. A dark cloud rose slowly and flames shot upwards, and the people fell into the river in a cloud of fire and lightning.

The tank or the bridge wired with explosives may be 'in charge', but that does not mean you have to follow its orders.

At the 'product' end of Hybrid Leadership we might consider the atomic bomb. When dropped on Japan the bombs represented not simply enormous death and destruction in an instantaneous flash, but perhaps more importantly, that the future was related to the success of American leadership and unrelated to what the Japanese may have regarded as their superior leadership. In effect, it could be said to have led the Japanese to surrender – although this point is itself controversial. Again, it was not simply the atomic bomb – the technology – that determined the surrender of Japan because significant internal negotiations occurred between the military and political authorities as to whether Japan should surrender or continue to resist. Nonetheless, it would seem clear that the atomic bomb was to some extent instrumental in 'leading' the Japanese to that decision. In effect, it was not just the willingness of President Truman, the formal human leader, to continue the deployment of the weapon if necessary, nor the assumption that Truman was the individual with the leadership character to go through with the threat, nor that his behaviour would be instrumental in any action, nor even that he was positionally 'in-front' of the American people in this, nor that he, and not 'the system', could continue the action. Rather it was because it was Truman situated in a particular Allied envelope of space and time with the requisite material and symbolic resources at his disposal, and because he faced the Japanese in another contiguous envelope, and because of their mutual interpretation of each other's situation. Truman's leadership did not win the war against the Japanese, the Allied – and primarily American – leadership was an effect of their superior hybrid.

In what follows the notion of hybrid leadership is evaluated against a case study where the very idea of leadership embodied only in human form was never really appropriate – D-Day, 6 June 1944 – hence the resonation with the former sub title: putting the 'ship' back into leadership. However, the different approaches of the combatants towards technology in general, and boat technologies in particular, generated quite different approaches to the problems involved.

Hybrid leadership on D-Day: putting the 'ship' back into 'leadership' II

D-Day was the most complex single operation of the Second World War, the most significant aspect of the Battle of Normandy, and the most important battle for the Western Allies against Germany. A 40-mile stretch of the Normandy coast was the site and the object was: 'to carry out an operation from the United Kingdom to secure a lodgement on the continent from which further offensive operations can be developed. This lodgement area must contain sufficient port facilities to maintain a force of 26–30 divisions and to enable this force to be augmented by follow-up formations at the rate of from three to five divisions a month' (quoted in Pitcairn-Jones, 1994: 11). Within 24 hrs the Allies had landed over 175,000 troops in eight divisions (five by sea and three by air), 1500 tanks, 3000 guns and 15,000 other vehicles.

It was not the largest single operation of the war. Operation Bagration, the Soviet offensive timed to coincide with D-Day, deployed 1.7 million troops, 4000 tanks and 6000 aircraft against the German eastern front. Within a week the Soviet offensive had caused the Germans to lose 154,000 troops, 2000 tanks, 10,000 guns and 57,000 vehicles (Kilvert-Jones, 1999: 28). By comparison, in the first *month* of the Normandy campaign the Germans lost just over 80,000 troops. Thus reflecting the overall war effort, it was the Soviet Union not the Western Allies that took far more casualties (probably around 8.5 million direct Soviet military casualties versus 210,000 Allied military casualties in Western Europe) and inflicted more casualties (70 per cent) upon the Germans (roughly 607 German divisions versus 176 by the Western Allies [Furtado, 1992: 57]). However, Normandy was a catastrophe for the Germans. By the end of August 1944, three quarters of a million German casualties had been incurred and one quarter of a million German troops captured, double their losses at Stalingrad (Reynolds, 1999: 32).

But it is the complexity of the D-Day operation that defies the imagination because everything had to be transported across the channel for D-Day and not simply pushed further west as with the Red Army's operations. Indeed, Rommel was well aware of the difference in the two fronts:

> Our friends from the East cannot imagine what they're in for here. It's not a matter of fanatical hordes to be driven forward in masses against our line, with no regard for casualties and little recourse to tactical craft; here we are facing an enemy who applies all his native intelligence to the use of his many technical resources, who spares no expenditure on material

and whose every operation goes its course as if it had been the subject of repeated rehearsal. Dash and doggedness no longer make a soldier. (Quoted in Kilvert-Jones, 1999: 32)

And as far as Churchill was concerned: 'This war is not … a war of masses of men hurling masses of shells at each other. It is by devising new weapons and above all by scientific leadership that we shall best cope with the enemy's superior strength' (quoted in Delaforce, 1998: 15). In effect, there was a clear recognition that the raw courage of human leadership-in-front was no longer adequate in the new war of hybrids. And what a hybrid! Planning Overlord was hardly a routine operation: it required plans to move a city the equivalent of Birmingham in the UK across the channel, under enemy fire, and keep it moving until it got to Berlin (Turner, 1994: 26).

Churchill began his search for a hybrid solution to the problem of invasion by recruiting Frederick Lindermann, Professor of Experimental Philosophy at Oxford University (Fort, 2003), Millis Jefferis, a major in the Royal Engineers, and Percy Hobart, a recently retired General of an armoured division, to his 'toyshop' and between the four of them many of Britain's 'new weapons' evolved.

The first problem facing the initial assault troops was the obstacles and mines that littered the beach area itself. Any attacking amphibious force would have to face row upon row of defences even before landing on the beach. First, at around 225 metres from the high-water mark (HWM), 3 metre high iron obstacles tipped with Teller anti-tank mines were supplemented by an occasional example of 'Element C': an array of large steel girders welded together to form a mined obstacle 15 foot long and 12 foot high. Second, at around 200 metres, there were rows of logs, supported by an 'A' frame and tipped with mines and driven into the sand at 45°. Third, at 120 metres, were deployed rows of 'hedgehogs' – constructions of metal rods designed to rip open the bottom of the landing craft.

If the invading troops got through this deadly maze they would then face rows of concertina barbed wire interspersed with minefields and tripwire mines of various kinds. Rommel had 6.5 million land mines laid along the French coast (one million a month for four months between February and D-Day), though he had originally wanted 20 million. Where mined beach defences remained submerged specialized underwater demolition teams were to be sent in to make sea-lanes safe and to mark them for the following landing craft. However, 'safety' had a cost: the casualty rate of these teams was amongst the highest of all. On Utah beach, the safest of all, only 13 of the 40 underwater demolition engineers survived the day, and only two of these were uninjured despite the use of Kapok Jerkins, a novel protective suit designed to resist the destructive power of underwater explosions (Neillands and de Normann, 1994: 156–7; Turner, 1994: 37).

Following the underwater demolition squads were the combat engineers. The engineering requirements for D-Day were two: first to open up 50-yard gaps in the wire and minefields to allow initial exits from the beaches. These were to be opened up by special engineering assault gapping teams. Second, behind the gapping teams, support engineering teams would widen the gaps, set up the communications to link the beach to the ships (including radios, semaphores and heliographs with coloured lights to inform the ships what to send in the next wave), and generally ensure an adequate traffic flow.

After D-Day the beach would be cleared by the engineering battalion beach groups who would also be responsible for establishing ammunition and fuel dumps. So important were the engineering tasks that 25 per cent of all the troops landed on D-Day were engineers of some kind. For example, on Omaha the first wave involved 1450 assault infantry and 546 engineers (including 126 American Navy demolition experts), though the normal proportion was 8 per cent (Ambrose, 1995: 143; Forty, 1995: 52; Fowle, 1994: 216).

Omaha was 7000-yard long with between 70 yards of sand at HWM and 400 yards at low water mark (LWM). It was covered by the fifth and sixth Engineering Special Brigade making up the 5632 members of the Provisional Engineer Special Brigade Group. Another 2500 engineers landed with other units. (Utah was covered by a single unit, the first Engineering Special Brigade.) Omaha's obstacles comprised two main lines: 250 yards from the HWM was a 50-yard deep line of Element C, Belgian Gates, covered with Teller mines. Fifty yards closer to the beach was a 50-yard deep line of wooden posts and ramps supported by three staggered rows of hedgehog obstacles. (Fortunately, there were no Teller mined posts on Utah) (Fowle, 1994: 215–16).

By nightfall, about 34 per cent of the combat engineers on Omaha were dead or wounded and 60 per cent of their equipment had been lost or destroyed (Neillands and de Normann, 1994: 193). Moreover, they had been unable to complete their task of blowing 16 gaps in the beach defences, though four had been opened. Partly this was because the initial bombardment left many defenders alive and fully capable of making the beach a no-go area. This then slowed the demolition down so much that the rising tide covered many other obstacles before they could be dealt with. Partly it was because the fire was so intense that many infantry soldiers crouched behind the obstacles thus preventing the engineers from blowing them up (Ramsey, 1995: 353).

Getting the troops and equipment to the beaches, rather than across them, was the responsibility of the Royal Navy and was achieved through an array of specialized boats and ships. The Landing Ship Tank (LST) was the largest, at 4000 tons and 327 feet long with a maximum speed of 10 knots. Depending on the precise size (the British built versions (the Mk1) were 288 foot long, the US built versions (known as the Mk2) slightly shorter) they could carry between eighteen and a dozen tanks, or between 500 and 1400 tons of stores, or 25 three-ton trucks. And since the ships were flat bottomed they could be landed directly on shallow beaches, usually grounding in a metre of water. The American version carried traffic lights for unloading instructions: red – unhook your vehicle from the chains it was held by for the voyage; amber – start your engine; green – bow doors open and go! (Bruce, 1999: 105). The first 200 LSTs to land in Normandy also carried emergency medical kits which were dumped ashore before any hospitals were set up (from D-Day+2). LSTs also ferried casualties back to England, some of whom were operated on in transit within a small operating theatre at the back of the tank deck.

LCLs (Landing Craft Large) were the next largest specialist vessels at 110 feet long, capable of carrying about 200 troops or up to 8 tanks or 75 tons of material. These were also capable of direct beach unloading. Wherever possible 'balanced loading' was adopted which ensured that, for example, guns and their ammunition went together to avoid the problem encountered in Norway – where anti-aircraft guns were shipped separately from their ammunition and the loss of one disabled the other (Doughty, 1994: 84). It was also necessary to 'combat load' the craft so that the materiel was unloaded with the critical elements first. This required some considerable driving skills in reversing heavy equipment up a small and steep ramp and guns in particular proved almost impossible to load except with the help of human muscle power. David Robertson, with the US one hundred and nineteenth Field Artillery was involved in such efforts when a Brigadier General arrived and demanded that the unit adopt standard loading procedures – at which point the supervising Lieutenant told the Brigadier to 'go away and leave these people alone'. He did (quoted in Bruce, 1999: 158).

In total, around 304 of the large landing craft of various forms were lost or disabled in the initial assault on the Normandy beaches, half to mined obstacles and the rest to artillery and accidents. The numbers included 131 LCTs (97 on the Anglo-Canadian beaches and 34 on the American beaches), and 21 LCLs [carrying 200 soldiers] (9 Anglo-Canadian and 12 American). The differential implies that the heavy US casualties on Omaha were caused more by problems on the beach rather than getting to the beach (Pitcairn-Jones, 1994: 107).

Indeed, while the troops tiptoed carefully around the mined obstacles, and even before they tried to cross the triple line of concertina barbed wire that was strung out along Omaha beach, the whole beach area would be under fire from the gun emplacements and the machine guns. Since these were often set at oblique angles, the defenders were protected from attackers' fire directly in front of them, while being able to provide enfilading fire along a pre-set angle of the beach to the side. Should the attackers appear to be gaining a foothold, the defenders could often retire through a maze of concrete tunnels back to safety some distance from the beach, often to the mortar units whose mortars were already zeroed in onto specific beach positions (Neillands and de Normann, 1994: 33–4). In fact one analysis suggests that the most lethal German weapon was the 81 mm mortar with an effective range of 2500 yards which caused three times more casualties than machine gun bullets (Ramsey, 1995: 527), and there are claims that two-thirds of all the Allied casualties in Normandy were due to mortars (Delaforce, 1999: 53). Most concerning to the Allied troops seemed to be the fact that the mortar shell, unlike most other shells, was almost inaudible in flight (Balkoski, 1999: 94–5). Certainly very few Allied soldiers were killed or wounded by the German's secret beach weapon – the Goliath (Leichte Ladungsträger [SdKfz 303]) which was a remote-controlled (wire guided) tracked container filled with 75 kg or 100 kg of explosives (Ramsey, 1995: 386).

The dangers of invading a fortified coastline had already been demonstrated by the failure at Dieppe in August 1942 and it had become clear, at least to some people, that human flesh was inappropriately vulnerable as a method of leading soldiers ashore under such circumstances. Instead, some form of hybrid leadership was necessary – not in the form of remote-controlled machines like the German Goliaths but through armoured assault vehicles. Here the two main Allied armies (Anglo-Canadian and US) used the same technology to get *to* the beaches but different technologies to get *across* the beaches. In both cases the technologies formed an inherent element of hybrid leadership – the beaches were not invaded by naked soldiers and not 'led' to and across the beaches by naked officers. But neither were they led by independent automatic machines. Instead they were led to the beaches by hybrid leaders comprised of boats with sailors and soldiers and they were supposed to be led across the beaches by hybrid leaders of tanks and their occupants, even though on Omaha beach the latter generally failed. It is this that largely explains the disproportionate losses at Omaha for there was little of the specialized armour used on the Anglo-Canadian beaches to lead the invasion – the so-called 'Funnies'.

One might be forgiven for thinking that leading the Normandy invasion in a boat of any kind on 6 June 1944 was an extraordinarily dangerous thing to do, but why make it worse by leading the invasion in a hybrid composed of wooden boats with unarmoured soldiers? What was even crazier was that this self-evidently weak hybrid could have been replaced by an armoured boat that would have offered far better protection, at least from small arms fire and shrapnel, though not from a direct artillery shell. So why did the Allies lead with such a weak hybrid?

Landing craft

With the US navy heavily involved in the Pacific Ocean against Japan, the British navy took prime responsibility for the transportation, and the operating procedures had been established for many years through the experience of previous amphibious operations: HWOST (High Water of Ordinary Spring Tides) marked the dividing line above which the navy's role ceased and the army's responsibility started.

Responsibility for actually providing the landing craft mainly fell on American shoulders, since most British capacity was involved in the repair and construction of merchant ships and warships. However, the American Pacific supremo, Admiral King, remained wedded to the Pacific theatre and ensured that most American-built landing craft were diverted there: for example, on 1 May 1944 only 2493 of the 31,123 existing US landing craft were destined for Operation Overlord (Botting, 1978: 48; Neillands and Normann, 1993: 67). Eventually, the overall US commander, General Marshall, intervened to force Admiral King to release some of the landing craft being stockpiled for the Pacific campaign but only on 15 April 1944 did King release a number of naval ships for support (3 battleships, 2 cruisers and 22 destroyers) (Lewin, 1998: 176).

Paradoxically, then, one of the most critical factors in determining the date of the invasion was the provision of such landing craft, allegedly because the difficulties of design and production ensured that not until 20 March 1944 were the theoretical numbers settled, and not until May 1944 were sufficient numbers of such craft actually available. Yet the numbers available in the Pacific were more than adequate for both theatres so the most significant problem was not the technical problem of production but the political problem of distribution. The numbers had to be huge because Eisenhower required 175,000 troops (of whom 2000 were allocated just for record keeping), 1500 tanks, 3000 artillery pieces and 10,000 vehicles to be on French soil in the first 24 hours (Neillands and Normann, 1993: 71; Turner, 1994: 54).

The naval plan required 4126 landing craft (of which 98 per cent actually sailed on the day), 736 support ships and 864 merchant ships. All of these were to be protected by 1213 warships of various sizes. Of the latter, 189 minesweepers would sweep the channel of mines (29 mines were swept) in the biggest minesweeping operation of the war to provide 12 safe lanes initially 15 miles wide broadening to 30 miles nearer Normandy (Pitcairn-Jones, 1994: 51).[14] There were also 6 battleships, 2 monitors (heavily armoured gunships), 23 cruisers and 56 destroyers that would provide fire power to destroy beach defences and gun-emplacements that might endanger the landings (Neillands and Normann, 1993: 69; Turner, 1994: 54–71). Specialized landing craft and transport vessels were also required in large numbers, and from the base line of just six in 1939, owned by the largest navy of the time, the British Royal Navy, the requirements were clearly large.

But perhaps the most pressing problem as far as the initial landings were concerned, was how to protect the troops as they disembarked under fire from the first personnel carriers to land (the larger landing craft were destined to land after the smallest assault craft). There was already plenty of information available from the failed Dieppe raid in August 1942 about what was likely to happen when unarmoured troops landed on exposed beaches facing a heavily gunned and emplaced enemy. Nevertheless the 1089 leadership hybrids that deposited the first vulnerable humans onto the beaches at Normandy were the American LCVPs (Landing Craft, Vehicle and Personnel) also known as the Higgins Boat and the British built version of the same boat, the LCA (Landing Craft, Assault). Both boats were fabricated entirely from wood with the exception of the bow which had some armour plating after the Dieppe fiasco had demonstrated that all-wooden landing craft were strangely ineffective against bullets and shells.

The Higgins boat derived from a boat designed by Andrew Jackson Higgins, an Irish American who set up Higgins Industries in the 1930s, to deal with the Louisiana swamps. The boat had a very shallow draft (18 inches) and a strong pine 'headlog' that could brush aside any floating debris in the swamp and allowed the boat to land onto sand bars without damage. It was relatively fast (12 knots) and manoeuvrable and could carry 36 troops or a jeep and 12 troops. Over 23,000 were built during the war; indeed by September 1943 Higgins industries had built almost 13,000 boats for the US Navy – almost 92 per cent of the total. At its peak Higgins Industries employed 20,000 workers and built 700 boats for the US Navy every month.[15] Higgins – whose creations included the catchphrase 'The man who relaxes is helping the Axis' – was much admired by Eisenhower, even if the former could demolish a bottle of whiskey a day, as the Commander once said of Higgins: 'He is the man who won the war for us. ... If Higgins had not designed and built the LCVPs, we never could have landed over an open beach. The whole strategy of the war would have been different.'[16]

The Anglo-Canadian LCAs carried twenty soldiers and were crewed by two Royal Marines, one to operate the ramp and the other to operate the engine and steering. LCAs were built across Britain in numerous factories, many of which had previously built furniture. The largest single producer in Britain was J. Bolson & Son's shipyard at Poole that had previously made leisure boats and yachts. At the height of production Bolson's produced one LCA per day and adopted what was, for then, a revolutionary production strategy: the assembly line and specialized division of labour was replaced by single work squads who produced a complete boat (Legg, 1994: 28). But it wasn't just the lessons of Dieppe that were ignored on the whole; the entire experience of the 'Island Hopping' strategy of the American Marines and Army in the Pacific provided not just further evidence of the problems but a possible solution: the amtrac.

(Not) learning from the Pacific

In the invasion of Betio Island in the Tarawa Atoll in the Pacific, between 20 and 23 November 1943, the US Marines faced 26,700 Japanese troops, 1000 Japanese labourers and 1200 Korean labourers ensconced, it was alleged, in the most heavily fortified area in the world. At just two miles long and one mile wide, the Japanese had installed 14 large coastal defence guns, 40 other artillery pieces and more than 100 machine guns firing through a four foot coconut log wall. In all there were 500 pillboxes. As the Japanese commander, Rear Admiral Keiji Shibasaki, boasted, 'A million men cannot take Tarawa in a hundred years' (quoted in Steinberg, 1998: 106). Some of the emplacements had concrete walls eight-feet thick which proved to be impervious to the largest naval shell fire despite the pre-landing bombardment from the sea and air that saw, on average, ten tons of high explosives fall on each of the 291 acres. If ever there was an impregnable hybrid, this was it.

The US Second and Eighth Marine Divisions were carried to the beaches either on the conventional wooden LCVP (Higgins Boats) or the newer LVTs (Landing Vehicle, Tracked). The LVTs or amtracs (amphibious tractors), or 'alligators' as they were known, had originated in civilian tractors built for working in the swamps of the southern states. In 1936 Donald Roebling, an engineer who had retired to Florida, witnessed a disastrous hurricane and re-designed a vehicle with his son, John, that they had first dreamt up in 1934.[17] The tracked vehicle, the 'alligator', was one of the few that could traverse the Florida swamps or the marshy everglades to rescue the beleaguered population on behalf of the Florida Red Cross. That rescue mission was covered by *Life* magazine in 1937 and the article was read by one individual who immediately saw a greater use for it: the Commanding General of the US Fleet Marine Force in the Pacific. Using diagonal track cleats and an aluminium construction, the Roebling alligator or amphibian was first prototyped in 1939 and could reach speeds of 10 mph on land and 25 mph in the water. It had a cruising radius of 400 miles and steered either by disengaging the tracks on one side or by reversing the tracks on one side. The prototype drew only 5 feet of water fully laden with well over 20 people and could drop 6 feet from land to water without capsizing. The provisional cost was put at £3600 and by 1940 the US Marine Corps was convinced the vehicle was critical for them. In November 1940 the US Navy and US Marine Corps ordered 200 to be made with light steel rather than duralumin and by 1941 the first 100 were delivered. By the end of the war 18,620 had been made.

The first military amtrac, LVT1, was one of 1225 built by Roebling and FMC (Food Machinery Corporation) in July 1941. It had a capacity of 24 troops plus a crew of three and it travelled at 6 mph in the water and 12 mph on the land. The slow speed of the vehicle and the short life of the tracks led to a two-month delay while the design was redeveloped at the California Institute of Technology. In June 1942 demonstrations of the new prototypes were held for the US Navy, Army and Marine Corps.

Most of the LVT1s went to the US Navy and Marine Corps but 485 went to the US Army and 55 were sent to the Anglo-Canadian forces. Its first operational use was at the battle of Guadalcanal on 7 August 1942 and some – especially those for transporting personnel rather than materiel – were fitted with appliqué armour (armour plate 'applied' to the existing structure). Of the 2936 LVT2s, 1507 were used by the US Navy and 100 sent to the Anglo-Canadian forces. From 1943 the LVT3s had their engines moved forward so that a rear-loading ramp could be used but the most popular British use was of the LVT4 which could carry 30 soldiers, had a rearward-loading ramp, and could mount four machine guns. Most of the LVTs used in Europe, however, known in Britain as the Buffalo, were unarmoured with a trapdoor exit at the front. As many as 500 were sent to Britain or Canada.

Tarawa, in November 1943, was the first assault which used amtracs in large numbers to carry troops (Bruce, 1999: 200, 273). Fitted with propellers and tracks these amtracs could travel at four knots in the water and 20 mph on land – and they had rearward facing doors. Critically, this meant they did not have to disgorge their vulnerable contents straight into the sights of enemy gunners at the water's edge, but could travel across some reefs, sand and barbed wire right up to the enemy emplacements and unload their occupants from the relative safety of the back of the vehicle. In effect, these amtracs operated as hybrid leaders, leading their humans to and across the beaches in a much safer environment than the wooden LCVPs.

The Marines' commander, General Smith, had demanded more amtracs to carry his troops forward but Admiral Turner, the amphibious force commander, had overruled his request, insisting that the LCVPs were quite adequate for the task. Given that Rear Admiral Kingman, the commander of the ships, had promised to 'obliterate' Tarawa before any Marine landed, Turner presumably thought Smith's request unnecessary. Nevertheless Turner eventually accepted the request and 50 more amtracs were delivered before the invasion bringing the total to 125 – just enough for the first three assault battalions, but leaving the follow up units to land in LCVPs.

The execution of the plan left much to be desired – and much to be learned for Overlord. The disembarking Marines were forced to delay their exit from the carrying ships when it was realized that they were directly under the bombing route. Then the failure to co-ordinate the naval and airborne bombardments led to a 35-minute gap between the two and a radically shortened aerial assault. As the Marines approached the beach, the fires caused by the bombardment prevented the naval ships from firing right up until the landing and, although Japanese communications lines were cut, precious little material damage had been done to the defenders. Thus at a distance of 3000 yards the line of 125 amtracs came under direct fire from the beach guns which destroyed half of them. Meanwhile, the LCVPs could not even cross the reef, leaving the follow-up forces to wade ashore or transfer into one of the few remaining amtracs returning from the beach. The only area where the defensive ring was penetrated was on Red Beach 3 where two destroyers put the large Japanese guns out of action, allowing the amtracs to move through the sea wall. Eventually, after three days of fighting, the defenders were overcome. Only 146 of the 4700 defenders survived (including just 17 Japanese). Of the 12,000 attacking Marines 1027 were dead or missing (as were 29 Naval personnel), 2292 were wounded. But significant lessons had been learned and on 1 February 1944 these new techniques and technologies were deployed against Kwajalein Atoll when all the infantry from the 7th Infantry Division landed in amtracs, and after three days and 334 deaths the atoll was captured (Steinberg, 1998: 104–19). For the rest of the Pacific war vital lessons were learned: amtracs were fitted with thicker armour and some upgunned to carry 37 mm or 75 mm guns in turrets while those invading Okinawa on 1 April 1945 often carried four 30 calibre machine guns.

Despite this experience only two amtracs were shipped to Normandy and both these appeared on Utah, although it had been clear from the Pacific and Dieppe, that conventionally propelled and unarmoured landing craft with bow-facing doors exposed the assault waves to considerable enemy fire, and – although no vehicle was immune to artillery fire – an armoured amtrac with a rearward opening door could lead troops across the most exposed part of the assault, the beach, much more successfully than an LCVP. Such vehicles were already available by D-Day because 500 LVT(A)1 – amtracs with an enclosed and armoured hull supporting a 37 mm gun – were supplied to the US Navy and Army between 1942 and 1944. Indeed, they were used again en masse at Saipan in the middle of June 1944 when 150 LVT(A)1s were deployed in support of the 600 LVTs carrying 8000 US Marines in the first wave on a four mile assault of the beach. Even more useful was the LVT(A)2 which was like the LVT(A)1 except the armour was increased and the 37 mm gun removed – thus providing a well-armoured personnel carrier – of which the US Army used 200 between 1943 and 1944. These had originally been used just for carrying stores and troops and were photographed in *Parade* on 15 August 1942 carrying troops – so their availability was clearly not unknown to the Overlord planners.[18]

Nor was the utility of this vehicle questioned by those using them in combat. When the ten-thousandth LVT rolled off the assembly lines at FMC on 14 May 1945,

Vice-Admiral Cochrane, Chief of the (US) Bureau of Ships, said:

> There is not the slightest shadow of doubt that the overwhelming victories of our forces at Tarawa, Kwajalein, Saipan, Tinian, Guam, Palau and Iwo Jima could not have been possible without the amtracs. It is only they that could navigate the coral reefs which the Japanese thought were their sure defence. It follows, therefore, that the war against Japan would be far from its present reassuring stage had it not been for the thousands of amtracs turned out by your company. (Quoted in Campbell, 1988: 35)

That lesson seems to have bypassed most of the Normandy planners, but not all of them. Major General Corlett, for example, had commanded the US Seventh Infantry Division against Japanese forces on the Kwajalein atoll which had fallen for a fraction of the cost in casualties of the attack on Tarawa and he had suggested the D-Day assault use the new amtracs (Parker, 1995: 335). But Corlett was, in his own words, 'squelched' by both Eisenhower and Bradley when he suggested it to them in a meeting (Kilvert-Jones, 1999: 76). A response that Corlett put down to himself being 'A son-of-a-bitch from out of town' (quoted in Balkoski, 1999: 124). Admittedly, it was probably too late to provide large numbers of these vehicles but even a few would probably have proved invaluable and two were certainly operating off Utah beach (one of them is still there). After all, at least 24 were stockpiled in England by 23 March 1944 (the photo of them was embargoed until after 6 June 1944) (*Wheels and Tracks*, No. 24, 1988: 26–7).

Even after Omaha the Western Theatre commanders avoided any significant deployment of amtracs, though three 'Buffaloes' as the British called them were used on 1 November 1944 by 41, 47, and 48 Royal Marine Commandos, supporting the First Canadian Army in clearing the Westkapelle end of the Dutch island of Walcheren which blocked the route to the sea from Antwerp (Bruce, 1999: 185). Thus the lessons of inadequate naval and air bombardments against deeply entrenched beach artillery and the advantages of using amtracs over unarmoured personnel landing craft to lead amphibious assaults were never learned by the Normandy military leaders – except perhaps by those who became casualties on the Normandy beaches on D-Day. For the latter in the American LCVPs rather than the Anglo-Canadian LCAs, being part of a leadership hybrid comprised of soft human bodies and only marginally stronger wood was just the first problem on D-Day.

As it was the US Fourth Infantry Division losses at Utah on D-Day were put at 197. The casualties at Omaha for the Fourth and Twenty Ninth Infantry Divisions were approximately 2000 on the first day (Kilvert-Jones, 1999: 10; Ambrose, 1995: 43). On Juno beach the Canadians suffered 805 casualties and there were another 243 casualties in this area from the British Commando units involved on or near Juno, to bring the total for the Juno area to at least 1204 (and this excludes casualties taken by the commando units operating inland) (Holt and Holt, 1999: 169, 181). On Gold beach itself the British suffered 413 casualties (Delaforce, 1999: 151). On Sword the beach casualty figures totalled 630. It is self-evident that some casualties would have been incurred under any circumstances imaginable but the point really is to consider whether different leadership hybrids could have significantly reduced the casualties. The casualty rate amongst the leading waves of infantry and engineers was the highest of all and, given the developments in the Pacific of the amtrac, it would seem clear that the leadership hybrids deployed by the Allies on D-Day left soldiers unnecessarily exposed: unarmoured humans make extraordinarily ineffective leaders on invasion beaches.

Conclusion

This chapter explored the possibility that leadership could be defined not just by the person of the leader but that such leaders first, need not be individuals and second, need not even be human. The first part of the chapter traced out the connections between leadership, followership, commitment and independence to construct a hypothetical schema of four ideal types of leadership: the 'white elephant', to represent the leader who is born a god, who is omnipotent, omniscient and as rare as an albino elephant; the 'cat herder', where leadership proved impossible in the face of individually oriented and independently minded 'followers'; the 'emperor', where an assumed superiority acted to generate irresponsible followers; and the 'wheelwright', founded upon the acceptance by the leader of his or her limitations, his or her need to learn how to lead through an apprenticeship, and rooted in a dependence upon the advice and support of responsible followers who were both committed to the community but retained their independence of judgement from the leader. The role of the last type was then explored in some detail through various examples where the role of the followers – responsible or otherwise – supported or undermined the success of their leaders through an accumulation of small acts. Indeed, it was suggested the leadership was better understood as the god of small things because of the importance of this relationship between leaders and followers.

Having argued that the notion of leader as person was severely constrained by the actions of followers I then proceeded to question whether even this expansion of the definition of 'person' was sufficient to explain leadership and proceeded to suggest that leadership, far from being the consequence of human acts, was much better explained through as a consequence of hybrids rather than humans. Indeed, it would seem that leaders *qua* humans are seldom 'naked' and usually enwrapped by significant forms of clothing and supporting by more or less robust technologies. And even if in the case of the Nigerian women protesters at the Chevron-Texaco Escravos site described in the first chapter they did enhance their leadership by threatening to remove their clothes, this was hardly likely to be effective on D-Day.[19] If leadership cannot be reduced to a naked and individual human then we should start to consider both the collective and the hybrid nature of leadership.

Casualties were always going to be relatively heavy on D-Day, though Allied casualties were smaller than expected by the planners. Nonetheless it is also highly probable that some of these resulted from the weak hybrids that led the troops to and over the beaches. It is inconceivable to think about how such an invasion could have occurred without some form of hybridity, though remarkably most of the texts consider leadership only in its human embodiment. Of course, this still implies that we have resolved the volitional problem of leadership – as opposed to sidestepping it – nevertheless, the point is to consider whether a volitional act by a naked human would have been sufficient in and of itself to have 'led' the Allies to success, or even the Germans to defeat. This, surely, is the point: what matters in this approach to leadership is not to be sidetracked into philosophical disputes about volition and causation and to focus on the pragmatic aspects of leadership: neither human-less networks nor thing-less networks could have succeeded on D-Day. Thus our discussion in the second part of this chapter has focussed less on the human element in leadership than on the way different leadership hybrids are constructed and deployed. In both the hybrids that led the first Allied assault troops to the beaches of Normandy – the LCVPs and LCAs (to say nothing of the hybrids that led them across the beaches) – significant weakness in the hybrids were cruelly exposed by the defenders and some of them were the consequences of political infighting and cultural blinkers rather than rational decision-making. But these cannot be separated from the technologies themselves because they form inherent parts of it; they are, indeed, hybrids of people and things.

Notes

1 Mission Command, which has long played a role in some aspects of the British Army, has recently become a critical aspect of the British military's Defence Leadership Centre doctrine. See Watters (2004).

2 See www.eng.fju.edu.tw/worldlit/lecture/Roy.ppt

3 Thanks to Jack Nasher-Awakemian for reminding me of this distinction.

4 See http://www.geocities.com/Athens/3682/clowdisley.html

5 See http://www.odyssey.dircon.co.uk/Victoria.htm It is to inhibit the powerful influence of rank that contemporary British Courts Martial precede the final verdict with a discussion of individual conclusions by the most junior officer first, and the senior officer last (thanks to Group Captain Graham Evans for pointing this out to me).

6 Edmund Burke (1729–97) is alleged to have said that 'all that is necessary for the triumph of evil is for good men to do nothing'.

7 See http://pw1.netcom.com/~asapilot/p90.html In 1994 Boeing published research into airline safety that used Hofstede's cultural categories to examine the link between culture and air crashes. That research suggested that those countries deemed to be high on power-distance and low on individualism (specifically, Panama, Colombia, Venezuela, China, Korea, Pakistan, Thailand) had an accident rate 2.6 times the average. See Phillips, D. (1994) 'Building a Cultural Index to World Airline Safety' *Washington Post*, 21 August 1994, p. 8. (Thanks to Adrian Wilkinson for alerting me to this research.)

8 'Provided Vincristine is administered intravenously (IV), it is a powerful and useful drug in the fight against leukaemia. However, if the drug is administered, in error, through an intrathecal injection (IT) the result is usually the death of the patient or if the patient does survive, then they typically suffer from severe neurological trauma.' *External Inquiry into the adverse incident that occurred at Queen's Medical Centre, Nottingham, 4th January 2001* by Professor Brian Toft. http://www.doh.gov.uk/qmcinquiry/

9 See http://news.bbc.co.uk/1/hi/health/1284244.stm

10 Hedge Funds (which started with LTCM in 1994) are limited partnerships with a maximum of 99 partners and are almost unregulated. About 4000 existed in 2004, financed by very wealthy institutions and individuals and with very high leverage/gearing. The debt to equity/capital at LTCM was between 50:1 and 250:1 while most operate at around 2:1.

11 See Heifetz (1994) on the issue of follower responsibility.

12 Much has been made of the oath of allegiance sworn to Hitler by all members of the German armed forces and the SS. Allegedly this prevented such individuals from abandoning their positions or even rejecting Hitler's increasingly erroneous orders. Yet the German Army's officer corps had previously demonstrated the fragility of such oaths when General Groener (who succeeded Ludendorff) told Kaiser Wilhelm II in November 1918 that he was no longer bound by his oath to the Kaiser – it was 'now just a notion' (quoted in May, 2000: 26).

13 Some of these rifles with a 90° bend in the barrel and a special mirrored sight were captured by US forces towards the end of the war. See Russell (1981: 183).

14 Kilvert-Jones (1999: 40) puts the number of minesweepers at 278.

15 See: http://www.higginsboat.org/html/higind.html

16 Quoted by Mike Whaley at http://www.softwhale.com/history/D-Day/Higgins-boats.htm

17 The earliest known amphibious craft was the 'amphibious battle wagon' designed by Agostino Ramelli (1531–1600). Several amphibious military vehicles were tested by the British and American forces in the 1920s, including an amphibious tank, the British 'Johnson Light Infantry Tank' in 1922 and Christie's two US models (*Wheels and Tracks*, No. 24, pp. 53–4 (1988).

18 *Parade* was an illustrated weekly published by British troops for British troops from August 1940 until February 1948. Examples can be seen in *Union Jack* (London: HMSO/Imperial War Museum).

19 Celtic warriors, however, did tend to fight naked in battle, at least until around 300 BC.

Leadership as results:
putting the subjunctive back
where it belongs

Introduction

This chapter is concerned with examining the perspective that takes results as the critical aspect of leadership. This model became very popular towards the end of the twentieth century, marked by the rise of all forms of audits and measurement systems that purported to improve the performance of leaders and their organizations. In what follows I approach this phenomenon by first evaluating the extent to which results can be traced back to the actions of leaders before proceeding to analyse the significance of results-based leadership for ethical behaviour, in particular in the case of two leaders usually lauded as embodying the highest ethical standards: Gandhi and Mother Theresa. The narrative then concentrates on an area that normally escapes from leadership studies: slavery. Using the slave revolts led by Spartacus in the Third Servile War against Rome, and the rebellions and resistance organized against Nazi slave labour, I argue that any simple notion of assessing leadership by its alleged 'results' is doomed to fail: the results of leadership are as contested as the definitions, and we would be better served by considering leadership as a subjunctive verb – as something that may, or may not, have results, rather than something that definitely does or does not.

Results, responsibility and culpability:
soft shell, hard shell

In Douglas Adams's *The Long Dark Tea-Time of the Soul* the first chapter ends with Kate Schechter at Heathrow Airport when an explosion knocks her unconscious. Chapter two begins thus:

> The usual people tried to claim responsibility. First the IRA, then the PLO and the Gas Board. Even British Nuclear Fuels rushed out a statement to the effect that the situation was

now completely under control, and that it was a one in a million chance, that there was hardly any reactive leakage at all, and that the site of the location would make a nice location for a day out with the kids and a picnic, before finally having to admit that it wasn't actually anything to do with them at all. No cause could be found for the explosion.

The point at hand is how quickly we attribute cause and effects, often with little or no evidence to support our attributions. Moreover, the precise cause and effects of leadership are also subject to reconstruction over time and in different places to the point where we can never really finalize the argument about leadership results with any kind of hermetic seal. Put another way, we might usefully configure the results of leadership through a subjunctive verb – something that *might* occur, rather than something that has or will occur, something for which leaders might, or might not, be responsible. Thus, as in Douglas Adam's novel, something happens and we need to find someone to blame or congratulate: we sack CEOs and generals if the stock falls or the battles are lost, even though it may have nothing to do with them. Indeed, as suggested in the previous chapter, leaders can be likened to saints and scapegoats in that they do not need to be physically or morally responsible for an event but we feel more secure if (1) we can establish a cause for an event and (2) we can establish an individual or group that we deem responsible for that event. In other words, we hold leaders *responsible* even if they are not *culpable*. The distinction between bearing the blame for others' mistakes and being personally guilty of making the mistake may be legitimate if the leaders are also directly involved in the recruitment, training and guidance of subordinates but often they are not and it is in this sense that leaders provide the ritual role of sacred scapegoat: someone needs to be sacrificed to the gods to assuage their wrath.

For Durkheim (1883) the sacred role of leaders also related to their function in society, as iconic embodiments of all that society held to be good and noble and as a yardstick for followers to measure themselves against. Without such leaders, Durkheim suggested, 'ordinary' people have no method of measuring themselves and no result to aim for. Hence the symbolic reward due to leaders – the respect of followers – was not to privilege them, nor was it necessary to encourage people to undertake the responsibility of leadership, instead the respect of followers was functionally necessary for followers in the same way that the sacred ritual of a funeral is necessary for the grieving but not for the dead. Indeed, the symbol of sacrifice is often manifest in the representations of the deaths of leaders – for example, Benjamin West's portrait 'The Death of Lord Viscount Nelson' specifically reconstructs the admiral's death to reflect the sacrifice of Jesus Christ. Thus when we are attempting to establish the importance of Leadership by Results it is worth remembering that 'Results' has multiple meanings and the word should not be reduced to some matrix of Key Performance Indicators.

The latter form of results-based leadership came to its apotheosis in the quality control movement, particularly in standards such as ISO 9000 and one of its predecessors BS 5750. Both of these systems of quality control had their origins in the attempts by various governments, but particularly the British, to maintain engineering standards in munitions factories in the Second World War. But what started out as a beneficial method of avoiding accidents at work and ensuring munitions did what they were supposed to, has, according to Seddon (2000), not only failed to deliver the promised improvement in quality but actually undermined the ability of organizations to improve quality by replacing an engineering standard with a management standard, a learning environment with one rooted in 'command and control'. In effect the focus of concern shifts from quality to the standard and thus satisfying the standard becomes more important than improving the quality of the product. The development of the 'audit society' (Power, 1999), itself rooted in 'the tyranny of numbers' (Boyle, 2001) has various manifestations of the debilitating effect of conformance, including universities who concentrate on satisfying government demands rather than those of their profession (research and teaching), hospitals that shift resources around in time to comply with specific medical audits rather than concentrate on medical improvements, and the removal of non-ISO 9000-registered companies from authorized suppliers' lists. In sum, achieving the *required* results may not be the equivalent of achieving the *desired* results and the same shift from trust to conformity often inhibits leadership.

One example from Seddon's (2003) renewed attack upon results-based models will suffice to cement the criticism that the problem is not the measurement but whose results are being measured? The answer is usually the managements' rather than the customers and the separation of the planning from the execution of work – in true Taylorist fashion – often leads to organizational misbehaviour designed to satisfy the management hierarchy and its fetish for results that can be easily measured rather than their desire to provide good service or products. Moreover, the consequence is often a determination to blame the poor performers rather than restructure the system that is itself usually responsible for the problems. The consequential fragmentation of the system generates extraordinary acts by the employees – but only in their ingenious methods of compliance and conformity not in service provision. For example, Seddon notes how a local authority developed a house repair system that required customers (tenants) to ring a call centre that diagnosed the problem, decided a Specification from the Schedule of Rates that determined how the trade workers would be paid and who would undertake it. This system was evaluated by results in terms of budget and 'time to repair', and the Best Value Performance Indicators (BVPI) that were mandated by central government were the percentage of 'emergency' repairs undertaken in 24 hours, the percentage of 'urgent' repairs done in seven days, and the percentage of 'non-urgent' repairs done in 28 days. The result was not an efficient and effective system for undertaking repairs as quickly as possible but a raft of skilful game playing devices to play the system: jobs were 'closed' and then 'reopened' to avoid delays being measured; jobs were reclassified to turn 'emergencies' into 'urgents' and 'urgents' into 'non-urgents'; a single repair often required different trades thus generating multiple BVPIs for the same repair. As a consequence 40 per cent of the calls to the call centre were complaints about the tardiness of repairs – even if the BVPIs showed the required progress. A reconstructed system that shifted the emphasis from 'working the system' to 'responding to demand' routed the calls straight to the responsible and appropriate trades workers who negotiated their own visiting schedules directly with the tenants and the elimination of the paper targets.

Another way of understanding this problem is to consider a biological analogy. Living creatures tend to exhibit either a 'soft-shell' or a 'hard shell' solution to the problem of protecting themselves.[1] Exogenous skeletons, that is, hard shells invest their trust in an external armoured body – such as a crab or lobster – which is very strong but liable to shatter and rupture if sufficiently damaged. Endogenous skeletons, that is, soft shells – like those of many animals – embody flexibility at the cost of sustaining reparable damage. In effect, the surface tissue is easily damaged but repairs easily too. Neither of these is essentially better than the other but some are more appropriate than others in certain circumstances.

Take the exoskeleton approach; here the object is to maintain the integrity of the boundary at all costs, even if that means losing the flexibility offered by the endoskeleton. In this case we might consider the results based approach of ISO 9000 and equivalents as concerned with maintaining the standard, the boundary, to the point where what the standard is for may be forgotten. In contrast, an approach more concerned with how organizations learn to cope with diversity and danger – even if that means accepting some damage and danger along the way – is closer to an endogenous skeleton. In short, while the endogenous skeleton approach is concerned with leading by learning, the exogenous skeleton approach is concerned with leading by maintaining the boundaries of acceptable and unacceptable action and results. Unfortunately, the learning that tends to accompany leadership by results is learning how to manipulate the system to ensure individual survival and prosperity, rather than learning how to enhance the survival and prosperity of the organization by the systematic application of knowledge.

But if leaders do not achieve anything can we regard them as leaders? This, of course, bears witness to the assumption that leadership is necessarily related to movement of some kind: leaders change things or stop things changing; those that fail to instigate change that is required or fail to stop change that is not required, are simply failed leaders. Hence for all that individuals or groups or hybrids may achieve positional leadership – 'in charge' or 'in front' – if the results of their position are negligible then they will not be regarded as successful leaders. And there clearly are examples where results have both improved and been associated with particular leaders. Perhaps one of the most visible is that associated with William Bratton, the 1994 New York Chief Police Commissioner whose policy of zero-tolerance and making individual officers responsible for the 'results' on their patch has, allegedly, turned New York from a city where, as Bratton recalled, 'the NYPD was demoralized and the ethos was: "Stay low and keep out of trouble"', to one where, by 2003 according to Howard Saffir (Bratton's Replacement), New York was the 'safest city in the world'. This had all been

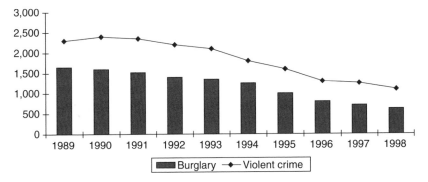

Sources: Bureau of Statistics, *Sourcebook of Criminal Justice Statistics*, 1990, 1997. Federal Bureau of Investigation, *Uniform Crime Reports*, 1996, 1997, 1998. Reconstructed from Brereton, 1999

Figure 3.1 Zero-tolerance and crime in New York city 1989–98 per 100,000 population

achieved by a judicious combination of focusing on the results, not the process, of policing using clear targets, using IT support to track crime, local accountability, rapid deployment, zero-tolerance, the saturation of crime 'hot spots', the removal of departmental barriers, and weekly meetings between precinct commanders when anyone of them may be called upon to explain any problem or anomaly.

There is little doubt that crime rates, including violent crimes, have dropped over this period but as Figure 3.1 above suggests, the fall in crime rates was already underway before Bratton arrived in 1994.

Furthermore, the crime rates have also dropped in cities that have undertaken radically different police methods such as San Diego, Los Angeles, the District of Columbia and Chicago (Brereton, 1999), as Figure 3.2 suggests. So the issue is not whether it is possible to lead by results but whether the results can be traced back to the leadership and whether the method tends to generate unplanned and deleterious outcomes.

Results and ethics: Gandhi and Mother Theresa

The difficulties of correlating results with the actions of leaders is often more difficulty than it might seem: it may be clear that the share price has risen, that the school's performance has improved, or that the army is victorious – but in what sense can we be certain that these successes were the direct result of the leader? And if we are certain that the leaders caused the results, rather than they were simply in post when the results occurred, is this necessarily beneficial? Take as an illustration the

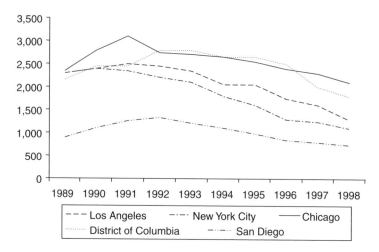

Sources: Bureau of Statistics, *Sourcebook of Criminal Justice Statistics*, 1990, 1997. Federal Bureau of Investigation, *Uniform Crime Reports*, 1996, 1997, 1998. Reconstructed from Brereton, 1999

Figure 3.2   Violent crime in US cities, 1989–98 per 100,000 population

response of Jeffrey Skilling, one time President of Enron to this question:

Questioner: What would you do if your company made a product that caused harm or even death?

Skilling: I'd keep making and selling it. My job is to be a profit centre and maximize return to the shareholders, it's the government's job to step in if a product is dangerous. (Quoted in Fusaro and Miller, 2002: 27)

The ethical consequences of this kind of, literally, irresponsible leadership have been well documented in relation to Enron (McLean and Elkind, 2003) and need not detain us here – you do not need to be an expert in Machiavelli to recognize unethical leadership. But what interests me here is a rather more complex issue: do ethical leaders necessarily generate beneficial results? Certainly Ulrich, Zener and Smallwood's very popular book, *Results-based Leadership* assumes that the adoption of a Balanced Score Card method of measuring results takes care of any ethical problems because it is *balanced*, and, as they suggest, Enron is a prime example of what can be achieved:

Enron has created significantly more shareholder value [than Florida Light and Power]. Why? Again, we suggest that Enron's leadership plays a significant role in achieving the larger multiple for the company's earning. Enron provides a prime example of a company whose leadership has created an organization that can effectively implement a strategy for meeting shareholder expectations and thus a larger valuation from and for those shareholders. Enron's thoughtful leaders deftly balance the many necessary results levers. (Ulrich *et al.*, 1999: 155)

Unfortunately this says it all – the results are only those of interest to the shareholders and the consequence, in this case at least, was the catastrophic collapse on Enron and the disgracing of its executives. In contrast, Florida Light and Power are still in business.[2]

Machiavelli would not necessarily have insisted on a negative response to the question connecting ethics to beneficent leadership: his concern was that leaders could only succeed if they recognized the kind of environment they worked in. Hence in an ethical world it was conducive to success to act ethically, whereas in Machiavelli's time, to have acted as ethically as the Christian scriptures and church leaders insisted at the time, would have doomed the population to the rapacious conquests of unethical invaders. Or, as he put it far more eloquently in *The Prince*,

> The fact is that a man who wants to act virtuously in every way necessarily comes to grief among so many who are not virtuous. Therefore if a prince wants to maintain his rule he must learn how not to be virtuous, and to make use of this or not according to need. ... Cesare Borgia was accounted cruel; nevertheless, this cruelty of his reformed the Romagna, brought it unity and restored order and obedience. On reflection it will be seen that there was more compassion in Cesare than in the Florentine people who, to escape being called cruel, allowed Pistoia to be devastated. (Machiavelli, XV, XVII)

In effect, Machiavelli is not suggesting that leaders should act immorally but that to protect the interests of a community a prince has to do whatever is necessary for the greater good. Thus the act should be contextualized and not analysed against some mythical moral world. The problem, of course, is defining 'the greater good' and relating this to the result. But what if we take leaders who are not tainted by ethical concerns but who have achieved clear results – can we not now say that the results-based leadership of these leaders are archetypes of this approach to leadership? Possibly, but the difficulty with this apparent move will be explored through two ostensibly similar cases: Mahatma Gandhi and Mother Theresa.

Mahatma Gandhi (1869–1948) rose from an obscure and unsuccessful small-town lawyer to become the self-appointed champion of the rights of Indian workers in South Africa to the nationalist leader *Mahatma*, 'Great Soul', leading the struggle for Indian independence from Britain through the use of non-violent resistance. In one sense his leadership by results is clear to see: India did gain its independence from Britain – but it isn't at all clear either that he was directly responsible for this or that the result resembled much of his vision for a future free India. So for example, his desperate efforts to prevent partition between India and Pakistan failed; his attempt to embody the leadership of all faiths was limited to the leadership of (some) Hindus; his attempts to stop violence between Hindus and Muslims either failed outright or were short-lived because over 1 million died in the ethnic violence accompanying partition; his economic ideals of autarchy and the rejection of a modern economy were, in turn, rejected by most people; his theories on women were not regarded by feminists as in anyway liberating; and the results of his strategy for limiting the effects of caste were themselves extremely limited. Thus on a strictly result-based analysis,

Gandhi seems to have failed many counts despite maintaining an ethical stand and being categorized as a successful leader. However, his real achievement cannot really be assessed in this way and his role is better articulated through the words of his erstwhile friend and then the Prime Minister, Nehru, speaking on the evening of Gandhi's assassination on 30 January 1948:

> The light has gone out of our lives and there is darkness everywhere … The light has gone out, I said, and yet I was wrong. For the light that shone in this country was no ordinary light … that light represented something more than the immediate present, it represented the living, the eternal truths, reminding us of the right path, drawing us from error, taking this ancient country to freedom.

This kind of epitaph spills over the edifice of any results' matrix and proclaims a value that is both beyond that matrix and subversive of it: some 'results' are extraordinarily difficult to measure but that does not mean they are irrelevant.

The case of Mother Theresa looks similar but generates a different lesson. Even if Gandhi's direct results are relatively poor compared to his hopes and dreams, he remains the consummate ethical leader whose iconic acts of bravery and non-violent resistance inspired, and still inspire, many political activists and leaders today. But can the same be said for Mother Theresa? Her beatification – the first step on the Catholic journey to sainthood – by Pope John Paul II occurred on 19 October 2003. According to the EWTN, the Global Catholic network, 'Mother Teresa founded the Missionaries of Charity and devoted her life to the care of "the poorest of the poor." She began her work in Calcutta, India and her sisters now continue work and ministry throughout the world bringing food, medicine, care and Christ's love to those in most need.'[3] She was born Agnes Gonxha Bojaxhiu on 26 August 1910, in Skopje, Macedonia, in the former Yugoslavia, joined an Irish Order of Nuns at 17 and moved to Calcutta in 1944 where she taught in a convent school. By 1950 she had left the convent to 'look after' the poor of Calcutta and established the Missionaries of Charity which expanded to over 450 centres in 133 countries led by 4500 nuns, tending the poor and the dying. She won the Pope John XXIII Peace Prize and the Nobel Peace Prize in 1979 'for work undertaken in the struggle to overcome poverty and distress, which also constitute a threat to peace'. A great leader indeed, if we are to judge her by these results.

One of these results must be her ability to secure benefactions. According to the official website,

> a chairman of a multinational company once asked, 'Mother, how do you manage your budget?' I asked him who had sent him here. He replied, 'I felt an urge inside me.' I said: other people like you come to see me and say the same. It was clear God sent you, Mr. A, as He sends Mr. X, Mrs. Y, Miss Z, and they provide the material means we need for our work. The grace of God is what moved you. You are my budget. God sees to our needs, as Jesus promised. I accepted the property he gave and named it Asha Dan (Gift of Hope).

However, according to Aroup Chatterjee, a doctor who used to work for Mother Theresa and author of the book *Mother Teresa: The Final Verdict*, Mother Theresa's main concern was not helping the poor but proselytizing the Catholic faith and accumulating huge sums to further the spread of the Catholicism, rather than to alleviate the poverty she found all around her. Similarly for Christopher Hitchins, Mother Theresa remained uninterested in solving the poverty of the poor and far more concerned to generate huge financial resources for the spread of the catholic faith.[4]

For our purposes which of these two images prevails is less relevant than that the image is clearly contested. Hitchins' account of her is entitled 'Hell's Angel' so it would be difficult to find two more diamterically opposed view of a leader. But, note that both positive and negative images accept her as a successful results-based leader, albeit that success is deemed positive by one account and negative by the other. But this is precisely the problem with notions of ethical leadership criticized in Chapter 1: what counts as ethical depends not upon the actions that are taken, nor even the context within which the actions occur, but rather the perspective of the perceiver. For dedicated Catholics successful proselytization is deemed by definition to be an ethical endeavour; but for believers in other religions or atheists it cannot be regarded in the same light: results-based leadership is not so much dependent on ethical behaviour as a component of it. This does not mean that Mother Theresa was an unethical leader – but it does imply that we cannot separate such assessments for their own cultural milieux: what counts as ethical leadership depends not upon some universal set of ethics and most certainly not on some alleged definition of 'Human Nature', but on what counts as ethical behaviour in that particular envelope of space and time.

In effect, it does not matter whether we regard the acts of leaders as unethical; what matters is whether the followers of those leaders regard their leaders as unethical; and if they do whether this is less relevant than the results of their leadership. Take slavery, for example, surely there are few people today who regard slavery as an ethical form of relationship, though many may have done so in the past. But since there are probably more slaves alive now than ever before at one time even this assumption cannot be true. As Bales (2000: 3) suggests:

> Across the world slaves work and sweat and build and suffer. Slaves in Pakistan may have made the shoes you are wearing and the carpet you stand on.[5] Slaves in the Caribbean may have put sugar in your kitchen and toys in the hands of your children. In India they may have sewn the shirt on your back and polished the ring on your finger. They are paid nothing.

But since the power of slaves is so severely inhibited by their condition and since there have been so few successful slave leaders, is there anything to be learned about results-based leadership by considering slavery? After all, since slavery was abolished by philanthropists and religious groups, rather than by successful revolts, what have slave leaders ever achieved?

Slavery and leadership

Slavery, coercion and results

Since slavery is essentially rooted in a coercive relationship what possible place does it have in leadership? Perhaps the first thing to question is whether leadership is associated with non-coercive relationships. Weber certainly argued that Charismatic authority was the only non-coercive form since followers wanted to follow rather than had to be forced or persuaded. But even the religious charismatics that Weber focused on rooted their authority in their gods, all of whom promised some form of punishment for non-believers. That being the case, and since slavery is such an endemic aspect of human history, to remove the leadership of slaves by slave-owners and their slave overseers because it is premised on a coercive relationship seems to remove a vast chunk of human history from our purview.

Even if slavery is one of the most coercive forms of 'leadership' does this imply that slaves are powerless? Well although slaves destined for the gladiatorial arena had little control over their future they still had some. Granted, those tied to a stake and eaten by wild animals had only their voices with which to protest or voice their belief in their gods but gladiators could always refuse to fight – and accept the consequences. For example, Seneca (4 BC–AD 65) noted how two German prisoners choked themselves to death on the sponges used in lavatories, while another put his head between the spokes of a moving wheel. Three hundred years later Symmachus (AD 345–410) describes how 20 German prisoners, destined for the gladiatorial arena, killed themselves just before their appearance (Wiedemann, 1995: 113).

Nonetheless, the power to commit suicide, to refuse to allow others to kill you, is significantly more limited than the power to organize a rebellion against the enslavers. The important word here is 'organized' because individual resistance does not necessarily require leadership since there may be no followers – and followers are the *sine qua non* of leadership. And because slaves have so few resources with which to resist their enslavers, leadership of resistance amongst slaves must rank amongst the most difficult of all leadership tasks – and one of the most difficult to trace by its effects because so few revolts were either successful or recorded.

In what follows I examine this most difficult form of leadership through examining slavery in Ancient Rome and Nazi Germany[6] and select particular aspects to illustrate issues important for leadership rather than just slavery in and of itself. What unites Rome and Nazi Germany beyond their reliance on slave labour is the red thread of Spartacus. As the leader of a slave rebellion in Rome of the first century BC he may well have threatened the very bedrock of Roman 'civilization', though ultimately he failed in this; and as a symbol of the resistance of the oppressed he became the political icon of the Spartacist League (subsequently the German Communist Party) in the heady days of Germany just after the end of the First World War. In turn the communists, especially in Hitler's construction of them as led by the

'Jewish-Bolsheviks', most represented all that the Nazis sought to exterminate after 1933. In both cases the leadership of slaves and prisoners proved only partially successful in terms of direct material results – neither Imperial Rome nor Nazi Germany were toppled by slave rebellions – but in both cases the examples of leadership provided hope to others that even military dictatorships are not omnipotent. This is a critical lesson for leadership by results: the results are often difficult to determine, are often rooted in narratives provided by the victors, and may occur long after the leader has theoretically 'failed'.

From the existing records it would appear that slavery has been an endemic aspect of most human civilizations. Gravestones in Lower Egypt, for example, suggest that a Libyan people enslaved a Bushman tribe in 8000 BC (Thomas, 1997: 25). Slaves are also depicted on memorials from the 'golden standard' of Ur in the middle of the third millennium BC and slave markets were a regular feature of early Babylonian society (around 1800 BC) where some slaves even owned their own slaves. Indeed, Lévi Strauss suggested that writing may well have had its origins in facilitating 'the enslavement of other human beings' (quoted in Dugan and Dugan, 2000: 166), and Marx was convinced that 'direct forced labour is the foundation of the ancient world' (1973; 245). So great has been the impact of slavery that Patterson (1982: vii) suggests 'probably there is no group of people whose ancestors were not at one time slaves or slave holders' (quoted in Blackburn, 1988: 263). The Ancient Egyptian empires also involved slavery, though they were less important than in their neighbouring societies (Roberts, 1993: 49, 65). Instead, the Egyptian elite, although owners of slaves themselves, tended to rely on indebted labour, often in huge gangs of 20,000 or more workers who migrated from the fields to the infrastructure as demand required (Mann, 1986: 151). Certainly the ancient Chinese societies of Eastern Zhou (beginning around 770 BC) turned prisoners of war into slaves owned by the aristocratic class and, by the Warring States stage (beginning about 470 BC), by the state itself (Yates, 1999: 19, 28).

Yet it remains the case that slavery is not a topic much visited by scholars of management or leadership. Recently, only Cooke (2003) has made a serious attempt to grapple with the relationship between slavery and contemporary management and his work is restricted to American slavery. Even here the scale of the issue is significant for 'by 1860, when the historical orthodoxy has modern management emerging on the railroads, 38,000 managers were managing the 4 million slaves working in the US economy' (Cooke, 2003: 1895). Thus the emergence of modern management and leadership can either be located in heroic American rail road engineers or in the cotton fields and rice swamps of American slave plantations. As Cooke makes clear, Chandler's (1977) account of the growth of contemporary management ignores American slavery because there was little separation between ownership and control and there were few large-scale plantations – though in between 1850 and 1860 the number of plantation managers almost doubled to 37,883 and by then 2279 plantations used more than 100 slaves. Braverman's (1974) alternative model denies slavery a role because it was not based on wage labour, but the disciplinary mechanisms used against slaves and the forms of resistance developed by them all have echoes in contemporary management. Indeed, in 1846 the Southern Cultivator explained in eerily Taylorist language precisely how to control slaves: 'the slave should know that his master is to govern absolutely, and he is to obey implicitly ... he is never for a moment to exercise either his will or his judgement in opposition to a positive order' (quoted in Cooke, 2003: 1911).[7]

Moreover, since slaves could not be coerced entirely their forms of resistance manifest an important aspect of the issue of power – it is seldom total. Writing in 1860 Olmsted noted not just that the slaves worked more efficiently if they were given an occasional day off, but that they 'cannot be made to do their masters will. ... Not that they often directly refuse to obey an order, but when they are directed to do anything for which they have a disinclination, they undertake it in such a way that the desired result is sure not to be accomplished' (quoted in Cooke, 2003: 1905).

The Ancient Greeks and Romans, of course, were slave-owning societies, though we do not know much about them before Herodotus, himself a slave-owner, began writing in the fifth century BC and by this time many places that Herodotus visited used slaves (Harvey, 1988: 42–3). The Greeks were surprised to learn in 300 BC from Megasthenes, a Greek ambassador to India, that no slaves existed in India. In fact there were indentured labourers in India at this time who were, in all but name, slaves (Roberts, 1993: 339).

Homer's period coincided with most slaves being captives from war and therefore mainly women, since their menfolk would have been slaughtered, but this practice was gradually displaced by one of enslaving men too, so that by the fifth century BC, the height of Athenian power, between 25 and 35 per cent of the population were slaves, undertaking a variety of tasks from working in the fields, to running messages, carrying water and preparing meals (Harvey, 1988: 49). Some acted as teachers and one of these was Aesop. The word *pedagogue* is derived from the Greek description of a slave who accompanied a wealthy boy to school and this is richly ironic given that the Ancient Greeks often justified slavery on the basis of their barbarian nature, that is, they lacked intelligible speech and reason. But in reality most Greeks probably did not concern themselves with justifications for slavery because slavery was apparently endemic throughout the world and more often simply a consequence of defeat in battle. Anyway, since many influential Greeks regarded ordinary labour as only marginally better than slavery, their concern for justifying slavery would have been minimal, after all, neither slaves nor those who were dependent upon another for their livelihood were 'free' in any sense recognized by Athenian citizens, who were, of course, all men.

The Romans called a slave *servus*, literally an object (*res*), a thing, as indeed did Aristotle before them, for he considered a slave to be 'an animated instrument' (*The Politics*, 1253b). Note here also that the Latin *servare* – to save, to conserve – had close links to the word for slaves, *servi*, because to enslave a military prisoner was literally to decide *not* to execute him, to save him or her from their 'deserved' death (Wiedemann, 1995: 103). Following this logic the Romans appeared to have recruited slaves into their armies for the Second Punic War between 218–202 BC (Santosuosso, 1997: 13, 150), but, importantly, Roman armies were not reliant upon slave or indebted labour for camp or fortification building, and instead were self-sufficient (Mann, 1986: 276). Such was the military success of Rome that by 50 BC of the 1 million people living in Rome, between 100,000 and 200,000 of them were slaves (Köhne and Ewigleben, 2000: 127).

Coincidentally, as naval warfare became predominant at this time, the Athenians reintroduced the practice of destroying a city after capture, executing the men and selling the women and children into slavery (Raaflaub, 1999: 142). Athens also produced both a philosophical justification, and a critique, of slavery. The justification came from Plato and Aristotle's argument that some people were 'naturally' suited to slavery,[8] though Greeks should not enslave other Greeks. As far as Aristotle was concerned, 'Humanity is divided into two: the masters and the slaves; or if one prefers it, the Greeks and Barbarians, those who have the right to command; and those who are born to obey' (quoted in Thomas, 1997: 28). In effect the issue of leadership was not restricted to any individual or class but common to an entire ethnic group, as long as they were Greek and male.

Athens also produced one of the first philosophical critiques of slavery in stoicism, though slavery here was defined as being in bondage to one's own faults and lusts, rather than relating to the legal condition of slavery (Ste. Croix, 1988: 29). Nevertheless, the stoics also suggested that humans and animals were differentiated by reason, and thus all humans were in this sense equal. It is but a short step from this foundation stone to argue that humans are all subject to the same 'natural law' and that arguments that distinguish between slaves and non-slaves on any fundamental basis are unjustified. The ideological problem facing slave owners was resolved by different forms; the Romans tended to suggest that providing the local civil law permitted slavery then slavery was legitimate; some early Christian authorities often sidestepped the problem by insisting that original sin was the root cause of the problem, but others in some of the monasteries took their religion rather more literally and enslaved themselves to a life of property-less poverty and prayer (Anthony, 1977: 15–38).

Yet one of the greatest threats to the Greeks derived not from philosophy but from the slaves themselves, in particular from Sparta. There the 'helots' or 'slaves' of Sparta not only outnumbered their Spartan rulers but themselves posed a considerable threat to Spartan domestic security. In fact the helots were bonded to the land not to individual owners and were thus closer to a serf than slave, and, unlike Athenian slaves, Helots could only be freed by the Spartan state and not by individual slave owners. But the relative absence of slave revolts in Athens and the constant fear of a Helot revolt amongst the Spartans tell us something about the importance of organizational factors for collective resistance: domestic slaves simply did not have access to the mechanisms normally required to organize collective resistance.

The Spartans had good reason to fear their own labour force – it seems to have been the only known society that required its principal judicial leaders to declare war on the Helots on taking office each year, making the killing of Helots beyond the criminal law. In Rome, the murder by a slave owner of the slave of another slave owner usually resulted in a fine of twice the value of the dead slave; after all the owner had some property rights in the deceased, if nothing else (Blackburn, 1988: 276). By contrast, Persians were forbidden to injure, let alone kill, their slaves for a single offence. But even such Spartan hostility could not guarantee quiescence: in 369 the Helots of Messenia successfully overthrew their Spartan controllers and established their own state (Cartledge, 1988: 38).

Only in Rome did freed or manumitted[9] slaves acquire political rights and their children, if born after freedom was attained, acquire Roman citizenship. Only freed slaves in Rome were likely to have any chance of acquiring wealth, and even slaves themselves (Ste. Croix, 1988). But we need not assume that rebellious slaves would be any better treated in Rome than in Sparta: in AD 61 the murder of Pedanius Secundus by one of his slaves resulted in the traditional punishment – all 400 of his slaves were executed, a punishment that persisted for another 500 years (Blackburn, 1988: 273).

But even if individual resistance to slavery was actually far more apparent than we might surmise, and certainly Bradley's (1994) summary of individual slave resistance from the works of Cato, Cicero and Pliny the elder, for example, implies that it was an endemic feature of slave relations, it is also clear that collective revolts aimed at overthrowing the Roman slave system were notable for their general absence. However, there had been two slave revolts (the First and Second Servile Wars) in Sicily (BC 134–32, 104–101) prior to the revolt led by Spartacus (known by the Romans as the Third Servile War) so it was not unheard of. The accounts of the revolt are both minimal and, of course, tend to be written by Romans like Sallust whose *Histories* was written 35 years after the events but have since been lost. However the works of Greeks like Plutarch's *Life of Crassus* and Appian's *The Civil Wars*, and the *History of Rome* by Florus (an African born Roman) from the early second century AD give us enough to consider the difficulties of leading such a rebellion against Rome.

Spartacus and leadership in the Third Servile War

Appian suggested that Spartacus was a Thracian[10] by birth and had served in the Roman army, possibly as an auxiliary, before being enslaved and then sold at auction into the gladiatorial school of Cnaeus Lentulus Batiatus in Capua. As we shall see in the case of revolts inside Nazi Concentration and Death Camps, the discipline, skills and cultural affinity spawned by military service provided some groups with a much greater capacity for organizing and leading collective resistance.

For Spartacus it is notable that the revolt spread from the gladiatorial school at Capua rather than simply from ordinary slaves, again implying that the cultural or community affinities of the 74 gladiators (Florus suggests 30; Plutarch suggests 78), together with their martial skills were important in their initial break out in 73 BC and escape to Mount Vesuvius, roughly 30 kilometres away. There the gladiators elected three leaders: Spartacus, Oenomaus and Crixus, and Lendering (2003) suggests they represented the three main ethnic groups: a Thracian, a Greek, and a Gaul respectively. After a local Roman militia was beaten off, Rome – already involved in major wars on two fronts (Pompey in Spain and Lucullus in Macedonia) – sent the Propraetor (Roman magistrate in charge of a province) Caius Claudius Glaber with a small legion of 3000 hastily conscripted and untrained soldiers. Glaber trapped the slaves on top of Mount Vesuvius but the slaves abseiled down vines, moved to the rear of the Roman camp and looted it, driving the soldiers back to Rome. Appian says many slaves and some freemen then joined them 'Since Spartacus divided the profits of his raiding into equal shares, he soon attracted a very large number of followers' (quoted in Shaw, 2001: 140). Moreover, according to Appian, Spartacus forbade the import of gold and silver into the slave camp to maintain a basic level of equality and to focus on collective survival, and tried with less success to prevent the mass looting undertaken by Crixus and the Gauls.

A Roman army of 6000 under the Praetor (Roman magistrate responsible for the administration of justice) Publius Varinius was then despatched bearing the symbol of the Roman senate, the *fasces*, but this too was destroyed and Varinius humiliated. As Florus suggests 'they (rebels) ranged over the whole of Campania. Not content with the plundering of country houses and villages, they laid waste Nola, Nuceria, Thurii and Metapontum with terrible destruction' (quoted in Lendering, 2003).

Apian suggests that the slave army rapidly increased to 70,000 in number and it spent the winter of 73 BC in the south of Italy before moving north, apparently seeking to escape over the Alps into Gaul (present day France, then not under Roman control). At some point in the journey the slave army was divided between Spartacus and Crixus. Rome sent two legions to defeat the slaves and although the 20,000 Gauls under Crixus were defeated, Spartacus' main army destroyed both legions (a legion varied between 3000 and 5000 men and was around 5000 at this time) and then killed some of the prisoners by crucifying them and making others fight each other in a makeshift gladiatorial arena in a parody of their own world. As Spartacus' army increased to 100,000, according to Appian, he defeated another Roman army of two legions led by Cassius Longinus at the battle of Mutina (now Modena). However, for reasons unknown, the slave army turned back at the foot of the Alps and returned to Rhegium (now Reggio Calabria) just off Sicily defeating yet another Roman army of two legions under Licinius Crassus on the way.

Crassus had already ordered the decimation of the army he inherited (one in ten drawn by lot executed by his comrades)[11] and as the slave army dithered for some reason at Rhegium, Crassus had fortifications built across the strip of land, effectively blocking the rebellious slaves in. After a brief foray against the fortifications Spartacus ordered the crucifixion of a Roman prisoner and then broke through the fortifications to reach the port of Brundisium (Brindisi) only to find that the Roman General

Lucullus was disembarking his army from Macedonia. In the chaos that followed an army of ten legions (around 50,000 soldiers) led by Crassus finally defeated Spartacus's army near the source of the River Silarus, killing perhaps 30,000 of the 36,000 who chose to fight (Appian puts the Roman losses at 1000). At the same time Pompey's army arrived from Spain to kill those fleeing from the battle northwards. Although 3000 unharmed Roman prisoners were subsequently discovered at the camp of the slaves, Crassus had all 6000 surviving slaves crucified along the 200 mile route of the Appian Way between Capua – where as Figure 3.3 below suggests, the revolt had started – and Rome, where the fate of the slaves was sealed (Bradley, 1998: 124).

The final aspect of the Third Servile War that throws a critical shadow over the entire episode is to note how important slaves were to the undermining of hubris – the Roman Senate authorised a 'Triumph' for Pompey for his previous success in Spain but not for the victory over Spartacus by Crassus who received the lesser award of an Ovation.[12]

That Spartacus did not set out from Capua with his fellow gladiators to seek personal immortality or overthrow slavery in the Roman world seems incontrovertible, but that his army of slaves survived for two years under harsh conditions and defeated as many as nine Roman armies is a testament to their collective military skill and his political leadership. But is it the achievements of Spartacus that encourage us to perceive him as a leader?

Under this line of enquiry we should note that Spartacus deployed an array of astute tactical moves that significantly enhanced his chances of a successful result even if he never achieved that. Thus he instilled discipline into the rag-tag army of slaves; he refused to allow Roman Army deserters to join for fear that they would jeopardize the solidarity of the slaves; and he ensured the equal division of spoils and

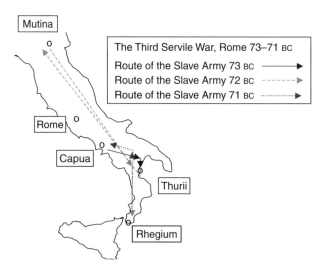

Figure 3.3 The Third Servile War

limited the acquisition of gold and silver for personal advancement. Moreover, some of his actions were resonant of Sun Tzu's admonitions about putting your troops into 'dead ground' where they have no option but to fight; thus he slaughtered his own horse on the eve of the final battle, made Roman prisoners fight each other as gladiators and even crucified Roman soldiers in full view of the Roman army knowing that the consequence could not be anything other than the prevention of surrender and the death of all captives. To have survived at all as a gladiator was an achievement in itself but to have led a rag-tag army of many thousands comprised of Gauls, Thracians, Greeks, Germans and probably many other ethnic identities for two years, most without any form of military training and against the greatest army the world had then known, was a significant achievement of leadership.

It is also worth pondering whether it was ever possible for a single leader, without formal authority and without the vestiges of a formal military hierarchy to 'lead' a 70,000 strong army of ex-slaves. Given the limits of the human voice the only way that Spartacus could have imposed his will upon such a large group before – never mind during – a battle, would have been to imitate the Roman system of trumpet calls and flags. We do not know whether the slaves used such methods to control the deployment of groups or whether it was simply a case of the mass bearing down in one gigantic tidal wave to overcome their Roman opponents, or be subdued by them.

Perhaps the slave army, imitating their origins as gladiators, embodied a form of organization that relates linguistically to that most feared of gladiators – the *retarius*. The *retarius* was a gladiator armed with a net and a trident and usually wearing a *Murmillo* helmet, common to Thracia from where Spartacus came of course. The *retarius* usually fought the *secutor* (armed with a semi-cylindrical shield and the sword common to Roman soldiers, the *gladius*) in a combat traditionally associated with the *retarius* as the pursuer and the *secutor* as the pursued (Connolly, 2003: 77–8). The *retarius* was the lowest ranked gladiator and was at a distinct disadvantage unless he (there were some women gladiators but they were more common in Britain than Rome) could compensate for his vulnerability through greater agility and speed. *Retarius* comes from the Latin *rete* – a net, or having veins, from which we derive the word reticulate: a network of parts; a net; having veins. Ironically, then, the net that the *retarius* used may have been how the slave army operated because it would have had to operate as a loose and decentralized network under distributed leadership rather than a well-oiled military machine under the central control of Spartacus. It is no doubt a great irony that we are only now returning to consider the value of the networked organization over 2000 years after Spartacus may have been obliged to develop it.

Whatever the organizational method that was deployed the result was temporarily at least successful. On the one hand he facilitated the short-term freedom of perhaps 70,000–100,000 slaves against the most formidable empire the world had then experienced. He also defeated the might of nine Roman armies with a rag-tag army that had virtually no military training, with limited weapons, and with a group of immense ethnic diversity and heterogeneous interests. Of course the revolt failed and slavery continued but it is at least questionable whether that defeat was inevitable and whether that implied failure for those who gained at least a couple of years of freedom rather than living and dying in chains.

Indeed, so great was his achievement that even his enemies explained his success through his similarity to them. For example, Plutarch (*Life of Crassus* 8) suggests that Spartacus was unusual for a Thracian:

> Spartacus was a Thracian from the nomadic tribes and not only had a great spirit and great physical strength, but was, much more than one would expect from his condition, most intelligent and cultured, being more like a Greek than a Thracian.

It may well be that Plutarch, like the Romans who fought and feared Spartacus, were loath to accept that a mere barbarian could have inflicted so much upon them and that attributing Greek-like characteristics to him may have rationalized their uncertainties. Plutarch also insists that Spartacus believed himself to be fated after an incident that occurred as he was sold at Rome:

> When he first came to be sold at Rome, they say a snake coiled itself upon his face as he lay asleep, and his wife, who at this latter time also accompanied him in his flight, his country-woman, a kind of prophetess, and one of those possessed with the bacchanal frenzy, declared that it was a sign portending great and formidable power to him with no happy event ...[13]

Leading slaves the Hollywood way

We shall never know whether Spartacus really believed he was fated to 'great and formidable power' though Eunus, the leader of the slave rebellion in the First Servile War seems to have been associated with a religious cult (Bradley, 1998: 58–9) and Arthur Koestler's novel about Spartacus, entitled *The Gladiators* (1999) and originally published in 1939, suggests that Spartacus may have been influenced by the messianism of the Hebrew prophets. However, Stanley Kubrick's movie version starring Kirk Douglas and based on Howard Fast's 1952 novel *Spartacus* implies that Spartacus eventually recognizes he cannot defeat Rome.

It might seem somewhat irrelevant to review the movie version to reconsider the leadership of Spartacus but there are important lessons in the making and editing of the movie for all students of leadership. Fast's novel envisions Spartacus as a proto-communist whose leadership is critical to taking the slaves to brink of destroying Rome itself. At the end of Fast's novel (1974: 272) Varinia, the wife of Spartacus and mother of his child, is explaining to Gracchus, a Roman Senator, what Spartacus wanted to achieve:

> *Gracchus*: But when he tore down Rome, what would he build instead of Rome?
> *Varinia*: He wanted a world where there were no slaves and no masters, only people living together in peace and brotherhood. ...
> *Gracchus*: So that was the dream of Spartacus ... to make a world with no ships and none to be whipped – with no palaces and no mud huts.

Koestler does not dispute Spartacus's proto-communist leanings but has a very different timbre to his novel of Spartacus. Koestler, an ex-member of the same German Communist Party that Luxemburg and Liebknecht founded from the Spartacist League, became massively disillusioned with it by 1935 and his novel resonates with the brooding inevitability of failure. Hence his book is primarily written as an investigation into what he called 'the law of detours' which compels the leader on the road to Utopia to be 'ruthless for the sake of pity'. In particular, Koestler relates this to an episode that remains confusing in the sources: what happened to Crixus?

All that we really know about Crixus is that he was one of the original three elected leaders and that he and between 20,000 and 30,000 Gauls had separated from the main slave army and were annihilated by a Roman army. However, Koestler suggests in his novel that Crixus was intent on pillaging the Roman lands while Spartacus was keen to lead the entire group to freedom to build the 'Sun Sate' – the slaveless utopia (Fast's version has Crixus intent on destroying Rome itself and with it the entire slave system). While Spartacus toys with the idea of executing Crixus to prevent the break up of the army he hesitates over the decision and Crixus leaves with one third of the army, fatally weakening Spartacus's position. As Koestler notes,

> [Spartacus] shrinks from taking the last step – the purge by crucifixion of the dissident Celts and the establishment of a ruthless tyranny; and through his refusal he dooms the revolution to defeat. In *Darkness at Noon* [Koestler's novel about Russian under Stalin], the Bolshevik Commissar Rubashove goes the opposite way and follows the 'law of detours' to the end – only to discover that 'reason alone was a defective compass which led one such winding, twisted course that the goal finally disappears in the mist'. Thus the two novels complement each other – both roads end in a tragic cul-de-sac. (1999: 317)

The result of Spartacus's weakness for Koestler is to let slip the chance of success, and the Roman blood-letting that follows the last battle captures not just the rebels but 'whosoever owned less than one acre or two cows [who] was suspected of revolutionary sympathies was killed or kidnapped; a quarter of the Italian slave population was extirpated. The rebels had squirted blood over the country, the conquerors turned it into a slaughterhouse' (Koestler, 1999: 305). Thus for Koestler Spartacus's leadership is almost an irrelevance because he is doomed whichever way he turns: if he is ruthless enough to save the revolution it will become directionless because the law of detours will make it so; but if he retains his ethical position the revolution will be strangled by its enemies.

In many ways Kubrick's film reproduces this fatalism and its accompanying irrelevance of leadership. For example, a scene in the 1959 movie *Spartacus* shows Varinia (played by Jean Simmons) trying to comfort Spartacus (played by Kirk Douglas) as he wrestles with the tragic realization that, despite all his victories, he must plan for a future battle against yet another Roman army.

Varinia: They've never beaten us yet.
Spartacus: No. But no matter how many times we beat them, they always seem to have another army to send against us. And another. Varinia, it's as if we've started something that has no ending.

This deeply pessimistic view of the possibility of leading slaves to freedom against the mightiest empire of the day was also deeply controversial at the time of making the movie. The facts were in dispute because several accounts of the revolt suggested that Rome was by no means secure and was very close to defeat itself at one time. And the precise words used by the actors in the movie were subject to immense controversy, as the director, scriptwriter and actors all fought over the way the narrative should be explained.

In the subsequent battle, the Romans defeat the slaves and in the aftermath, Spartacus and his closest friend, Antonius (played by Tony Curtis), discuss the purpose and possibilities of the slave revolt.

> *Antonius*: Could we have won, Spartacus? Could we ever have won?
> *Spartacus*: Just by fighting them, we won something. When even one man says, 'No, I won't', Rome begins to fear. And we were tens of thousands who said it.

This scene, which appears to offer a rather more optimistic account of the leadership trials of Spartacus, was subsequently retaken to create a very different interpretation for the first public showing.

> *Antonius*: Could we have won, Spartacus? Could we ever have won?
> *Spartacus*: No! That was the wrong fight. We were doomed from the beginning. But it was a beautiful thing.

In the event the negative reaction of the audience to the second take forced the reinsertion of the original take but it's important to reflect here on the leadership role of the film makers in constructing radically different images of leadership in the film itself. While Dalton Trumbo wrote the screen play his left wing sympathies had ensured he had done little significant worked during the previous decade of McCarthyism and although John F. Kennedy's personal endorsement of the film had undermined the attempt by the right wing journalist Hedda Hopper and the American Legion to boycott the film, Universal Studios remained sensitive enough to the political context to tread very cautiously through the various rewritings of the script, including cutting three battle scenes and a dozen dialogues that implied that the slaves were very close to eliminating Rome altogether.[14]

The upshot is that the movie *Spartacus* is not simply an essentially contested account of the leadership of a little known slave but itself the result of essential contests between different leaders. It might be appropriate, therefore, to leave this account by relating it to the moment in the movie when the Senator Crassus demands to know the identity of Spartacus in return for sparing the lives of the remaining 6000 slaves. The historical accounts suggest that Spartacus's body was never found but the movie account is important for its playing out of the essential contested nature of identity, for one by one the slaves responds to Crassus' demand by getting to their feet and shouting 'I'm Spartacus!'

We will never know who the real Spartacus was – but that is the point: it doesn't necessarily matter and the ambiguity of his character also facilitated the legacy of resistance to slavery and oppression that has inspired countless individuals and groups ever since. One of those groups also reinforces the limits of the 'results' of his leadership. The Spartacists were a group of revolutionary socialists led by Rosa Luxemburg and Karl Liebknecht whose actions in the chaos of early post–First World War Germany were intended to tip Germany into a revolutionary cauldron that would result in the end of capitalism. The Spartacists – or Spartacus League as the party was actually called – were founded in 1915 primarily as a consequence of the support for the war by the Social Democrats, a heterogeneous left wing political party whose members included Luxemburg and Liebknecht. Luxemburg was imprisoned for her opposition to the war and wrote the Junius Pamphlet[15] whilst in prison which called for the German Army to mutiny.

On their release from prison in the general amnesty of November 1918 they were both instrumental in the formation of the German Communist Party in December 1918, which was essentially composed of Spartacists. In January 1919 the most radical Spartacists, against Luxemburg's advice, attempted to turn the widespread workers unrest into a revolution in Berlin against the government of Ebert, a Social Democrat. Ebert immediately withdrew to Weimar and allowed the right wing Freikorps (comprised mainly of ex-soldiers) free reign to put down the insurrection. On 15 January Luxemburg and Liebknecht were arrested and taken to the Adlon Hotel to be held as prisoners and both were murdered that night; Luxemburg was found in the *Landwehr* canal in May, long after the *Freikorps* had put down the attempted revolution with great violence and bloodshed (Nettle, 1969).

After a lengthy period of disarray the German Communist Party recovered under Thurman's leadership and went on to gain four seats in the Reichstag in the 1920 election, 62 in 1924 and 54 in 1928. Not until the 1930 election did the Nazi Party secure more votes that the Communist Party but by 1933 the latter had been abolished having spent most of the previous decade towing the political line from Moscow that the Social Democrats were actually Social Fascists, that is little better than the Nazis, and believing that the inevitable failure of the Nazis would leave the Communists free to pick up where the Spartacists had left off in 1919.[16]

The 'Results-based' approach to leadership then, suggests that Spartacus was on one side, like that of the German Spartacists, manifestly a failure: his actions facilitated the deaths of thousands, few slaves achieved the freedom they had presumably joined the revolt to acquire, and Rome as a slave-based imperial power persisted for a further five centuries after his death. On the other hand the results of his leadership have inspired many to resist what they perceive to be equivalent forms of oppression. Yet the most famous inheritors of that iconic leadership also failed and once again left a trail of dead in their wake. On these grounds we might conclude that Spartacus was a failed leader but this implies that no further 'inheritors' will ever arise and, if they do, they will also fail. In short, irrespective of any existing empirical example of failure, it could still be said that a results-based analysis of the leadership of Spartacus remains potential significant.

But if Spartacus provided the symbolic leadership to create the Spartacist League and the early German Communist Party, he also provided the excuse for Hitler to reengage with slavery and several examples of leadership under conditions reminiscent of those facing Spartacus.

Slavery and leadership in Nazi times

The enslavement of prisoners of war or conquered people has, as we have seen, a long tradition in human history. But the enslavement and extermination of a proportion of one's fellow citizens is unusual, and the policy of destruction through labour (*vernichtung durch arbeit*) at a time when a labour shortage existed is positively irrational, at least in economic terms. That atypicality reached its apotheosis in the twentieth century under the Nazi regime in Germany, though Stalin's assaults upon the Kulaks and various 'enemies of the revolution' puts him in strong contention for a place in this hall of infamy. Stalin also imposed the 'Not One Step Backwards' order (no. 227), which effectively ensured that anyone retreating would be shot by their own side, but this is a different form of coercion from the one we are dealing with here (See Beevor, 1998: 85). This section, though, will concentrate on the issues of leadership for the 7.5 million foreign labourers in Germany, most of whom worked as slaves under Hitler, as well as the 6 million Jews who died, some through over work, but most of whom were simply murdered, and the several million Prisoners of War (POWs). Very often the groups overlapped, so that, for example, POWs who were Jewish ended up working as slaves in German industry, so what follows analytically separates what was often a collective group.

Foreign workers/slaves

It is clear from the accounts of survivors that resistance to the Nazi regime on the part of foreign slave labourers, Jews and POWs was endemic but usually individually based and seldom organized as a means of undermining the Nazi state. Herbert's (1997) review, for example, suggests that work avoidance routines and feigning sickness were common amongst the foreign workers, many of whom were slaves, but that resistance was primarily aimed at buttressing personal survival rather than regime change. Indeed, the consequence of poor productivity amongst foreign workers was a vigorous debate amongst the Nazi hierarchy as to how to increase work effort and this included improving food, enhancing punishments and even generating some provision for 'wages' beyond that deducted for tax, board and lodging which normally ensured that no 'wages' were paid. As a letter found on a French civilian worker in May 1944 suggested, there were Ten Commandments for the 'perfect French worker':

1. Walk slowly in the workshop
2. Walk quickly after knocking off
3. Go to the toilet frequently

4. Don't work too hard
5. Annoy the foreman
6. Court the beautiful girls
7. Visit the doctor often
8. Don't count on vacation
9. Cherish cleanliness
10. Always have hope. (Quoted in Herbert, 1997: 329)

Hitler's slave labourers were not the first to enter Germany in the twentieth century, for slaves had been used by Germany in the First World War, though they were not described as slaves. But the conscripted Poles were little short of slaves. From 26 October 1939 all Poles between 16 (soon reduced to 14) and 60 were 'subject to compulsory public labour' and something like 85 per cent of those eligible were forced to move to Germany. In all, just fewer than 30 per cent (1,659,764) of the foreign workers in Germany were Polish, and many lived in large camps near industrial sites. Berlin alone had 666 camps for foreign workers. All Poles had to wear a large purple 'P' on their clothing and were forbidden from mixing with the German population to the point where sexual relations with a German was punishable by death. Even this threat did not deter everyone: between 1942 and 1943 over 5000 Germans were arrested every month for sexual liaisons with foreign workers (Goldhagen, 1996: 314). Executions were the preserve of the Gestapo and used for murder, political offences and sex with a German, but few if any cases originated with them, and at least half were initiated by 'ordinary' members of the public (Gallately, 2001: 153–5).

By early 1944, the addition of Italian POWs increased the numbers of foreign workers to 5.7 million, of whom 1.9 million were women. Initially women that were pregnant were sent back, but when the Nazi authorities believed that women were deliberately getting pregnant to avoid work a new policy was developed: children of 'good racial stock' were to be brought up in special German, often SS-related, institutions; children of 'inferior racial stock' were sent to 'homes' which, as expected, had very high mortality rates. In addition, there were 1.3 million surviving POWs. One-third of the foreign workforce worked in agriculture (mainly French and Polish, providing 50 per cent of the workforce in many places), one-third in heavy industry (providing 33 per cent of the workforce) and the rest in light industry. In sum one-fourth of the workforce in Germany were foreign by the end of the war – a proportion that Herbert (1994: 233) suggests allowed the war to continue for at least 18 months longer than would otherwise have been possible.

But despite the paranoia of the Nazis that the foreign workers would forment a revolt to coincide with D-Day – probably using leaders parachuted in by the Western Allies – there were very few organized acts of collective resistance. Partly this was because the regime was so dominant and repressive that personal survival almost always took precedence over political action. Partly it was because only after the German defeats of late 1942 and early 1943 did it become apparent that the Allies might actually win the war, thus providing a long-term political purpose to the resistance. At that point many foreign workers were routinely executed after Hans Kammler, from the SS, suggested it would be a good idea to 'decimate' foreign workers as the Soviet forces drew closer, simply to ensure 'general security and good order' (Gellately, 2001: 240–1, 254–5).

Jews

The focus on personal survival was made all the more difficult for Jews, not simply because of their appalling material conditions but because, had they known it, there were very few who survived. Once it became apparent what was likely to happen to them Jews became very active in their resistance but initially the apparent irrationality of the controllers made resistance difficult. For example, on Primo Levi's entry to Auschwitz, which carried the infamous *Arbeit Macht Frei* (Work Gives Freedom) over the entrance, he was made to strip off his clothes and to take particular care of his shoes. These were carefully placed in a corner, alongside those of the other prisoners and then something happened that Levi could not, at first, understand: 'Someone comes with a broom and sweeps away all the shoes outside in a heap. He is crazy, he is mixing them all together, ninety-six pairs, they will be all unmatched' (Levi, 1987: 29). But work for Jews, according to Goldhagen (1996: 317–18), seldom had any rationality, let alone economic utility. It was usually associated with low productivity yet incessant and impossibly high work rates, normally involved some retributive element, was associated with boundless cruelty on the part of the Germans, and, unlike the work of non-Jewish prisoners, was usually fatal. As one inmate recalled:

> Then we went to 'work.' In our wooden shoes we were chased by blows from rods into a corner of the field and had to fill sometimes our caps, at other times our jackets, with stones, wet sand or mud, and, holding them with both hands and running under a hail of blows, bring them to the opposite corner of the field, empty the stuff, refill it and bring it back to the opposite corner and so on. A gauntlet of screaming SS men and privileged prisoners, armed with rods and whips, let loose on us a hail of blows. It was hell. (Quoted in Goldhagen, 1996: 294)

Levi was 'lucky' in the sense that he was not imprisoned in Auschwitz until early 1944, and thus avoided the fate that most Jews met, but the large scale corralling of Jews had begun on a systematic basis in December 1939 when Polish Jews were herded in a ghetto in Lodz, with the intent of removing all their remaining wealth in exchange for food prior to expulsion. A similar pattern occurred in the Warsaw ghetto which housed almost half a million Jews by early 1941 – 30 per cent of the population lived in 2.4 per cent of the area. With the food ration of Jews set at 300 calories a day (compared to 634 for Poles and 2310 for Germans) it quickly became apparent that starvation would soon engender wide-scale deaths and hence disease that might spread back into Germany. In Lodz, a centralized economy was developed, employing 80,000 Jews making material for the *Wehrmacht*, but in Warsaw a more decentralized economy was just beginning to flourish in the June of 1942 when policy changes in Berlin induced the 'evacuation' of both ghettos and the beginning of the end of the Jews.

Initially Himmler had sought a policy of 'destruction through labour' of the Jews and, with Heydrich, foresaw using Polish Jews to build an *Ostwall*, marking the new boundary of Greater Germany. However, the failure of the offensive against the USSR and the entry of the USA into the war persuaded some Nazis that, although Jewish labour would be required for the war effort, 'destruction through labour' would ensure the achievement of two contradictory policies: the elimination of the Jews and the expansion of the war economy simultaneously. The policy initially and temporarily foresaw the replacement of Polish and Soviet labour in Poland by Jews, while the former groups were sent to Germany itself. But Himmler became dissatisfied with its results, and those seeking to exploit the Jews, rather than eliminate them, lost ground in the debate until very late in the war (Browning, 2000: 59).

In the event, by late 1942 only those Jewish workers regarded as absolutely essential to the armaments factories were (temporarily) spared and sent to SS-run factory camps. Elsewhere Polish and Soviet workers displaced Jews and not the other way around. For instance, by June 1943 only 21,000 Jews remained in the Galicia district's SS work camps, the other 434,000 had been transported to extermination camps or were already dead. And after the uprising in the Warsaw ghetto in April 1943 Himmler, with Hitler's full support, ordered the closing down of all further Jewish work camps and the removal of all but a few of their inmates who remained in Lublin. In all, 300,000 Jews in Poland who were fit enough to work – and therefore supposed to be 'destroyed through labour' – were just destroyed. As Goldhagen (1996: 296) suggests, in the light of murdering 2 million Polish Jews, the irrational 'waste' of labour in a state under war conditions defies the imagination – except for those whose preference was not to win the war but to destroy the Jews.[17]

However, the value to the German war effort of POW and Jewish labour should be balanced by the problems induced by such labour and it is in this context that we need to evaluate the role of leadership. For example, few Jews were used in the armaments industry until late 1943 to early 1944, when the greater German borders began to shrink and the supply of foreign labourers started to dwindle. At this point, for example, thousands of concentration camp inmates were transported to the Harz Mountains to build underground armaments factories. By late 1944, 600,000 inmates were 'available' for work: 140,000 on the secret armaments projects, 130,000 on construction projects for the *Todt* organization (who for example, built some of the Atlantic Wall defences), and 230,000 in private industry. Between October 1943 and March 1944, 3000 Jews from the Buchenwald camp died in building the V2 rocket complex at Kaunstein in Thuringia, and that after 1000 had died in the journey. By March 1945 40,000 prisoners worked in the Dora-Mittelbau I camp producing 600 rockets per month (Burleigh, 2000: 775).

However, contrary to popular assumption, sabotage and other forms of resistance existed and significantly hindered the German war effort. In Dachau, for example, inmates managed to ensure that skilled workers were seldom sent to arms factories where their skills would prove useful to the Germans, while those with the skills and the political will to sabotage production were directed to the automatic rifle production line. The Combat Group Auschwitz managed to reduce armaments production by 50 per cent while the Mauthausen Messerschmitt plant was forced to train up unskilled labourers because a prisoner-clerk in the administration had 'inadvertently' sent all the skilled craft workers to other camps. Another Mauthausen plant, the Steyr munitions plant, was effectively put out of action for several days at a time by various groups of prisoners: French, Italian, Spanish and Polish, the latter by failing to harden the metal in the guns so that, although they all passed the quality inspection, few would have fired effectively for any length of time. The Gustloff Works near Buchenwald was forced to re-engineer nine month's supply of automatic carbines after sabotage, and although the production capacity was set at 10,000 a month – and 15,000 a month was possible – only 8000 a month were ever produced. So problematic did the situation become that the Nazi authorities began recruiting Soviet and Eastern women workers (who comprised half the foreign workforce from 1943) precisely because they believed them to be less likely to engage in acts of resistance than Jewish men (Herbert, 1997: 340–93).

In fact the Nazis had only to look in their own backyard to see that quiescence was not inexorably related to women. Indeed, the only public demonstration against the deportation of German Jews during the entire Holocaust occurred on the evening of 27 February 1943 when 200 'Aryan' or Gentile wives of the 1700 Jewish men in 'mixed' marriages in Berlin protested outside the holding building in Rosenstrasse against the arrests earlier that day and likely deportations of their husbands. What was to be 'the final roundup' of the remaining Jews in Germany turned into a fiasco for the SS and the Gestapo who threatened to shoot the protesters; the numbers of women grew through the following week to 1000 as did the continuous chant: 'Give us back our husbands!' [The 7000 Jews without 'Aryan' partners were deported to Auschwitz without any German civilian protests though it transpired that 35 of these had 'Aryan' wives. The Gestapo would not allow these to be freed since they would have knowledge of the extermination programme, but they were redirected to a Labour camp]. On 6 March after a week of embarrassing protests Goebbels reluctantly ordered the release of the 1700 men and plans for transporting other intermarried Jews from the rest of Germany were dropped (Johnson, 1999: 422–6). As Stoltzfus (1996: 245) concluded:

> Goebbels feared that Germans, angered by forced deportations of their partners and children, would begin to question and complain. Unrest about the fate of the Jews could severely hinder the domestic social unity necessary for fighting the war. A parallel development was the increasing need for secrecy surrounding the Final Solution, the revelation of which would have damaged the public morale that the regime strove to nurture, especially during the war. A public discussion about the fate of the deported Jews threatened to disclose the Final Solution and thus endanger that entire effort.

Clearly, we have great difficulties in reconstructing the role of leadership in leading the resistance against Nazi assaults on and exploitation of the Jews, but we know enough to suggest that men and women, individually and collectively, Jewish and Gentile, played a role in that resistance. However, if Jews had a significant motivation to resist it was usually the groups with the most organizational resources that led the most successful forms of resistance: the POWs.

POW's

The invasion of Russia in 1941 did not induce any concern amongst the Nazi establishment for what would be done with the Soviet POWs; they were expected to be shipped north to Siberia and were therefore of little initial interest. The inevitable result was a very high mortality rate: over 60 per cent of the 3.3 million Soviet POWs captured during 1941 were dead before the end of the year. Of the 5.7 million Soviet POWs in total, 58 per cent (3.3 million) died in German captivity. Yet for the Nazis, the problem was not Soviet mortality as much as a German labour shortage. With so many German men in uniform, and by late 1941 little prospect of the Soviet war ending quickly, German industry began to slow down under pressure of a million vacancies, though the proportion of German women employed never varied from about a quarter throughout the war. Göring's response on the deployment of Russians, *Russeneinsatz*, was unequivocal:

> The place of German skilled workmen is in the armaments industry. Shovelling dirt and quarrying stones are not their job – that's what the Russian is for. ... As a matter of principle, the German worker is always the boss of any Russian. ... The Russians can arrange their own food (cats, horses, etc.) ... Range of punishment: from limitations on food rations to execution. (Quoted in Herbert, 1994: 222–3)

But since most POWs had already died, and few of the rest were fit for work, German labour shortages continued. In February 1942 the decision was taken to use Soviet civilians under the Reich Main Security Office (RSHA), led by Fritz Sauckel, and 'Eastern Workers' (*Ostarbeiter*) were formally recognized. These workers were to wear an OST badge at all times, to be divided by sex and separated from all other groups, especially German workers. They were to be kept in camps, always guarded and occasionally allowed escorted excursions as a reward. A rigorous punishment regime was introduced, including withdrawal of rations, imprisonment and flogging (Herbert, 1994: 220–6).

Some division of labour was introduced: French and Polish workers were primarily deployed in agriculture for example, and 'volunteers' were paid similar rates to German workers, but few foreign workers entered German industry until the failure of the war in the USSR by November 1941 made it necessary. Of course, what also became essential was to replace the Jews that had been transported to the extermination camps in Poland. The Germans then required the Soviet authorities in occupied territory to provide conscript labour but this proved difficult and the resort to force and wide-scale kidnapping became common. It brought some considerable success: at an average of 40,000 per week over 1.3 million civilian men and women, in conjunction with just under half a million Soviet POWs, were transported from the USSR to Germany between April and December 1942.

However, despite the numbers involved two problems became self-evident. First, the losses on the eastern front – particularly from Stalingrad in early 1943 – developed into a running haemorrhage on German men. Second, as Figure 3.4 below suggests, the productivity of all foreign workers, but particularly Soviet workers, especially their POWs, proved inadequate to the demands.

For example, by April 1942 Krupp in Essen was already reporting that 30 per cent of the Soviet POWs which had been healthy on arrival were already too ill-nourished to do any work, despite being given exactly the set amount of food. Like most things, conditions and food depended upon the place in the Nazi racial hierarchy: thus Western workers did significantly better than eastern workers, and the food of the latter could be dire. In the summer of 1943 one report recounted the food intake of eastern workers as:

Breakfast:	1/2 litre of turnip soup
Lunch:	1 litre of turnip soup
Dinner:	1 litre of turnip soup + 300 grams (six thin slices) of bread
	+ weekly ration of 50 grams of margarine
	+ weekly ration of 25 grams of meat. (Quoted in Herbert, 1994: 246)

By increasing the rations and 'privileges' – and the punishments – some increase in productivity was reported from late 1943, but still the problems persisted. Of the 181,764 Soviet POWs in German mines in early 1944, fully 18 per cent (32,236) had 'left' by the middle of 1944, the vast majority returned to their POW camp through ill health. This was hardly surprising: a Red Cross report in September 1944 noted that the POWs were regularly flogged, lived and worked in damp conditions without boots, had one blanket to sleep in but lots of rats to sleep with, were inspected by a doctor at the rate of one every 18 seconds and had inadequate food. Rather better

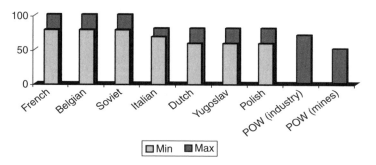

Source: Reconstructed from Herbert (1994: 231)

Figure 3.4 Productivity of foreign workers and POWs compared to Germans (100), 1943

conditions were available in industry – though foreign workers were forbidden to enter air-raid shelters. But the best place was agriculture, for the extra rations usually ensured a higher survival rate (Herbert, 1994: 238–45).

American POWs with Jewish origins fared little better than Polish or German Jews. For example, the 80 who worked at the Berga work camp were forced to dig tunnels for an underground armaments' factory. Their hours varied from 8 to 12 a day but no breaks were allowed and no food or water provided during the shifts and they were not allowed to wear coats against the cold. Yet, despite the daily beatings and incremental exhaustion the POWs still managed individual and collective forms of resistance, from stealing the pipe and whip of a particularly hated guard to going on strike, to singing American songs: all of these incurred some form of punishment but the POWs persisted with their actions. Many of the POWs died, less from the bullets or gas inflicted on their colleagues, but from the diseases induced by overwork, poor conditions and malnutrition (Bard, 1994: 76–90). And, had they known it, many American Jews were themselves victims of American technology, for IBM sorters, tabulators, printers and the punch card technology that allowed the Nazis to find and trace all their victims, were provided with the help of IBM's founder, Thomas Watson (Black, 2001).

In late 1943 the collapse of the Italian regime persuaded the German authorities to mobilize all those Italian soldiers who refused to continue the war. That turned out to be the majority and half a million were transported into Germany to work. About 45,000 Italian 'military internees' died through starvation, inadequate medical attention or were simply murdered by the Germans including 9500 of the 11,500 Italian occupation force on Cephalonia.[18] And many of the executions, of civilians, POWs, Jews and 'undesirables' were carried out in full view of the German public, with little if any dissent and a significant degree of support.

But whatever the level of persecution and retribution, there was always some degree of resistance. Perhaps the most important resistance as far as the war effort was concerned, occurred in the Dora camp near Buchenwald, where prisoners worked on the V-1 and V-2 rockets. The camp resistance organizations sent electrical engineers to change the voltage in the relays that operated the steering mechanisms in the tail, meanwhile Russian POWs urinated on the transformers and carried out acts of sabotage on an individual basis, and groups of Russians, Yugoslavs, French and Czech POWs did likewise. A group of Italian POWs made a public stand against being forced to work on the rockets that led to seven of them being executed. And betrayal was never far away: of the 400 people arrested between November 1944 and March 1945 for suspected sabotage, 118 were hanged (99 Russians, 16 Poles, 2 Czechs and 1 Lithuanian). Quite what effect this sabotage had is obviously difficult to establish, but the sacrifice of these slave labourers does not seem to have been wasted. Suffice it to say that 20 per cent of the 11,300 V-1s failed to launch, and 5000 of the 10,800 V-2s either exploded on take-off or in mid-air, or fell into the North Sea. A quality check on 8 December 1944 of 150 items established that 22 failed and the failures were regarded by management as the direct result of sabotage (Langbein, 1994: 279–316).

In terms of a resistance movement amongst the foreign workers and POWs, the most important seems to have been the Fraternal Cooperation of Prisoners of War (*Bratskoje Sotrudnichestovo Vojennoplennych* [BSV]). This was formed in early 1943 by Soviet officers held as POWs in Munich with the help of 'Josef Feldman' who was a civilian interpreter in the camp but in reality was Georg Fesenko an NKVD (Soviet Communist Party secret police) officer who had escaped from Germany and returned on a secret mission on behalf of the Soviet Communist Party. The BSV acted as a typical secret political party with a strict leadership hierarchy but split into cells that remained ignorant of each other's identities. The group acted to train and arm members for the future Soviet invasion and aided escape attempts before finally being uncovered by the Gestapo in February 1944. By May of that year 383 members of the BSV had been arrested and executed, mainly in Dachau.

Other organized political groups included the Committee for Struggle Against Fascism (*Komitee Kampf gegen den Faschismus*) in Dusselfdorf that aided escaping Western pilots, organized sabotage and gathered intelligence and overall the Gestapo were adamant that the political resistance was almost always led by Soviet POWs. It generally was, but there were no organized attempts to lead an uprising, and although many 'foreigner gangs' emerged as the war drew to a close they were restricted to ensuring their own collective survival rather than facilitating the end of the Nazi regime. But it was perhaps the combination of the two most important 'resistors' that produced the greatest embarrassment to the Nazi Regime: the leaders of the rebellion at Sobibor Death Camp who were Jewish and POWs simultaneously.

Jews and Jewish POWs: escape from the Sobibòr deathcamp[19]

Sobibòr was situated in eastern Poland in the Lublin district, very near to a railroad line but a long way from prying eyes. Over a quarter of a million Jews were murdered in Sobibòr's gas chambers, primarily of Polish nationality but including some from the Soviet Union, some Czechs, French, Germans and Austrians as well as around 35,000 Dutch Jews.

On 14 October 1943 half of the 600 inmates broke out and though only around sixty survived to the end of the war, it was one of the most significant examples of resistance within the extermination and concentration camps. The camp, an area approximately 400 yards by 700 yards, had three gas chambers 'housing' up to 180 people each, and was surrounded by a triple layer of barbed wire, a 15-yard deep minefield and watchtowers. It was built in March 1942 by slave and local Polish labour, and it began murdering Jews in April of that year under the Aktion Reinhard Program. This was named after the assassinated Nazi Reinhard Heydrich and was aimed at clearing the two and a quarter million Jews of the General Government region in Poland in the three new death camps at Belzec, Sobibòr and Treblinka.

Sobibòr was commanded by Franz Stangl and guarded by between 20 and 30 SS men, supported by a number of Ukrainians. Since the Ukrainians developed a penchant for escaping too they were only armed with five bullets each. Up to 300 Jews serviced the gas chambers and 1000 serviced the rail yard and the accommodation. As usual with the death camps everything was done to ensure a smooth transition from rail wagon to gas chamber, so all the Jews were told when they had arrived was that they were at a transit camp. They were then required to undress, and separated into men, who were murdered first, and women and children. A train of 20 wagons could be 'processed' in under three hours.

Generally it seems that the 'processing' went without a hitch until June 1943, just after the death camp at Belzec was abandoned (because its wooden gas chambers could not cope with the increased flow of victims) when the 600 prisoners left at Belzec were transferred to Sobibòr where they were immediately shot. However, in clearing the bodies a note was found in a pocket that warned the inmates of Sobibòr of their own impending doom. The note said:

> We worked for a year in Belzec. I don't know where they're taking us now. They say to Germany. In the freight cars there are dining tables. We received bread for three days, and tins and liquor. If all this is a lie, then know that death awaits you too. Don't trust the Germans. Avenge our blood!

After this it was obvious that no one would escape Sobibòr alive and immediately two prisoners escaped. The SS then summarily executed 20 prisoners as a warning to the rest. Nevertheless, on another occasion five Jewish prisoners, including two women and two of their Ukrainian guards escaped but three were shot in the pursuit and hundreds of prisoners were subsequently executed as a reprisal.

Such a brutally repressive system clearly generated enormous problems for those leaders of the resistance inside Sobibòr. Initially, Leon Feldhendler, the former chair of the *Judenrat* in Zolkiew (Poland) (the Jewish Council that acted as community leaders under German control) led the planning for the break out and it was agreed that only a mass break out was viable, since any smaller escapes would have led to further reprisals against those left behind. Several plans emerged: one to get the young Jewish boys who acted as servants to the SS to murder them; another proposed setting fire to the camp; and a third proposed digging a tunnel, but all three were rejected as unfeasible and it became apparent to Feldhendler that no one in the leadership group had the military training or leadership ability to make the plan work. Then a (Jewish) Dutch Naval Officer, probably called Joseph Jacobs, was engaged to lead the project. Unfortunately the plan was leaked to the Germans by one of the Ukrainian guards who had apparently agreed to assist the Jews, and Jacobs and 72 other Dutch Jews were executed as a reprisal. Two more escape attempts were foiled in September 1943 and then finally Feldhendler made contact with an officer from the Soviet Red Army, Lt Alexander Pechorsky who had arrived with 100 other Jews who were Soviet POWs. Pechorsky took over the project using Feldhender as his second in command and a plan was hatched for ensuring the escape of all 600 inmates (including 100 women), this time without involving the Ukrainian guards and using both a tunnel, the killing of the SS, and a mass break out.

Heavy rain in early October washed out the tunnel and Pechorsky then had some difficulties dissuading a group of eight prisoners from escaping on their own. The planning for a mass break out continued and a group of 40 prisoners agreed to go for 13 October when each of the SS guards would be asked to go to a workshop on a mundane task and then killed by small groups of trustworthy prisoners between 15.30 and 16.45 hours. Simultaneously all the telephone and power lines would be cut and the camp transports sabotaged while ammunition and guns were stolen and distributed. Next, the usual roll-call would be organized and the prisoners marched off towards the main gate, but this time with the conspirators in the front rank who would seize weapons from the arms shed on the way and fight their way past the Ukrainian guards. Then each prisoner would make his or her way across the mine-fields to the forests to meet up with the local Partisans.

Unfortunately an unexpected inspection occurred early on 13 October and the break out was postponed to the following day. At the allotted start time on 14 October 11 SS men were inveigled into the workshops and killed while phone and power lines cut, the camp vehicles immobilized, and six rifles stolen. But as the roll-call lined up the still unaware majority of prisoners, a German lorry appeared and its driver, seeing a dead SS man, opened fire on the crowd and was himself promptly killed, along with the commander of the Ukrainian guards. At this point the remaining Ukrainians began opening fire and pandemonium broke out as the prisoners scattered through the gate and across the fences, many dying from gun-shot wounds or from mine detonations.

Pechorsky, correctly assuming that there would be no mines around the living quarters of the SS, broke through the fence at this point and led a group into the woods. Three hundred of the 600 prisoners escaped on the day and 100 were killed in the attempt, while a further 50 were killed in the following few days. All those that remained in the camp – whether they took part in the attack on the guards and the break out or not – were summarily executed over the next 24 hours.

Assuming that the prisoners would move east in a single group to get over the River Bug, the Germans immediately moved around 400 troops in the direction but most of the prisoners had actually gone north in small groups of around 10 people towards the forests. Pechorsky, however, led his group (which may have taken most of the weapons) across the River Bug on October 19. By 22 October Pechorsky had met a group of Soviet Partisans while Feldhendler stayed in the forest for a fortnight before joining a different group of Partisans. Of the 200 that made the initial successful escape only 50 survived until the end of the war; Feldhender was murdered on 2 April by Polish fascists, just a month short of the end of European hostilities. Pechorsky survived to return to the Soviet Union. Sobibòr camp was destroyed by the Germans shortly after the break out.

We will not belabour the point here that resonates with Spartacus's leadership in the Third Servile War against Rome: under the most difficult of material conditions it proved possible not simply to invoke small-scale acts of individual resistance to the Nazi regime but also to create organized resistance and sabotage. That organization required some kind of leadership and it tended to occur not simply where the 'need' was greatest – amongst those Jews destined for oblivion – but where the cultural proclivities of the group coincided with the prerequisite military and political skills. The groups most able to resist tyrannies tended to have similar experiences and a level of military experience that generated sustainable leadership cadres. Individuals could say 'no' and take the consequences from their oppressors, but organized groups could make their oppressors take the consequences too. In terms of results the leadership of slaves, POWs, foreign workers and Jews achieved some destabilization and inhibition of the German war effort – though at best it was modest. But in terms of establishing an icon of heroic resistance their achievements were much greater.

Conclusion

What can we conclude from this review of Leadership as Results? Well several aspects are worth highlighting.

First, it is often impossible to establish the causal link between leader and results, even if followers and subordinates prefer to attribute the latter to the former because this provides a useful scapegoat or a valuable role model to embody.

Second, even where the results can be related to the actions of a leader this does not necessarily bode well for organizations: if the results that are monitored are chosen because they are easy to measure and/or because they reflect the needs of the managerial hierarchy or partial elements of it, rather than the whole organization, the customers, clients or followers, then the consequence may distort organizational behaviour as members are encouraged to 'play the system' rather than support the system. Under such conditions the organization adopts a 'hard shell' strategy and seeks to defend the monitored boundaries rather than a 'soft shell' system that seeks to learn and grow.

Third, and turning to the case studies of slavery, even under the most arduous conditions imaginable and against overwhelming force, it is possible for subordinate and heterogeneous groups to resist their oppressors and leadership does seem to have played some role in those results: instigating the rebellion, facilitating its survival, ensuring its elimination and perpetuating its memory. However, the results of leadership are extraordinarily difficult to quantify, not just in terms of establishing whether the aims were achieved but in terms of a much longer term and subtle impact: Spartacus's rebellion failed in its own terms of securing freedom for the slaves who fought against Rome but in terms of generating a symbol of resistance against oppression that motivated subsequent leaders and followers it may well be judged a success.

Fourth, our accounts of leaders and leadership are never raw but always cooked, that is they never arrive as neutral transparent accounts of the truth but always constructed from particular perspectives and using particular forms of evidence. In this case we have a double cooking because not only do we have contested accounts from the original sources – and nothing from the losing side at all in the case of Spartacus – but we have contested accounts in the novels of Spartacus and even within the writers, editors and producers of the movie. Similarly, as Goldhagen's work has demonstrated the relatively nearness in space and time to the Nazi era is no proof against contested accounts of leadership and responsibilities.

There is no objective solution to this problem, there is only ever-present vigilance and scepticism – but that does not imply cynicism. We may disagree radically about the nature, role and value of leadership but it is too important a topic to be left to leaders to resolve on our part.

Notes

1 Thanks to Steve Rayner for suggesting this analogy.
2 See http://www.fpl.com/
3 http://www.ewtn.com/motherteresa/Beatification.htm
4 http://www.secularhumanism.org/library/fi/hitchens_16_4.html
5 Unless, of course, you are standing on a Rugmark carpet, a symbol that the carpet was not manufactured using slave labour and a quality assurance system for improving the lives of carpet makers by allocating 1 per cent of the wholesale price of the carpet to a fund to support child labourers. In 2000, about 30 per cent of handmade rugs and carpets sold in the UK had a Rugmark (Bales, 2000: 241). B&Q and the Cooperative sell Rugmark carpets. For more information see www.rugmark.net
6 My accounts of African and Contemporary slavery can be found in Grint, 2003.
7 F.W. Taylor, despite his upbringing by abolitionist parents, was notoriously racist (see Kanigal, 2000).
8 Aristotle's defence of slavery as 'natural' to some people was extensively used to justify slavery in South America by the Spanish slave owners (Ste. Croix, 1988: 29).
9 From the Latin manümittere, to release, from manü (from one's hand) and emittere (to send away).
10 Thrace was centred on what is now Bulgaria but then also included Romania, parts of Serbia, Greece and Turkey and was successfully controlled by Rome by 46 BC.
11 Decimation or *fustuarium* is described by Polybius.
    'This is inflicted as follows: The tribune takes a cudgel and just touches the condemned man with it, after which all in the camp beat or stone him, in most cases dispatching him in the camp itself. But even those who manage to escape are not saved thereby: impossible! for they are not allowed to return to their homes, and none of the family would dare to receive such a man in his house. So that those who have once fallen into this misfortune are utterly ruined . .... If the same thing happens to large bodies, and if entire maniples desert their posts when exceedingly hard pressed, the officers refrain from inflicting the bastinado or the death penalty at all, but find a solution of the difficulty that is both salutary and terror-striking. The tribune assembles the legion, and brings up those guilty of leaving the ranks, reproaches them sharply, and finally chooses by lot sometimes five, sometimes eight, sometimes twenty of the offenders, so adjusting the number thus chosen that they form as near as possible the tenth part of those guilty of cowardice. Those on whom the lot falls are bastinadoed mercilessly in the manner above described.' (Plutarch *Life of Crassus* quoted in http://itsa.ucsf.edu/~snlrc/encyclopaedia_romana/gladiators/ spartacus.html#anchor5371) The 90 per cent who survived the decimation were still subject to public humiliation and were forced to eat barley instead of wheat and to sleep outside their tents at night (Goldsworthy, 2003: 162).
12 The criteria for a 'Triumph' included a 'decisive victory' (at least 5000 killed) over a foreign enemy [which is why Crassus had no joy from defeating Spartacus]. An 'Ovation' – a 'lesser victory' or one against a 'base or unworthy foe' – involved the general walking into Rome, wearing a plain toga with a wreath of myrtle not laurel on his head, without carrying a sceptre and usually without a procession of soldiers behind. See http://www.ku.edu/history/index/europe/ancient_rome/E/Roman/Texts/secondary/SMIGRA*/Ovatio.html

13 Plutarch, *Life of Marcus Licinius Crassus*, quoted at http://ancienthistory.about.com/library/bl/bl_text_plutarch_crassus_spartacus.htm

14 Duncan Cooper's 'Who Killed Spartacus?' and 'Spartacus: Still Censored after all these years' are the best source for the political intrigues over the filming of Kubrick's Spartacus. They can both be found at http://www.visual-memory.co.uk/amk/doc/0103.html

15 Available online at http://www.h-net.msu.edu/~german/gtext/kaiserreich/lux.html

16 *Spartacist* remains the name of the theoretical and documentary repository of the International Communist League (Fourth Internationalist).

17 It was not just with regard to the labour of Jews that Hitler's 'irrational' judgement prevailed. In the second half of 1944, when German losses were mounting very seriously on both fronts, Hitler allowed the withdrawal of 187,000 German troops to take part as extras in the film *Kolberg* – the story of an epic defence by a small Baltic town against Napoleon, or in the words of the Reich propaganda ministry, a film to 'demonstrate … that a people united at home and at the front will overcome the enemy' (Kershaw, 2000: 713).

18 The executions were the background to Louis de Bernières' *Captain Corelli's Mandolin* (1995).

19 This section is heavily reliant on the Proceedings Of The Fourth Yad Vashem International Historical Conference, Jerusalem, January 1980. These are available at: http://www.us-israel.org/jsource/Holocaust/reinhard.html

Leadership as process: leadership as a reflection of community

'THE CHILD is father to the man.'
How can he be? The words are wild.
Suck any sense from that who can:
'The child is father to the man.'
No; what the poet did write ran,
'The man is father to the child.'
'The child is father to the man!'
How *can* he be? The words are wild.
Gerard Manley Hopkins[1]

Introduction

This chapter is concerned with the process of leadership, and in particular the process by which leaders learn to lead. In the first part I examine various learning theories and consider their utility in the leadership arena. On particular theme that I pursue here is what I call 'inverse learning', that is, reversing the conventional direction of the learning from 'teacher' onto 'pupil' to 'pupil' onto 'teacher'. In this case it implies that leadership may be most appropriately learned from one's subordinates. Thus, just as adults learn to become parents by interacting with their children so leaders learn to lead by interacting with their followers. In effect, children teach their parents how to parent while followers teach their leaders how to lead. In the second part this inverse learning model is applied to an RAF leadership course because it most clearly contradicts the traditional process of military leadership: a formal hierarchy of ranks supported by an extensive network of procedures and rules is designed to ensure subordinate learning through subordinate compliance, and no inverse learning is necessary. In the event I suggest that the leadership learning occurs through inverse learning and within a Community of Practice but that the limits of the community actively limit the practice and hence the leadership learning; in effect, leadership becomes a reflection of the community within which it operates.

Learning to lead

The claim that leadership is critical to all organizational success (and failure) is almost as commonplace as the claim to have discovered the secret of its success. For McCall (1993) this implies that organizations should first identify and then nurture all those with leadership potential but this is easier said than done: how do people with leadership 'potential' realize it, how do we realize who has leadership potential, and how do leaders learn to lead? As suggested in Chapter 1, this partly depends on how we define leadership and if leadership is defined as an inherited characteristic then we either need to be much more careful about our choice of parents, or we need to think through the consequences of this. It could be, as Cameron (in Doh 2003: 59) suggests, that in these circumstances we should concentrate on laboratory experiments to assess potential. But if leadership is a natural talent then we probably need not engage in any selection or evaluation because a Darwinian selection will surely leave us to be led by the best. Sometimes these contradictory approaches are conflated; for example, in 2003 a BBC television programme ironically entitled 'Born to Win' involved 20 'high potential' young athletes who were actually being 'coached' to win, rather than simply 'selected' through the survival of the fittest.[2]

But of course, as Doh (2003: 54) reminds us, even if we can learn to lead that does not mean that leadership can be taught: it is possible that the process of learning is simply too complex, unconscious or non-replicable to teach. Yet Doh's review suggests that it can be learned and some aspects of it can be taught. Conger (in Doh 2003: 59) for example, suggests that leadership comprises 'skills, perspectives and dispositions', hence while 'many skills' and 'some perspectives' can be taught or enhanced many 'dispositions' cannot. That might simply be a self-interested response: if we can't teach any element of leadership then leadership educators will shortly be looking for employment.

Chief amongst candidates for learning is probably experience: the 'school of hard knocks' or the 'university of life' as it is conventionally referred to (Davies and Easterby-Smith, 1984; Hughes *et al.*, 1999: 89–96; McCall *et al.*, 1988; Yukl, 1998: 475–90). But this is primarily restricted to how leaders can learn from their own superordinates, from coaching and observing, not from their own followers. Even experience may be of limited value if every experience and every individual is unique so that no model of learning can predict anything of value, except that next time everything will be different. To some extent this assessment locks into some aspects of Complexity Theory in so far as the uniqueness of events and the indeterminacy of the future effectively disable the construction of any significant pattern learning. It also reflects Soren Kierkegaard's assumption that 'Life can only be understood backwards, but it must be lived forwards.' Or in Walter Benjamin's image of the Angel of History, the angel faces the past but is blown into the future. In other words, little of our past experience provides us with the wherewithal to become successful leaders – that has to be acquired through novel experiences.

Or it could be, following Popper's 'falsification' claim, that while we can disprove (leadership) theories and models we cannot prove them. Thus just as the hypothetical black swan invalidates thousands of sightings of white swans as a theory of swan colour, so we may never be in a position to validate any theory or model of leadership, for while it may work a thousand times we cannot be certain it will work on each and every occasion. We might pragmatically conclude that, since the sun has risen every-day since records began it will probably rise again tomorrow, but this is not the same as an objective proof of the inevitability of the rising sun. More importantly, if we are not able to establish why a particular leadership event turned out the way it did we should be very wary of simply repeating the process in the hope that there will be a replication of the ending. Here, luck may effectively step between the theory and the practice to unhinge our learning and 'lead' us astray. The Roman Army, for instance, was adamant that practice was far more important than anything else and luck was something to be extremely wary of. As Josephus (1981: 197) suggested in his review of the Roman war against the Jews:

> Nothing is done without plan or on the spur of the moment; careful thought precedes action of any kind, and to the decisions reached all ranks must conform. … They regard success due to luck as less desirable than a planned but unsuccessful stroke, because victories that come of themselves tempt men to leave things to chance, but forethought, in spite of occasional failures, is good practice in avoiding the same mistake.

Luck or leadership, it is self-evidently the case that leaders throughout history have succeeded, and failed, without recourse to any leadership text or attendance at a leadership course, though some of our most significant exemplars have had the most impressive education. Alexander the Great, for instance, was tutored by Aristotle and carried a copy of Homer's *Iliad* with him. But many historical leaders were illiterate, had little or no formal education, and yet managed to learn to lead.

However, I want to suggest that this mysterious inculcation of leadership skills and qualities may derive, at least in part, from an aspect of leadership that all leaders have, irrespective of their identity, time, space or culture: followers. By definition if a leader does not have followers then that individual is not a leader, so some form of relationship between leader and followers is inevitable. Indeed, one could argue that having followers is *the* critical definition of leadership. I want to suggest further, and in an inversion of our common assumptions about this relationship, that it is followers who teach leadership to leaders. In effect inverse learning occurs in that the relationship of 'teacher' to 'pupil' is the reverse of that normally assumed and often an inversion of the formal hierarchy that exists between 'teacher' and 'pupil'. Moreover, it is not just experience that counts, but reflective experience. But before we get to that point I first want to assess the extent to which this inverse learning is replicated in an area where all of us have some experience: the parent–child relationship.

Inverse learning: the child is parent to the adult

This counter-intuitive position is mirrored in the way most parents learn to be parents: their children teach them. Or as Gerard Manley Hopkins suggests, 'The CHILD is father to the man.' Hopkins probably means that the 'child' will mature into the man but here I would consider how the child can teach its parent to be an adult. Although many books and web pages exist on parenting (there were 12,356 books on Amazon.co.uk and 5,900,000 web pages relating to 'Parenting' on 6 October 2003; on the same day there were 13,494 books on leadership on Amazon.co.uk and 12,600,000 web pages; the apparent irrelevance of 'followership' can also be gleaned from these data: on the same day there were just three books and 14,600 web pages), it is worth pondering the degree to which most of us who are parents or have or had living parents learn to be parents from books or equivalent media? Of course, parents help their own children to become parents but increasingly in the UK, for example, families are far more geographically mobile than they used to be so that parents are decreasingly able to help their own children become parents. The requirement for advice is clear, not just from the huge numbers of books written and sold on parenting (including business-related models such as Jay's *Kids & Co* which promises to deliver 'Winning Business Tactics for Every Family') but, more recently, on the development of parenting websites. For instance, http://mumsnet.com/s/mn and http://www.babycentre.co.uk currently get more than 1,000 postings a day. Both these websites eschew the conventional 'expert evidence' or 'guru guides' to parenting and instead are firmly based in the interactive sharing of information by parents for parents, or, in reality, mothers for mothers (Moorhead, 2003: 12). In other words, less experienced mothers learn to be more competent mothers partly through learning from more experienced mothers. Nor is this explosion in advice restricted to mothers for there is now evidence that fathers are becoming more involved in parenting. For instance, 75 per cent of men under 55 now attach more importance to their home–work balance than their fathers – though 33 per cent said that work seriously interfered with their private life and 25 per cent admitted that they had neglected their children recently – and half said they would still not trade promotion for more time with their family (Gwyther and Hoar, 2003). There is also a new monthly magazine entitled *Dad* to rival the best-selling parenting magazine *Mother & Baby* that has a monthly circulation of 80,000 (Janes, 2003: 14).

Nevertheless, a large proportion of the learning to be a parent can only come from the experience of 'parenting'. After all you cannot know whether somebody else's method works until you try it on your own child. And for that to occur successfully an infant is required. In theory parents teach their children how to act as children but of course the latter have a way of ignoring much of this worthy advice. If this was not the case then no parent would ever have misbehaving children, no child would have a tantrum on the supermarket floor, no teenager would experiment with alcohol or drugs and none would come home late or leave their room looking like a burglar has just ransacked the place. Since this does occur regularly the superior resources of parents (physique, language, legal support, moral claims, source of pocket money, threats of grounding and so on) have only limited effect. What is more important is to understand why this is the case and how it relates to leadership.

The critical issue, then, is that parents have to learn how to be parents by listening and responding to their children. The end result is that we are taught to be parents by our children: if they don't feel comfortable with the way we are holding them as infants they cry and we adjust our hold; if they are hungry they cry and we feed them; if they are tired they cry and we rock them to sleep. And when – not if – we get it wrong they tell us, either by crying or struggling or sulking or whatever. Of course, we then have to decide what to do, whether to 'teach them' some self-control or whatever but whether that works or not is not solely in our control and we often have to negotiate our way through this continually changing relationship. Indeed, although experience might make parenting easier – the more children you have the easier it might become – this need not be the case, either because each child–parent relationship is different, and/or because each new child alters the pattern of prior familial relationships and/or because some people have problems learning to become parents. What might be critical here is the extent to which parents receive feedback from their children.

It may also be that parents learn most from relationships with their children that are not hugely asymmetric. In other words, where children are dominated by their parents – or vice versa – neither side in the relationship necessarily learns much or matures. Indeed, it may be that one of the reasons why so many parents do seem to make a relatively good job of a very difficult task is because children are often more open and honest in their feedback than adult followers or subordinates: if parents are not doing something 'properly' – as defined by the children not by the parents – the parents will soon hear about it. This is evident both with toddlers who can be excruciatingly honest in their conversations and when we meet the children of people we perceive as formidable leaders: so often their children seem capable of saying things to them that we poor followers dare not even think about saying to them. As Argyris (1985) insisted many years ago – and as so painfully revealed by Jim Carrey, playing Fletcher Reede in the 1997 movie *Liar Liar* – we are extraordinarily good at not telling each other the truth. And since it also seems apparent that most learning occurs when people do get accurate feedback, and that such feedback gets less likely as individuals move up the organizational hierarchy (Kaplan *et al.*, 1987), it may be that many people are better parents than organizational leaders.

So while we might think we are just teaching our progeny to be children they are simultaneously teaching us to be parents through this inverse learning. Since individuals are constantly developing this also implies that the relationship between parents and children changes, so that while parents may find themselves (micro)managing at some points, eventually the children mature and leave home, possibly to become parents themselves. If this is to be a successful process it is more than likely that the child has been given increasing levels of responsibility, a process that is often inverted once students become employees – with predictably 'childish' consequences (Argyris, 1985). Nevertheless the point is that while parents should not attempt to solve all their children's problems but get them to resolve their own problems, leadership is often configured as a problem-solving activity. Hence, leaders are people who construct and implement innovative solutions to organization problems on the part of their subordinates – and in turn the subordinates learn little from the process except that the responsibility for problem-solving lies with their leaders. Heifetz (1994), in contrast, suggests that this merely perpetuates the problem of irresponsible followers, and therefore leaders should reflect problem solving back onto their followers because only through a collective effort can a collective problem be resolved.

The follower is teacher to the leader

If we map this inverse learning model onto leadership the implication is that while leaders think they are teaching followers to follow, in fact it is the followers who do most of the teaching and the leaders who do most of the learning. Here then we might reconstruct Gerard Manley Hopkins: 'The follower is teacher to the leader.' It also highlights an interesting reflection on the etymological origins of leadership and its potential bearing on the parenting metaphor. If the English word 'management' derives from the Latin *manus*, the hand that controls, and 'leadership' from the Old German *leider*, to guide, to show the way, then the more leaders shift back into controlling the more likely followers are to resist. Inevitably some leaders fail to learn and some followers fail to teach but it may well be that one of the secrets of leadership is not a list of innate skills and competences, or how much charisma you have, or whether you have a vision or a strategy for achieving that vision, but whether you have a capacity to learn from your followers. And that learning approach is inevitably embedded in a relational model of leadership. I also want to suggest that the asymmetrical issue is critical to successful leadership. That is to say, where the relationship between leaders and followers is asymmetrical in either direction: weak/irresponsible leaders or weak/irresponsible followers, then success for the organization is likely to be short-lived because feedback and learning is minimized.

This dyadic exchange model between leader and follower is hardly novel (Graen and Scandura, 1987; Yukl, 1998: 149–74) but the relationship is usually construed as focusing upon the change required of the follower. For instance, Driver (2002: 107) suggests that 'In these dyadic exchanges, leader and follower negotiate which behaviours constitute behaviours that are routinely expected of the *subordinate* versus behaviours that are outside of the usually prescribed tasks' [my emphasis]. And much of this 'negotiation' relates to the role modelling undertaken by leaders, rather than role change that results from the interaction. To that effect, Driver (2002: 116) concludes that 'the two learning roles [single loop and double loop] negotiated in leader-member dyads are associated with different individual learning outcomes on the part of the *follower*' [my emphasis]. In other words, the changes are required of the follower not the leader. Here I want to suggest the opposite – that is, it is the leader who has to learn how to lead as much the follower who has to learn how to follow. In effect, learning is not so much an individual and cognitive event but a collective and cultural process (Weiss, 1990). This bears echoes of the Community of Practice arguments of Wenger (1998) that I shall pursue later in this chapter.

In what follows next I illustrate some examples of this inverse learning model, or lack of it, by reference to historical examples of successful and failed leadership. Obviously we should remain wary of assuming that these necessarily prove the case and I use them only as illustrations for constructing an alternative understanding of how leaders might learn to lead.

Teaching children to lead

The assumptions that learning is a collective and cultural process, and that leadership can be honed through such a format, is hardly novel. The Spartans, for instance, placed all their male children from 7 to 18 into the Agoge (*agôgê*) (literally 'raising', as pertaining to animals), an institution that combined education, socialization and training to turn boys into warriors. The primary aim of education for boys was the creation of a loyal dedicated army and at the age of 13 they were commanded by one of the *irens* – 20-year-old junior leaders whose experience in command was designed to instil Spartan leadership qualities amongst a large number of warriors. The younger boys were also required to go through the *Krypteia*, or 'period of hiding' when they lived alone or in small self-led groups living off the countryside and killing helots (Spartan slaves) who were regarded as particularly strong or likely to harbour leadership ambitions themselves. At the age of 18 a select group was appointed to the elite Royal Guard and thence to formal military leadership positions (Cartledge, 2002: 49–51).

The clearest connection to a more recent Spartan approach to teaching leadership was probably the organizations making up the Hitler youth movement (see Knopp, 2002). In the Adolf Hitler Schools in particular, German boys were groomed for leadership on the battlefield and in the homeland. While one third of Germans born between 1921 and 1925 died in the war, only 50 per cent of those attending the Adolf Hitler Schools survived. By 1935, 50 per cent of all Germans aged between 10 and 18 were in the Hitler youth and 90 per cent of all those born in 1936 were recruited.

In fact membership remained voluntary until 1939 but few resisted. It was organized on military lines with groups of 150 comprising a company (*Fähnlein*) down to the ten-boy *Kameradschaft* (*Jungmädelschaft* for girls). 'Leadership of the young by the young' was Hitler's slogan and nothing was left to chance: 12,727 Hitler youth (*Hitlerjunge*) (14–18) leaders and 24,660 *Jungvolk* (10–14 years) (*Jungmädel* for girls) leaders were put through 287 leadership training courses in 1934 alone. Once through the course of physical training, ideological conditioning, and military training, these young leaders were provided with manuals for their own followers, complete with introductions, songs and texts for each lesson. For example, a favourite song went:

> The world belongs to those who lead;
> Those who follow the sun.
> And we are the marchers;
> None can halt us …
>   (Quoted in Knopp, 2002: 12)

No discussion or dissension was permitted but the most important experience seems to have been the week-end and summer camps where the community building developed in earnest, usually by ensuring that everyone from the age of 12 took turns to lead his *Kameradschaft* or her *Jungmädelschaft*. 'That way', wrote a member of staff at a boy's school, 'he learns to give orders and gains the subconscious strength of self-confidence which is necessary in order to command obedience' (quoted in Knopp, 2002: 139).

After successful completion through the *Jungvolk* and *Hitlerjunge* the chosen few went onto to one of the *Ordensburg* (SS Colleges) where Sparta remained an ideal. 'What we trainers of young leaders want to see', said one trainer in 1937, 'is a modern form of government modelled on the ancient Greek city-state. The best 5 to 10 per cent of the population are selected to rule, and the rest have to work and obey' (quoted in Knopp, 2002: 119). These 'leaders-in-waiting' then spent one year in the SS College at Vogelsang learning 'racial philosophy', a further year at Crössinsee 'character-building', and a final year in Sonthofen on administrative and military duties. It was at the 1935 passing out parade that Robert Ley, the Nazi Party head of organization commented:

> We want to know whether these men carry in themselves the will to lead, to be masters, in a word: to rule. The NSDAP [Nazi Party] and its leaders must want to rule … we take delight in ruling, not in order to be a despot or to revel in a sadistic tyranny, but because it is our unshakeable belief that in all situations only one person can lead and only one person can take responsibility. Power rests with this one person. (Quoted in Knopp, 2002: 128)

Teaching adults to lead

For the Nazis the ultimate 'one person', of course, was Hitler and, despite all the feedback requirements instilled into the Nazi youth leadership schemas, as the war progressed Hitler increasingly distanced himself from subordinate feedback and this played an important role in his nemesis. For instance, it is clear that from 1939 to 1941, the invasion of Poland, Europe and the USSR, Hitler engaged in conversations with his generals and listened to them, even if he did not always take their advice. And only on one occasion did Hitler personally intervene in the invasion of Poland – to be overruled by Von Rundstedt. But once the invasion of the Soviet Union faltered in the winter of 1941 Hitler both began 'managing' the armed forces at the micro-level and simultaneously stopped listening to his generals. Thus as the war progressed Hitler's conversations became increasingly one sided and the information he received stopped coming from Constructive Dissenters and instead came from Destructive Consenters. That is to say, as the independent thinkers were removed from his circle of advisers so the quality of the advice sank to the point where the only advice he received was that he wanted to hear rather than which he needed to hear (Grint, 2001).

In contrast, Churchill, never one to withhold his own advice to others, began as prime minister by recruiting many of the individuals he knew to be the most independent and free-thinking. Hence, he asked Earnest Bevin, one of the leaders of the General Strike in 1926 that Churchill had previously sought to crush, to join the war cabinet as Minister of Labour and National Service. Indeed, he even worked with Chamberlain and Halifax, two of his bitterest political enemies. Similarly, in the military sphere, Churchill retained Alan Brooke despite their famous disagreements and furious disputes, because Churchill recognized that only such people had the fortitude and stubborn independence to give him the honest advice that he needed (Haffner, 2003; Roberts, 2003).

Another parallel should suffice to confirm this learning issue: Admiral Nelson and the Emperor Napoleon. Nelson was far more successful when operating with his 'Band of Brothers', his favoured group of captains, as at the battles of the Nile (1798) and Trafalgar (1805) for example, than when on his own – in the 1799 Naples fiasco and at Tenerife (1797) and Boulogne (1801), or when he ignored the advice of others, for instance at Copenhagen in 1801 (Grint, 2001; Kennedy, 2001). Napoleon did likewise: in his early major battles at Lodi (1796), Marengo (1800), and Austerlitz (1805), Napoleon listened to his generals and engaged in conversations about strategy, but by the time of his later defeats at Moscow (1812) and Waterloo (1815) he had all but abandoned any thoughts of taking advice from subordinates and insisted that only his personal planning and direction could achieve victory. As Marshal Ségur's diary noted in Russia, 'His pride, his policies and perhaps his health gave him the worst advice of all, which was to take no-one's advice (Weider and Guegen, 2000: 139). And by the time of Waterloo Chandler (1966: 161) insists that Napoleon was 'discouraging even his ablest generals from indulging in original thought'. Nor had British officers had much initiative before this. Wellington, for example, refused to allow his generals to design their own operations (Kier, 1997: 149).

In the First World War British military leadership expanded such a philosophy of destructive consent to the point where seasoned commanders in the field failed to question their superordinate commanders, even when the latter was demonstrably wrong. For example, Haig demanded changes in Rawlinson's original plan for the Somme offensive and Rawlinson accepted the changes, even though the latter knew they were unwarranted and rash in the extreme (Ferguson, 1998: 305–6).

The German prototype of training leadership through early practice and feedback, followed by the selection of the 'fittest', was in marked contrast to the British predilection for Carlyle's 'Great Man' theory, where (super)naturally talented individual heroes single-handedly turned the wheel of history, an approach still evident in the association of leaders with eras and events: Bismarck's Germany, Victorian Britain, Thatcherism and so on. But in Britain more generally Carlyle's model emerged as the amateur gentleman leader, who was both born to rule and, of course, primarily responsible for leading the British troops during war. As Gronn (1997: 4) suggests, the British, or rather English, elite sought to create a class of leaders with each new generation through a deft combination of institutions and culture:

> Family socialization of status hierarchy and authority norms; reliance on surrogates (e.g. nannies) to reinforce prescribed roles; intense peer socialization in preparatory and secondary boarding houses; a classics curriculum; a highly competitive, tribal games regime to instil muscular Christian virtues and character; and, finally, higher education in liberal-humanism at Oxford or Cambridge universities.

Laski captured the result perfectly 'a gentleman *is* rather than *does*; he maintains towards life an attitude of indifferent receptivity. He is interested in nothing in a professional way. He is allowed to cultivate hobbies, even eccentricities, but he must never practice a vocation' (quoted in Gronn, 1997: 4). Gronn (1997: 5) further suggests that this system generated a leadership 'prototype' – 'a cluster of characteristics forming a pattern or central tendency' and this prototype then became deeply embedded in the social mores of the British establishment, supported and validated by the education system, reference groups and mass communications.

For Gronn (1997: 5–6), following Barnett (1984) and Wiener (1982), the consequence of the leadership training developed through the nineteenth century was to leave Britain with a group devoted to loyalty, hard work and practicality – but little or no capacity for imagination and little interest in or support for science and technology: thus its difficulties in the early part of the First World War and the 1930s in particular, and the decline of Britain's technological lead in general. And where business and stalemated war required entrepreneurial and imaginative thought, instead it generated 'guardianship', a code of ethics that favoured responsibility and romantic idealism over innovative structures, procedures and strategies.

On the one hand that romantic idealism 'worked', that is, with few exceptions British soldiers followed their leaders: in the face of appalling danger thousands of formal leaders (officers and NCOs (non-commissioned officers)) and millions of their followers became casualties of an extraordinarily effective process of leadership. And on the other hand it 'failed', that is, the very inability of the leadership to rethink or modify their strategies in the first half of the war resulted in the same appalling casualties.

But how was the process of military leadership taught then? Sheffield's (2000) review of leadership in the British Army in the First World War suggests that what counted as good 'leadership' was closely aligned with the social origins and cultural predilections of a large proportion of the officer corps: the aristocracy. But with that privileged background came the social responsibility – *noblesse oblige* – that had kept the British aristocracy firmly in control of the country long after the French aristocracy had literally lost its collective head in the French Revolution.

The British soldiers these officers led, however, derived from the very lowest social classes so that the social gap between officers and soldiers in the British Army was probably as high as any other. Potential officers who were not 'gentlemen' – and increasingly they were not as the war progressed – had first to assuage any concerns that they would not embarrass themselves or their fellow officers in the mess or in front of the soldiers. But beyond the assumption that leadership was the equivalent of social class, leadership training did occur at GHQ Cadet School. From 1916 – after it became apparent that bravery and social class was an inadequate basis for leadership – officer cadets took it in turn to command their fellow cadets and were evaluated by their instructors and peers. Nonetheless the primary emphasis was on affirming the importance of paternalism. As a standard lecture insisted:

> Your first job is to get to know your men, look after them, study their interests and show you are one of them, taking a share in their pleasures and interests as well as their work. If you do this you will find that when the time comes they will follow you to hell. (Quoted in Sheffield, 2000: 58)

Leadership, then, was not something that subordinates might engage in – as the German Army had long been developing – but it was essentially rooted in a process of exchange: paternalism was exchanged for loyalty, dignity for deference. In effect, the leaders were obliged to treat their soldiers as they would to their own children and the soldiers would be obligated to obey their officers as *loco in parentis* in return. As one subaltern from the 1/King's suggested in 1914: 'How like children the men are. They will do nothing without us … You will see from this some reason for the percentage of casualties among officers' (quoted in Sheffield, 2000: 86). Hence privileges acquired by the officer corps were not necessarily resented by the soldiers, as long as the privileges did not undermine the social obligations of the officers to look after their men, and that often implied very small things, such as remembering a soldier's birthday, enquiring about his home life and making sure they were all fed as well as possible.

Nevertheless, even after commissioning a young subaltern had a lot to learn about leadership on the front line from the people who did most of it: the senior NCOs (the Sergeants and Warrant Officers). Indeed, the experience, prestige and value to the army of such NCOs was in marked contrast to that appertaining to a new subaltern, whose life expectancy at three weeks was much less than that of his NCOs. As Sheffield notes, many senior NCOs were responsible for 'nursing' their green lieutenants into the role of formal leaders, and that sometimes meant disobeying them – as did Sergeant Denmark when ordered by his new officer, Lt. Campbell, to stop unloading a wagon under fire and report immediately to him. 'Who's taking charge here, are you Sir, or am I?' responded the sergeant; the Lieutenant had the good sense not to compound his previous mistake (Sheffield, 2000: 124).

Between the wars the British army officer corps changed little; it was still a life of privilege based on inherited wealth and rank and it was irredeemably the cultivated amateur that dominated the mess. Indeed, it had to be because the pay was considered more of an honorarium than a salary; it was an institution that gentlemen attended (on a part-time basis) while they waited to inherit their estates. Thus 'training' was entirely unnecessary because an officer's life was merely an extension of the public school that most officers had already attended. Riding was the only really essential skill for a British army officer, not because it improved the ability of the cavalry but because it symbolized all that a gentleman needed to lead soldiers. The abject irrelevance of all that was not encapsulated by equine matters was most starkly revealed in the January 1939 edition of the *Cavalry Journal*. As the editorial stated, 'It is rather difficult to find very much to write about in this editorial' (quoted in Kier, 1997: 135).

And while the British strenuously avoided anything so controversial as politics and religion over dinner, the army officers mess went one better, prohibiting any discussion about military matters and concentrating on what was important: gentlemanly pursuits, sports, character development and 'good form'. One hospitalized officer recalled hearing his Colonel exclaim when he spied two military books by the bedside: 'What the devil are you reading those for?' He would certainly not have been reading them to enhance his decision-making capabilities because subordinate officers had virtually none to enhance. Hugh Dowding confirmed this, recalling the great contrast between the theory of freedom of thought – which allegedly distinguished the British from the rest of the world – and the practice that inhibited all unconventional ideas. 'As for expressing an opinion which differed from the general point of view', one officer remembered, 'that would be unheard of. … It would be considered very bad manners not to agree with the senior officer' (quoted in Kier, 1997: 130). Göring had come to the same conclusions when on an exchange visit with a British regiment before the First World War where officers were banned from 'talking shop' in the mess, were mesmerized by parade bashing, bored rigid by field craft training, and were certain that war was won by bravery not tactics or management (Blandford, 1999: 113).

Constructive dissent and destructive consent: the calchasian strategy

Perhaps most of the Allied military leaders engaged in the early part of both World Wars might have benefited from rereading their classical forebears. For example, the Roman armies were not only extraordinarily successful in time and space but they also operated on the battlefield with a process of political control that few contemporary commanders would care to repeat, for their ultimate leaders were professional politicians not military commanders, though they would have had some military training. Thus although, for example, the American President remains in command of the US armed forces this does not involve physically leading any battles. So how did the political leaders of Roman armies learn to lead? In many ways the answer is that they learned not to take the lead. In the words of one Roman general to Onasander, a military writer in AD 53, on how a 'politician' could lead the army, he should

> either choose a staff to participate in all his councils and share in his decisions, men who will accompany the army especially for this purpose, or summon as members of his council a selected group of the most respected commanders, since it is not safe that the opinions of one single man, on his sole judgement should be adopted. ... However, the general must neither be so undecided that he entirely distrusts himself, nor so obstinate as not to think that anyone could have a better idea than his own; for such a man, either because he listens to everyone and never to himself, is sure to meet with frequent misfortune. (Quoted in Peddie, 1994: 18)

Indeed, so concerned were the Romans to remind their most successful generals of their own limits that even those awarded the honour of a *Triumph*, a major battle honour, were also forced to endure reminders of their mortality. Thus although they were allowed (for one day only) to enter Rome at the head of their armies, dressed in a gold fringed purple toga, painted red like the god Jupiter, and pulled by a white-horsed chariot, they nevertheless always had a slave standing behind, holding a golden crown over them but whispering continuously in their ear *Respice post te, hominem memento te,* [Consider what comes afterward, and remember that you are but a man]. In short, the adulation of the Roman people that attributed god-like qualities to their *Triumphator* was tempered by the lowliest person reminding the general that he too was only mortal and, unlike the gods, neither infallible nor omnipotent. And if this wasn't enough the *Triumphator*'s soldiers marched behind him singing lewd songs and making crude jokes about him all with impunity for the day and all intended to deter their leader from seeking immortality.[3]

The assumption that no individual leader can possibly be the repository of all wisdom and that inverse learning was critical for leaders exists well before Onasander's time and at least as far back as Sophocles. For example, in his play *Antigone*, Creon, the King, initially declares that Antigone (his niece) will be executed by stoning for burying the body of her brother, Polyneices, a declared traitor, against Creon's direct order. Antigone, determined to save the soul of her dead brother, refuses to accede to Creon's demand that his body be left unburied and justifies her behaviour on the grounds that she is obeying the laws of the gods not human law. When Creon's own son, Haimon, appears romantically involved with Antigone, Creon first changes his sentence of death from stoning to entombing and then rescinds it altogether, but it is too late and his indecision and vacillation initiates not just the suicide of Antigone but the death of Haimon and the consequential suicide of Creon's wife, Eurydice. Yet there is more to *Antigone* than simply a story of indecisive leadership, for it also exposes an issue that sits at the heart of leadership and sits like the cancer of self-doubt. For as Haemon says to Creon:

Haemon ...   The Man
                who thinks that he alone is wise, that he
                is best in speech or counsel, such a man
                Brought to the proof is found but emptiness.
                There's no disgrace, even if one is wise,
                In learning more, and knowing when to yield.
                See how the trees that grow beside a torrent
                Preserve their branches, if they bend; the others,
                Those that resist, are torn out, root and branch.
                So too the captain of a ship; let him
                Refuse to shorten sail, despite the storm –
                He'll end his voyage bottom uppermost ...
Chorus   My lord, he has not spoken foolishly;
                You can each learn some wisdom from the other
Creon   What? Men of our age go to school again
                And take a lesson from a very boy?
                                          (*Antigone*, 1962: 25)

In effect, Haemon suggests that Creon cannot be omnipotent and therefore should take advice from one of his followers. This is a critical lesson for leaders: unless a leader is omnipotent – and none are – he or she will make a mistake at some point that could endanger the organization. So the issue is not 'how should an organization find a leader who does not make mistakes' but what kind of organization generates a process of leadership that prevents leaders making mistakes or at least mitigates their effects? As Collins and Poras (1996: 42) suggest in their discussion of the US Constitutional Convention in 1787, 'the crucial question was not "Who should be president? Who should lead us? Who is the wisest amongst us? Who would be the best king?" No the founders of the country concentrated on such questions as "What *processes* can we create that will give us good presidents long after we're dead and gone? What type of enduring country do we want to build? On what principles?" '

In short, since leaders cannot be omnipotent the process of leadership through continuous learning is as applicable to leaders as to followers. But this is to challenge the very legitimacy of Creon's leadership, for to be a leader, in Creon's eyes, is to be superior to one's followers and subordinates. Thus for Creon to admit to an error is to imply that he should no longer be the leader, and his refusal to accede to Haemon's logic condemns all the major characters to death or misery.

The Spartans institutionalized such a restraint on their royal leaders through the five annual elected Ephors, overseers, who swore to support the two kings but only if the kings maintained the rule of law. Thus if one Spartan king insisted on leading the army in battle, as he was permitted to do, two of the five Ephors always accompanied him and reported back on his conduct (Cartledge, 2002: 49–51).

This institutional constraint on leaders was also embodied in the advice given by a courtier to his prince in Castiglione's great sixteenth century work, *The Courtier*:

> Of this it commeth, that greatmen, beeside that they never understande the truth of any things, dronken with the licentious libertye that rule bringeth with it and with abundance of delicacies drowned in pleasures, are so far out of the way and their mind is so corrupted in seeing themselves alwaies obeyed and (as it were) woorshipped with so much reverence, and praise, without not onlye anye reproof at all, but also gainsayinge, that through this ignoraunce they wade to an extreeme selfe leekinge, so that afterwarde they admitt no counsel nor advise of others. (Castiglione, 1994: 297)

Note that in each of these cases, the Roman army, the Greek King Creon, the Spartan Ephors and Castiglione's prince, the learning occurs not through some unspecified 'experience' but from the process of listening – or in some cases not listening – to followers, through inverse learning. As Alvesson (2003) has suggested, far from leadership being located within extraordinary individuals it is rather the extra-ordinarization of the mundane, especially listening, that makes followers follow leaders. These leaders learn from their followers; indeed, they have to learn - leadership from their followers before they can attempt to exert leadership over them.

Finally we might relate this recruitment of 'enemies' to the experience of Agamemnon, King of Mycenae, in the Trojan War. In Greek mythology Calchas, the son of Thestor (a priest of Apollo) is a soothsayer that Agamemnon approaches in an effort to ensure victory over the Trojans. Calchas then visits the Oracle and declares that victory can only be achieved at significant cost to Agamemnon that includes: the sacrifice of his daughter Iphigenia, and that the task will take ten years and that no victory will ensue unless Achilles fights for the Greeks. In fact Calchas subsequently tells Agamemnon to build a wooden horse if he wants to defeat the Trojans and ultimately foresees his own death. However, two points are important here: first, Agamemnon has to take on trust the words of a Trojan, a former enemy; second, that the message Calchas relays is distinctly bitter – success has a cost.

The hubris of leadership, of course, has always been regarded as a fatal weakness for many, but the point is to understand what it is about hubris that so undermines leaders. Cohen's (2002) review of the relationships between political and military leaders in wartime confirms that in the cases of Lincoln, Clemenceau, Churchill and Ben-Gurion it is only when political leaders engage in the process of constructive dissent with their military leaders that a successful strategy is likely to prevail. Very often, it would seem, it is the military subordinates who must teach their political superordinates and wherever the relationship becomes too asymmetrical – in either direction – problems develop.

Leading to learn

I suggested above that perhaps leadership might be best learned from followers because it is through an iterative relationship between leader and followers that the latter teach the former to lead: a process of inverse learning. However, leadership is not something that only affects, or is effected through, isolated individuals and their atomised group of followers. On the contrary, leadership is essentially a social activity and leadership may best be learned within a 'Community of Practice' (Wenger, 1998: 4). For Wenger, learning starts with the assumption that 'engagement in social practice is the fundamental process by which we learn and so become who we are'. His approach is rooted in four premises:

1. The centrality of our social nature;
2. Knowledge is recognized as competence with respect to valued activities;
3. Knowing is a matter of engaging actively in the pursuit of such activities; and
4. Our experience of, and engagement with, the world generates meaning.

Learning is therefore a social process not an individual activity – despite the fact that we tend to teach and assess learning on an individual basis divorced from any 'lived experience of participation' (Wenger, 1998: 3). Participating implies not just an active learning mode and not just a social event but rather an engagement in a social practice that constitutes a social community and thus an identity. Communities of Practice are thus both informal and omnipresent, as families, work groups, street gangs, and in this case as a syndicate of sergeants on a leadership course. The implication is that learning occurs most effectively when the participants 'engage in and contribute to the practices of their communities' (Wenger, 1998: 7). In other words, learning occurs all the time and not just when we are sat in a lecture theatre or reading a textbook. The consequence of social learning is a social practice that embodies the folk-wisdom to allow community members to resolve their locally generated problems, though much of this practice is tacit knowledge it is essentially related to practice and does not divide mental from physical activities, 'theory' from 'practice'. In this sense Wenger's use of the term 'practice' is actually closer to the original meaning of 'praxis' – translating an idea into action. Hence even the construction of theory is both a social accomplishment and a social practice. And just as the social practice is a consequence of negotiations so too is its meaning, not merely in a linguistic sense but in a sense of a social process, a participatory practice that is more than mere engagement in a practice because it encompasses the lived experience that constitutes identity. As Wenger insists:

> Since the beginning of history, human beings have formed communities that accumulate collective learning into social practices – communities of practice. Tribes are an early example. More recent instances include the guilds of the Middle Ages that took on the stewardship of a trade, and scientific communities that collectively define what counts as valid

knowledge in a specific area of investigation. Less obvious cases could be a local gardening club, nurses in a ward, a street gang, or a group of software engineers meeting regularly in the cafeteria to share tips.[4]

The other half of a Community of Practice, according to Wenger, is manifest in reification – the materialization of abstractions – in other words, the way we make things represent ideas to the point where the thing appears to embody our own projections onto the world. Flags, for example, are reifications of identity, just as rank badges are, but so are classifications of people or things. These reifications capture and congeal human experience in material form that may be process or product, but either way they are the reflections of participatory practice. Wenger also insists that participation without reification generates too few anchors to link the practices together, and if there is reification without participation then social meaning cannot be generated and a community cannot be built: participation and reification are a necessary duality not a 'simple opposition'.

But a Community of Practice does not arise simply from physical proximity; that may be perceived as a community but unless there is 'mutual engagement' of participants that community will not develop a Community of Practice. Nor does an information network or social category mirror or generate *a* Community of Practice. Indeed, a Community of Practice is not a utopian ideal where mutuality and love prevail but one defined by shared practice and collective repertoires rather than harmonious relationships.

In what follows I use ideas from inverse learning and Communities of Practice to consider how Senior Non-Commissioned Officers (SNCOs) are taught to lead in the Royal Air Force (RAF). In what follows I describe my experiences of following two (overlapping) Intermediate Management and Leadership Courses (IMLC) undertaken in September and October 2003.

As suggested above, although experiential learning is critical here, it does not necessarily mean that the more experience one gets the better we become. It might be thus, and ordinarily we might expect it, but whether we learn from our experience depends upon the form of reflection engaged with. In other words, unreflective learning is hardly likely to improve our performance. If I practice scoring a goal every day for four hours but cannot see where the ball is going I am unlikely to improve much because I cannot reflect on my performance. In contrast, Jonny Wilkinson, England's rugby fly half in 2003, spent several hours a day practising his kicking and finished each session with a requirement to gain 6 consecutive perfect kicks; if there was an error he started all over again until he secured the magic total of six. Equally critical to the experience of performing the kicks however, was the reflection, both personal and from his kicking coach, David Alred who also trained with him every day (Williams, 2003: 2–3). Wilkinson might also prove a useful example of another issue: whether we are born of greatness or acquire it through education and experience. Surely if Wilkinson were born to the greatness he enjoyed after scoring the winning points in the 2003 Rugby World Cup in Australia he would not need to spend so long practising his greatness – it would simply be available to him, naturally. That Wilkinson's practice suggests that he does not believe this is merely confirmed by Phil Wilkinson, Jonny's father, who complained ironically that 'Christmas Day does tend to interfere with his training regime'.[5]

In complete contrast, former England football managers Terry Venables, Bobby Robson, Glenn Hoddle and even the former captain Alan Shearer have all suggested that you cannot practice for the football equivalent of rugby's place kicking – a penalty shoot-out – because it is based wholly on luck rather than skill. As Venables responded to a question about why he hadn't required the English players to practice in the same way that the German players had to – 'Are you telling me that it is not a lottery? I can't accept that.' It should be no surprise then when Gareth Southgate missed a penalty in the semi-final of the 1996 European Championship – it was the first he had ever taken in a serious game![6] Subsequent research has shown beyond any doubt that practice, while it does not make perfect, makes for a significant improvement (Whitefield, 2002). However, equally critical is the point that these practices tend to be communal – either everyone in the team tends to practice or no one does. By implication, the English World Cup winning rugby squad may not practice goal kicking all the time but they do engage in a phenomenal amount of practice (Catt, 2004).

I also suggested that a crucial element in the learning process was the feedback provided by the followers and it is this feedback that enables the leader to make sense of the action and interaction. This sense-making activity (Weick, 1995) occurs in all of us but is particularly present amongst formal leaders – the primary sense-makers. This sense-making activity is generally a pragmatic activity designed to deal with an extraordinarily complex world which is, in reality, too complex to grasp. As a consequence we tend to operate within an 'enacted world' – one that makes sense to us at the time and place we find ourselves in. Thus even if this proves to be inaccurate it is something we can work with and within: the world does not present itself as a series of tidy problems but as a raft of uncertainties and confusions that we have to make sense of and in making sense of it we reduce it to manageable proportions and problems.

Fisher *et al.* (2002) have suggested that this sense-making capability is best exploited 'at the point of action' in which the learner is posed specific forms of questions to help them make sense of the 'action' and simultaneously to embed the learning. Of course that 'help' need not be through an appointed coach, instructor or mentor and may more usually occur through interaction with peers. As Archer (2003: 8) suggests, students and peers often learn more from each other than from any teacher or superordinate. And very often that learning is facilitated by the kind of questions that encourage self-reflection, self-questioning, and self-understanding. As we shall see this model of leadership learning – do-review-apply – under the sense-making guidance of an experienced instructor and supported by a heterarchy of supportive peers, lies at the heart of the Intermediate Management and Leadership Course (IMLC).

IMLC

The aim of the Air Command Squadron (ACS) is 'to provide effective leadership and management training to RAF NCOs, shaping their beliefs, attitudes and skills to meet the future needs of the RAF'; while the IMLC is designed to further the management and leadership experiences and skills of 'acting sergeants', that is those individuals who already have the temporary rank of sergeant but whose confirmation of rank depends upon passing the IMLC. Each course lasts for three weeks and comprises a mixture of classroom and outdoor activities, in which the theory and practice of management and leadership – as the RAF currently perceive them – are taught by experienced SNCOs, primarily flight sergeants, with the occasional help of a warrant officer or commissioned officers of various ranks.

Each IMLC is split into four syndicates with each instructor, a flight sergeant, typically responsible for eight students, that is, acting sergeants. I followed two different courses over a period of five weeks in late 2003; the first was led by 'Wilf' the second by 'Geoff'. Both syndicates had more than the normal eight students because of the backlog of students that developed through commitments to operations (the firefighters' strike, and operations in Afghanistan and Iraq). Each course has a Course Commander (CC) who is one of the flight sergeants who has the coordinating role but does not take a particular syndicate except as a stand-in. The role of CC rotates and in my case Chris was the CC and stand-in for Geoff whenever Geoff was away. Most of the course takes place at the syndicate level where facilitated classroom discussion and outside exercises are combined, but occasionally lectures are provided for either half or all the course simultaneously. My role was essentially limited to observer with very limited and occasional participation. It is of course impossible to assess whether my presence affected the courses but my impression was that the participants and course instructors were relatively free of any distortion induced by me.

Every morning in the first two weeks starts with parade drill, something that many participants had not undertaken on a regular basis for some time. The primary purpose of this was not to ensure their drill remains at a certain level but that each sergeant got a chance to take the parade; a new and often nervous leadership task for most and one that perfectly captured the essence of the Community of Practice and learning philosophy: the parade leader may theoretically be 'in control' of the parade – but if the leader makes an error in the drill orders the followers are unlikely, unwilling or unable to comply with the leader's orders. Thus the followers teach the leader how to lead through the formers' feedback. Moreover, since this is an active process in which all participate, either as leader or follower, a Community of Practice is built up over time to embody collective knowledge and support the acquisition and recognition of competence.

Some days were spent entirely in the class rooms but often there were periods spent outdoors on physical activities, 'low ropes', orienteering, setting-up direction beacons, pine pole exercises, putting up and taking down tents and so on. The last two days were all outside. A series of tasks were set throughout the course including public speaking which, for example, developed from an unassessed five-minute speech on a topic of the participants' choice to the syndicate, to a ten-minute speech on a topic chosen by the instructor to the syndicate, and finished with the more pressured environment of a collective presentation to the whole programme including selective officers as well as a selection of newly trained recruits. Similarly a series of active 'leads' were required by everyone in increasing levels of complexity and time (called First Step, Mid-Step and Final Step) and while some of these were indoor exercises, most were outdoors involving some form of physical activity. First Step was not assessed and, from a learning perspective, the more mistakes made the better for all to learn. Mid- and Final Step were assessed by the flight sergeant in charge of the syndicate and, if necessary, by the Warrant Officer Training Standards. In between these 'leads' there were many 'theory' sessions provided either by lecture or, more usually, by group discussion and video, concerned with issues such as leadership, management, morale, drug abuse, Form 6000s (annual appraisal forms), 'defence writing' techniques and so on. Additionally, a series of video sessions were run in which the syndicate members took it in turn to interview and be interviewed in a series of scenarios, all of which were likely to arise back at their respective RAF stations.

This complex and busy schedule was run along typically robust military lines in terms of timings, self-discipline, forms of dress, attitudes and behaviour but underpinning it was a well-honed learning philosophy that embodied two critical components:

1. Leadership is a collective resource not an individual property. By that I mean that no individual was expected or required to know how to handle each and every situation that they were faced with – but they were expected to use their colleagues as resources to supplement their own knowledge and to control and coordinate the team. Thus when faced with a task the leaders were expected to delegate tasks wherever possible but to remain the coordinator of the followers' efforts rather than their executor. In effect, leadership was learnt by leaders accepting their own limitations and relying on their followers to compensate for these limitations.

2. Leadership skill is acquired primarily through the direct experience of leading but not just through the act of leading. Instead this has to be supplemented by the provision of honest and supportive criticism from instructors and team members and in an atmosphere that encourages self-reflection rather than denial and self-justification. In effect, learning to lead can be achieved through leading to learn. However, both learning and leading are social rather than individual activities and for both to be successful there is a requirement for a significant support network – a 'community of practice' (Wenger, 1998).

For instance on day one of the first course the instructor (Wilf) is setting up some ground rules for everyone to work with over the next three weeks and the issue of honest feedback is raised by one of the course participants:

> *Wilf:* What kind of honesty are we talking about here? It's no good – just because you want to be liked – you have to be honest with each other and with me – if you just sit there and be a passenger for three weeks, then come the final exercise you might get caught out. I'll stay behind every single night for as long as it takes to get you through this course but you need to be honest with me if you need help.

Wilf then runs through the programme and reminds them that most of the assessment occurs outside when they take up their leadership roles, their 'leads'.

> *Wilf:* I know some of you are worried about the public speaking sessions but don't be. I shall make notes in your folders on your performance but the pat on the back will not be a 'recce' for a knife! [Laughter]. Now remember the most important thing for the leadership Mid-Step exercise and the Final Step exercise is to help people who are given the lead but don't try and take over. Don't leave them if they're floundering but don't take over their lead. This is the most stressful time – a few sphincters will be going! [Laughter] A few teddies will be thrown out of the pram – but don't take things personally.

The role of questions to force, or at least encourage, reflective learning becomes quickly apparent when the syndicate is attempting to complete a Form 6000 – an RAF appraisal form – for their direct reports. The Form 6000 requires them to complete both numerical scores and a narrative on several development areas for each individual report and the time necessary to complete them has led to some making do simply with a numerical grade without any illustrative examples of behaviour.

> *Wilf:* So why can't you provide an example?
>
> *Sergeant N:* Well, I can't think of any.
>
> *Wilf:* Well if you say this person is the dog's bollocks but you can't think of a single example to support that – he can't be can he?
>
> *Sergeant N:* But most of my time is taken up with 6000s – it's taking me away from my primary task!
>
> *Wilf:* No, your primary task now as a senior manager is to focus on the troops – they should be concentrating on the primary task and you should be concentrating on them.

Sergeant N was clearly bemused by this response at first but over the next few days he did seem to accept that the task of a sergeant was not to undertake the technical jobs that he had done as a corporal or a technician. A similar example occurred in Geoff's syndicate. Sergeant J had provided an example to illustrate the numbers given on the Form 6000 but Geoff wasn't happy with it.

> *Geoff:* What have you written?
>
> *Sergeant J:* Well I've written: 'He has an interest in buildings.'
>
> *Geoff:* Yeh well I have an interest in brain surgery but what does that mean in practice? [Laughter].

The result of these sessions on the Form 6000 is a collective understanding of the right way to complete an appraisal and an acceptance that the form is not just a bureaucratic imposition but the primary route through which subordinates can improve their performance and secure promotion. In short, the result is a reified 6000 – a materialized standard that embodies collective practice and provides some participants with some purchase on what had previously been merely an abstraction. But if the distributed knowledge of former generations of the RAF is encapsulated in the 6000, that belonging to the syndicate under observation became manifest in the First Step exercises.

Leadership, delegation and a duty of care

One of the first 'leads' in First Step was a mental maths problem and provided an early opportunity to consider how important the distribution of knowledge was. Sergeant P was chosen and given a sheaf of papers to quickly look through while the rest of the group waited.

Sergeant P:	Who's good at maths? [two hands are raised] Do this please. [He hands them a card and the rest of the syndicate coalesce into different problem solving groups.]
Sergeant P:	Any one got any problems? [Silence]
Wilf:	1 minute guys … 10 seconds … time's up. Wilf gets them to write the answers on the board and most are right but a couple are wrong.
Wilf:	So Chris, what was all that about then?
Sergeant P:	Delegation – I just asked who was good and gave them the card.
Wilf:	So you didn't brief anyone about the task first?
Chris:	No I didn't think I had time.
Wilf:	So why do we delegate?
Group:	Spread work … Save time … Spread experience.
Wilf:	OK but note that Delegation is not Abdication. How many have worked for bosses who didn't delegate? [all hands rise]. So sometimes the boss signs work off as his own but it's really yours? [All nod] How does that make you feel?
Group:	It pisses me off … Yeh, yeh.
Wilf:	So don't do it yourself then! Delegation gives subordinates status, value, they feel important, they get confidence and they feel trusted. You must utilize others' experience. … When I was on Fresco [Fire fighters Strike duties][7] I had 30 RAF and 30 Paras and this Army lieutenant comes up to me and says – looking at my guys – 'I don't want any shit from this lot!' So I said 'Hold on – you don't need to talk to me like that – just talk to me.' Army leaders take everything on themselves but they can't do it. I just delegate and they get on with it. This is the most difficult part of the lead exercises – delegation – don't go 'hands-on', stand back and manage the process. So what shouldn't you delegate?
Sergeant N:	Shit-jobs!
Wilf:	Yeh, like sweeping out the hangar – 'I'm not doing that', 'I've done all that.' I think if the guys are really busy you should help. I know the bosses don't like

<table>
<tr><td>Sergeant N:</td><td>to see you doing it but it's good when you do it. Some of the older sergeants have lost the ability to make tea and do photocopying but when I got promoted I decided to keep doing it.</td></tr>
</table>

Sergeant N:	Yeh I do it still, not because I want to be liked by the lads but because I'd have liked someone do it for me.
Wilf:	And what else should you be delegating?
Sergeant P:	Complete tasks – otherwise there's no job satisfaction.

This exercise and debriefing set the pattern for the rest of the course. 'Leads' were not expected to know everything but to delegate tasks and retain coordination, control and decision-making. But delegation was clearly distinguished from abdication of responsibility and Wilf's sweeping example, supported by the 'old hand' of the group – Sergeant N – reaffirms that superior rank does not mean that maintaining a good relationship with one's subordinates is irrelevant. Note also that Wilf's approach combines the questioning techniques that demand self-reflection of the group with practical examples and illustrations. Furthermore, the interjection by Sergeant N reaffirms that this is a community issue and not something restricted to beneficent instructing staff. Indeed, the 'community' is built or undermined by precisely this practice of undertaking jobs traditionally restricted to subordinate ranks.

The clash with the Army lieutenant reveals another critical aspect of leadership training: leaders have to protect their followers from others, they have a duty of care towards them. Indeed, this seems to provide an important foundation stone for the exchange at the heart of leadership here: paternalistic care is provided in exchange for acquiescence to rank. This is anything but new; as Sheffield (2000) argued convincingly, the relatively good relationships between British soldiers and officers in the trenches on the Western Front in the First World War were primarily rooted in the exchange of paternalism for loyalty.

But it is not just the relationship between RAF leaders and followers that is underpinned by paternalism because the contemporary RAF has a large number of civilian employees that sergeants have unlimited responsibility for but limited control over. The second course I followed was run by Geoff and in this exchange he is facilitating a discussion on 'Working with civilians'.

Geoff:	Civil Servants comprise 18% of the Service so all of you will have to manage them at some time.
Sergeant W:	Can we bollock them?
Geoff:	You can't *bollock* them – you have to *counsel* them [laughter]. You can't take formal disciplinary action against them but you shouldn't need to if you're using your management skills properly … You can get the best out of your civilians and RAF staff if you are concerned about their welfare. Your attitude is critical. They have a lot of knowledge and you can only get at it by being concerned about them.

Leadership and discipline

The importance of the duty of care does not translate into a liberal 'touchy-feely' approach to managing subordinates, this is, after all, a military establishment and the instructing staff are typical of the 'robust' SNCOs that Kipling long ago proclaimed as the 'backbone of the British Army'.[8] But it does imply that leaders are responsible for what followers do – even if they were not aware of that responsibility. For example, Chris took the syndicate for a facilitated session on discipline.

Chris:	What do you all think of the state of discipline in the RAF today?
Group:	Gone downhill … People are scared of it these days [general murmurings of agreement].
Chris:	Yeh but you have to impose yourself. I mean whose fault is it if discipline is lax?
Sergeant N:	Ours.
Chris:	Yes exactly.
Sergeant T:	Yes but they don't expect it any more so you can't enforce it can you?
Chris:	Well you should go across to the recruit training because believe me, when they leave here after 9 weeks they are disciplined. But by the time they get their trade it's changed – they know what they can get away with. What happens if you say to someone 'Do that again and I'll charge you' – and they do it again and you don't charge them?
Sergeant N:	Everyone knows the Sarge is an easy touch.
Chris:	Yes, so it's up to you to stop it. So how do we define discipline?
Sergeant D:	The enforcement of personal and external standards?
Sergeant W:	The ability to obey orders?
Chris:	So how can we maintain it if we don't have the standards ourselves? How many of you have still got pride in the Service? [About half raise their hands].
Chris:	Well we may think differently but we've got to give our subordinates a chance and you've got to get used to confrontation. Your guys are looking to you to sort this stuff. If someone knocks at your door and you say 'Come in' – what have you done? You haven't given yourself time to prepare have you? So what happens if you say: 'just wait' or 'stand there' – what's happened? … You've told him who's in charge haven't you? And think about your body language – I know when I enter a room whether I'm going to win just by looking at body language. But top tip – know you're people, they're not all the same and therefore you need to treat them differently. It's our responsibility to set as well as maintain standards.

The ability to maintain discipline without resorting to authoritarianism, or worse, is not only tested in the field exercises but in the video interviews that occur towards the end of the course. One in particular is set up to test the toughest disciplinarian in the group: in this syndicate Sergeant I. As Geoff indicated before the exercise, the learning involved is in and through the community, rather than just the individual taking the lead: 'I need to use the appropriate people so the group can get the most learning from each situation. There's no point in putting a weak student in with Chris for example, he'll tear them to shreds and that would destroy his confidence and teach the group nothing.'

The scenario involves one aptly named 'Corporal Ironfist' whom, the scenario suggests, is perceived to be bullying his 'flight'. While Sergeant I goes to the interview room the rest of the syndicate eagerly await viewing the coming altercation on the Closed Circuit TV. Unbeknown to Sergeant I, Corporal Ironfist will not be played by another member of the syndicate, as is the norm, but by Chris the Course Commander, who bears a remarkably physical resemblance to the archetype embodied in the script – well over six foot, muscular, tattooed and with very short cropped hair. While Sergeant I is left to ruminate on his coming confrontation it becomes clear that Corporal Ironfist is in the vicinity because his voice booms through the television monitor:

Corporal Ironfist [outside the room]:	Get back to fucking work! He bangs loudly on the interview room door and immediately enters, carrying a large stick. He sits down without being invited and leans across to Sergeant I.
Corporal Ironfist:	Hi Sarge. What's going on?
Sergeant I:	[Clearly taken aback by the entrance of Corporal Ironfist and trying to recover]: I'll ask the questions.
Corporal Ironfist:	Excuse me Sarge [He stands up, goes past the Sergeant's desk to the window behind him and opens it as someone (Geoff) walks past]. Oi – you lot get back to fucking work!
Sergeant I:	[Standing] Sit down! Sit down!
Corporal Ironfist:	But Sarge those lazy fucking bastards – they're doing my head in! I mean they're a right shower. If I didn't chase them all day long I don't know what would happen!
Sergeant I:	Have you finished?
Corporal Ironfist:	Yes Sarge, but Sarge they need a right good bollocking.
Sergeant I:	I don't want to hear you giving them a bollocking in public.
Corporal Ironfist:	But Sarge listen, you've only been here for three months and …
Sergeant I:	That's got nothing to do with it.
Corporal Ironfist:	But the other sergeants never complained.
Sergeant I:	That's not the point. I'm in charge here now and the way you treat people is a disgrace.
Corporal Ironfist:	But Sarge in a few years I'm going for my third stripe and I've got a top flight you know.
Sergeant I:	Your flight only works because they're scared of you. You cannot shout at people all the time. You've got six months to change your ways.
Corporal Ironfist:	But Sarge if I go all pink and fluffy the boys will take the piss!
Sergeant I:	I'm not expecting miracles. I'm expecting to see some change though. Now go back to work.

After much laughter, both in the viewing room and at the end of the interview between Ironfist and Sergeant I, the latter returns to the viewing room for a debrief from Geoff.

Geoff:	So how do you think that went? [Laughter].
Sergeant I:	Well when I saw who it was I thought – fuck me! [Laughter].
Geoff:	Well you might have started by taking the stick off him! You need to remain assertive but not aggressive – I mean when you told him he was an 'absolute disgrace' – do you think that helped?!
Sergeant I:	No, not really.
Geoff:	Well you have two routes to go down here. You can either take the bullying, harassment and legal route or you can try and get him to self-identify the problems. Don't take him on and tear him a new arsehole! That's just as bad as his bullying isn't it? [Sergeant I nods.]

What is most intriguing about this is how close it comes to traditional archetypes of military discipline, and how well the players can pick up their roles. Yet underlying the humour there are serious points to be made: that bullying is not leadership; that being assertive is critical but it is not the same as being authoritarian; that it's very easy to fall back into the 'old ways' unless people are constantly reminded of the dangers and – if all else fails – that the law will not support rank if it's abused.

Overlaying all this is the engagement in a practice that supports the production and reproduction of the community of sergeants; the 'band of brothers' (and sisters since both syndicates included women). However, a significant degree of learning undoubtedly occurs between the sergeants and beyond the gaze of their flight sergeant. In the case of Corporal Ironfist, after Geoff had debriefed Sergeant I and reinforced the learning points he wanted to embed, the group of sergeants were asked for comments but none provided Sergeant I with any criticism, constructive or otherwise. Indeed, they collectively congratulated him on 'standing up' to Corporal Ironfist. In sum, the learning that Geoff was trying to instil into the group – bullying is not leadership – was blunted by the learning instilled by the sergeants' Community of Practice – bullies should be bullied back.

The limits on 'formal' learning imposed by the 'informal' Community of Practice also became manifest in one element of the Final Step exercise in which one lead requires all the syndicates to work together to coordinate the deployment of a system of ground signals that will enable a pilot to drop an item accurately on the target. In this case the target beacon, along with the aerial and the marker panels were all deployed correctly (in line) at a specified angle down a gentle slope over a 500 metre area. However, with just a few minutes to go before the aircraft was theoretically due an 'officer' arrived on the scene demanding to know who was in charge. The 'officer' was in fact another of the instructing staff dressed as an officer and the issue was whether the lead sergeant responsible for deploying the marker panels and the target beacon would maintain his stand against an intemperate officer.

Officer:	Sergeant – the central of the three marker panels is out of alignment and will confuse the pilot, get it moved 5 metres to the left.
Sergeant:	[Looking askance because the marker panels are perfectly aligned]. But it's right as it is sir.

Officer:	No it isn't, it's clearly wrong – now get it moved.
Sergeant:	But sir it looks right to me.
Officer:	Are you questioning my authority sergeant?
Sergeant:	No sir but … well … it looks fine to me [looks round for support from the group, but doesn't get any].
Officer:	I will ask you to move it just one more time sergeant.
Sergeant:	OK sir [the sergeant runs down to the marker and moves it left the required 5 metres so that it is now clearly out of alignment. He then returns to the officer.] OK sir?
Officer:	Sergeant, you were right the first time; why on earth did you change your mind? Have the courage of your convictions man. [He turns and marches off, leaving the sergeant baffled and bemused].

This incident was the most extreme case of challenging the participants to maintain their position in the face of pressure but it was not an isolated case and each one was designed to reinforce the confidence of the leader and the group in their own acts and not to rely upon, nor wilt before, the onslaught of apparently superordinate authority that they knew to be wrong.

The second example of integrity testing occurred earlier on the same day as we passed another syndicate marching back towards its original destination; Geoff asked their instructor (Dale) what was going.

Dale:	Well Sergeant J's got the lead and she's very decisive but often wrong – she could be a bloody officer! Well when she made the mistake I said she could either write the Course Commander a note explaining what she'd done or she could march the entire syndicate back to where they came from to do the task properly – so she's marching them back … I can't believe it … morale's absolutely rock bottom now.

It turned out later that when the task was completed the syndicate let her know their collective mind in no uncertain terms, once again reinforcing the notion that this was a community team at practice not a team practising to be a community. However, the gender of the errant leader in the previous example was not a contributory factor to the team's problems, as we shall see in the next example.

Gender and leadership

The first syndicate I followed had two women and eight men [the second had just one woman] and two of the early exercises generated important lessons for the group to consider. Both involved cooperation and competition and the first task was instigated without any context by Wilf.

Wilf:	OK, here's the task. You have a large tyre inner tube and you have to get the whole group through the hole. You have ten minutes to tell me how long, exactly, it will take you.
Sergeant A:	It's not a race so we could get this perfect! [Laughter].

Sergeant D:	Why don't we just try it and see?
Sergeant N:	You are talking about this hole Wilf? [Pointing to the inner tube].
Wilf:	As opposed to what hole? [Laughter].
	The group take it in turns to get through the hole as two people hold it, and raise and lower it alternately. It takes 31 seconds the first time and 24 seconds the second time.
Sergeant W:	Is it meant to be a race?
Wilf:	I don't know – is 24 seconds good enough?
Sergeant D:	No come on we can beat this.
	They do it in 22 seconds
Wilf:	Anything you want to know?
Sergeant N:	Yeh, why are we doing it?
Wilf:	Because I'm telling you to. Do you want to know about the other syndicate's times?
Sergeant N:	Yeh
Wilf:	A syndicate of eight can do it in 8 seconds.

At this point the two women in the syndicate begin to demand more effort from the group, though some of the men became uninterested. Wilf comments to me on the lack of leadership amongst the group and the resulting lethargy. One of the women asks Wilf whether they have to do it quickly.

> *Wilf:* You don't have to. All I'm telling you is that your time is average. It's entirely up to you.

The women then take formal control and demand great efforts and the time is reduced to 13 seconds. Wilf concludes by asking them to think about the importance of competition to performance and about the role of leadership in securing that performance, in this case by the two women sergeants.

The role of gender in leadership resurfaces the following day when the group engage in their first attempt on the Low Ropes, an array of ropes slung tautly between various trees just above ground level with various exercises that require balance, team work and leadership but do not endanger anyone – though one of the current syndicate broke his collar bone six months ago on this exercise! Wilf explains the requirements and the limitations of the exercise and asks for questions.

> *Sergeant N:* Is anyone in charge?
> *Wilf:* No

The two women agree that they should be in the middle because they don't have the physical strength to do this kind of thing and the men all accept this. In fact the two women then seem to remain in control through most of the exercises and frequently lead the group but it's very much a group effort and lots of advice is given. When they finish Wilf debriefs them collectively.

> *Wilf:* I was impressed with the low ropes – but there were some points when you got stuck weren't there? [Group nods].

Wilf:	Now I could have just stood there and done nothing – but what good would that have been?
Group:	None!
Wilf:	So when you get a lad who can't do it what do you do?
Sergeant P:	Shout at them! [laughter].
Wilf:	And if they still can't do it?
Sergeant P:	Shout louder! [laughter]
Sergeant N:	Yeh but when you said 'hold hands' we were off. Yeh we could have become demoralized then if we'd kept on failing.
Wilf:	Yeh, so it's a fine line between giving people the space and time to do it and helping them when they're stuck.
Wilf:	And what did the girls start out saying first of all?
Sergeant S:	That they wanted to be in the middle.
Wilf:	And where did they end up?
Sergeant S:	Leading us! [laughter].

Impact, delegation and distancing

The importance of using delegation as a mechanism for keeping clear of the task execution – so that the 'lead' could always have the space and time to maintain control, coordination and an overview – was constantly reinforced. Heifetz and Linsky (2002: 51) use 'getting off the dance floor and going to the balcony' as a metaphor for this task that enables leaders to keep asking themselves 'what is really going on here?' The confusion of the dance floor and the 'fog of war' are useful images for what occurs under the pressure experienced by leaders and the need to distance themselves, not from their followers, but from the 'doing'. On the first Mid-Step exercise, the first assessed task, Geoff gathered the syndicate for a quick briefing inside and reminded them of the briefing technique they have been taught to use when time is short: SMEAC – Situation, Mission, Execution, Ask questions, Check understanding.

Geoff:	When you have a task and it goes wrong, nine times out of ten it goes wrong because the brief is wrong. They (followers) don't know what the task is and they don't know what they have to do. SMEAC is good when time is short.[9]
	SMEAC: Situation, Mission, Execution, Ask questions, Check understanding.
	Situation: The overall issue.
	Mission: the details – say this twice, repeat it to reinforce it.
	Execution: How can we do this? If you haven't a clue ask for help, split them into groups and ask them to plan the execution. Then start delegating the tasks.
	Ask questions.
	Check group understanding.
	So, you may not have an idea, but rest assured someone in the team will; take them on one side if you want and ask them. Then get them all back together and say: 'OK, this is what we're going to do and then confirm with them that they understand. Think about your limitations. Once you've been through it

ask for questions. If you've got one or two that's OK. If all hands go up you have a problem. Then ask them about the limitations so you can confirm everyone knows ... As a team commander I don't want to see you doing everything – handling the equipment – because you lose focus, stand back, delegate and keep an eye on the big picture. If you see something going wrong step in, address it and step out again. Don't get sucked in. An important thing is a sense of impact at the start. You set the tone, raising your voice is fine. Don't walk to the group, get them to come to you – then they know who's in charge.

We then went outside to the wooded exercise area where Geoff ran through the Health and Safety requirements of working with ropes, hammers and so on and he asked for limitations that related to Health and Safety from each individual and they responded with examples. Then he picked Sergeant P for the first lead.

Geoff:	Stuart, you're first. I'll read the exercise to you, then give you the card and see if you have any questions. OK? [Stuart nods].
	OK. There a radioactive isotope over there [points] you have to render it safe using this equipment [reads it out] and these are the limitations: you cannot put the isotope down once you have lifted it, you musn't go within one metre for more than 90 seconds, there is a minefield between you and it. ... You have 30 minutes to complete the task. I'm giving you 5 minutes to think about the task and then you're off. OK? [Stuart nods] Tell me when you're ready [3 minutes]. Any questions Stu?
Stuart:	How likely is it that all the equipment is used?
Geoff:	That's entirely up to you. [5 minutes later] Ready?
Stuart:	Yep
	Stuart starts walking towards the group who are about 15 metres away talking under the trees (it's beginning to rain), then he looks at Geoff – presumably remembering Geoff's warning on making an immediate impact – and stops:
Stuart:	OK team on me! They run over and he explains the task slowly and carefully. At this stage I'll nominate a time-keeper – Jules that's you. Any questions? OK give me a limitation each. He runs through the group and some respond with a limitation. OK let's have a 2-minute planning session in two groups.
Geoff [aside to me]:	Stuart didn't repeat the mission nor get all the limitations out of the group in the session.
Stuart [to group]:	Can we have a group chat now?
Geoff [aside to me]:	That's too weak – should have been 'Come over here now!'
	The 'group chat' turns into a general discussion.
Geoff [aside to me]:	It's a bloody committee!
	Stuart then imposed order and asked for suggestions. Two are offered and Stuart selects one and they all pick up the equipment to practice the task.
Geoff [aside to me]:	He hasn't delegated anyone yet.

	Lots of people are standing around while two of the syndicate are tying up logs.
Geoff [aside to me]:	There's only 16 minutes left and look at them! He's not applying any motivational skills.
	Eventually, and after several failed attempts, the task is complete and the 'isotope' made safe. Geoff debriefs them:
Geoff:	Any injuries? [none] OK Stu how do you think that went?
Stuart:	Well we spent too long wondering about how to get it into the box.
Geoff:	Did you repeat the mission twice?
Stuart:	I can't remember.
Geoff:	I don't think you did. Go through the mission twice, go through the resources and the limitations. You appointed a timekeeper – that was good. Then you went through the limitations but you didn't cover them all again in the questions. Then you planned for 2 minutes – that wasn't enough was it? You should have had 4 or 5 minutes planning. Then they both came back with ideas. Did you get in to a pissing contest, a committee?
Stuart:	Yes it did.
Geoff:	Make it abundantly clear that you are in charge. 'Tell me – one at a time.' Say 'Shut-up. I need to listen to X.' Otherwise you're in meltdown. Did you delegate the task?
Stuart:	There didn't seem to be enough to do to delegate.
Geoff:	So what could you do? You could have said: 'Right you four go and get a drink or you're on safety.' Don't say 'someone get the logs.' Say: 'you, you and you, go get the logs.' 14 minutes in did you use any motivational skills?
Stuart:	No I don't think I did.
Geoff:	So motivate them – 'good knot Jasper' and so on. So there wasn't much urgency was there?
Stuart:	No, we were all standing around … it's hard to motivate them.
Geoff:	So when you had the log over the minefield who should have decided whether it had gone far enough?
Stuart:	The person with the best view.
Geoff:	So who should that have been?
Stuart:	Me.
Geoff:	Yes, it's your responsibility unless you delegate that task. And at the end of the task what were you doing?
Stuart:	I was holding the rope.
Geoff:	Yes you should have been monitoring the situation not holding the rope!

Here, then, Geoff used a combination of questions and assertions to probe Stuart's leadership, to evaluate his performance and to suggest practical ways to improve, and all without the stereotypical military 'bollocking' that the sergeants may either use themselves or have had to endure when they were corporals or below. Again, it's worth emphasizing here that although the approach is clearly prescriptive – there is a better way to lead than relying simply on your own resources – it remains very flexible because the *resources* that can solve the problems are those of the group not the individual leader, though the individual leader retains the *responsibility* for making the ultimate decision. That is to say, it is not what Hodgson (1999: 129) calls learning to lead by the equivalent of 'painting by numbers' because that would imply a 'correct' solution to the problem, whereas this approach concerns maximizing the possibilities of solving the problem rather than searching for the 'correct' one.

However, it is not fool proof. On one occasion with Wilf's course an assessed 'lead' on the Final Step involves setting up a Helicopter Landing Site (HLS). This is relatively easy to undertake but there are several aspects that are likely to go wrong. The appointed lead in this case had no knowledge of HLSs but, unbeknown to him, one of the team was an expert. The lead appointed a Second in Command (2^{IC}) without this knowledge and as the lead began to specify how the task should be done the 'expert' suggested otherwise:

Sergeant P: OK, this is how we'll do this [points to his diagram]
Sergeant M: That's not how you do it!
Sergeant P: And what do you know about it?
Sergeant M: I do this for a living!
Sergeant P: Who's in fucking charge here? I'm in fucking charge ... so that's how we're doing it.

The task is completed but improperly. Afterwards Wilf debriefed the lead

Wilf: Why didn't you make use of the man's knowledge rather than ignore him, and why bollock him in front of the team? And then you got it all wrong!
Sergeant P: I didn't realize you could have more than one 2^{ic} Flight. I won't do that again.

The problem of learning to lead is exacerbated by those with minimal experience as an acting sergeant before they attend the course. For instance, Sergeant J has only been acting for a few weeks, while the majority have been in post for months and occasionally more than a year. Geoff chose Sergeant J for the second Mid-Step exercise and by this time it was pouring down so they all donned their waterproofs and carried on. They failed in the task because the team hadn't understood the limitations properly and Geoff debriefed them in the relative warmth of the tent.

Geoff: So what went wrong then?
Sergeant J: Don't know really ... just ran out of time.
Geoff: Well your brief was too brief and missed out on the limitations. Hence you got penalized. Did you have a Q&A session at the end of the briefing?
Sergeant J: No – I asked if they all understood.
Geoff: Yes but you didn't know whether they really understood did you? And where was the motivation? It's pissing down – you should have been saying: 'I know it's pissing down boys but you're doing well etc.' Anyway you forgot to tell them that equipment can only go forward not back – that's why I penalized you. I'm not bothered whether you complete the task or not – but with that

	brief they couldn't have succeeded. Beyond that your delegation was OK but did you motivate people?'
Sergeant J:	No.
Geoff:	Well that's honest, at least. Remember what I said before – if it's going to screw up its because of the briefing – this was a classic case. When things went wrong Sergeant J you got quieter but we need the opposite – not Mad Max, but vociferous – *real* leadership.
Sergeant J:	But …
Geoff [smiling]:	No 'Buts'. When I give you constructive feedback don't fucking argue with me! [laughter].

It should be obvious by now that laughter plays a crucial role in this course – as indeed it does in most organizations (Collinson, 2002). Like all military situations the barrack room banter plays a functional role in defusing tension and in enabling troops to distance themselves from some of the things they are faced with. Nevertheless, underlying the humour here are real lessons in learning and leadership. To argue with the instructors feedback is to break the agreed ground-rules that honest feedback is vital and the ability to learn from it is an essential component of leadership and learning to lead. However, it is noticeable that the honesty of the feedback is usually restricted to Geoff the instructor – the other members of the syndicate were manifestly willing to accept and even support the poor leadership of Sergeant J because they all knew that they could be next in the 'firing line' and would have to call on Sergeant J and all the others for support. In effect, the *practice* of the community became rooted in a peer pressure that demanded support of anyone engaged in the *process* of leadership, even if their *practice* was poor.

A similar experience occurred during one of the interview video sessions. The least experienced and most nervous member of the syndicate (Sergeant J) is supposed to play the part of the sergeant who is interviewing a woman (Sergeant D) who has just arrived on camp. In the interview, which lasts around 20 minutes, at least 90 per cent of the time is taken up with the sergeant telling the new arrival about himself and the camp. In theory this should be evenly split to allow the sergeant to get to know the new arrival. When the interview stops, but before the interviewer and interviewee have returned to the viewing room, the group spend several minutes laughing at the events and the poor display of leadership by the sergeant:

Sergeant J:	He's as mad as a box of frogs isn't he? [laughter]
Sergeant N:	Yep – he's perfect officer material! [laughter]

Sergeant D returned first from the interview and the group demand to know what she thought of her 'interview', especially her chance to tell him all about herself.

Sergeant D:	Well, I certainly gave him a bloody good listening to! (laughter)

Again, with the exception of Geoff, no one on the group made any comment to Sergeant J about the problems of his performance on his return – the convention (though not the intention of the course designers and trainers) was not to criticize each other, at least not in public, and any valuable learning from such criticism was lost in the practice of the community. This should not be a surprise: ever since the Hawthorne experiments in the 1930s (Grint, 1998: 119–23) it has been obvious that social norms are extraordinarily powerful in the construction of everyday life and it would be bizarre if a training course was free from such normative patterning. Indeed, that is how communities are created and reproduced – through social norms. In this case learning to lead is both created and inhibited by the community within which it is practised. Or paraphrasing what Edmund Burke is alleged to have said, 'It only requires the good follower to do nothing for leadership to fail.'

Conclusion

I began by noting that although many leadership experts insist that we can learn to lead, or at least learn some aspects of the process of leadership, this does not necessarily mean that leadership can be taught. A parallel was drawn between learning to be a leader and learning to be a parent and I suggested that rather than parents teaching their offspring to become children it is often the other way round: children teach their progenitors to become parents through inverse learning. Of course, numerous forms of advice exist for new parents: their own parents, parenting books and websites, friends and so on but ultimately it may be that the most important teacher is the allegedly helpless and dependent creature in your arms, and through trial and error over a life time parents gradually acquire parenting skills thanks to their teachers: their children. If Gerard Manley Hopkins is right – and he acknowledges it is a counter-intuitive argument and is more concerned with the way the same individual matures from child to adult – then we may have to rethink how leaders learn too, for it may be that their greatest teachers are their followers.

This hypothesis was then examined through reference to a small number of exemplars from history whose own successes and failures do indeed seem to mirror Gerard Manley Hopkins poetic innovation. Moreover, although parents may suggest that a compliant and obedient child is the ideal to aim for, in reality any asymmetric relationship is likely to be problematic: irresponsible parents or children are a likely result of this leadership process. Similarly, where leaders secure domination over their followers their followers tend to become 'irresponsible', to provide destructive consent rather than constructive dissent, that is to reactively allow their leaders to make mistakes rather than to actively inhibit this. Thus it may be better for leaders to recruit and retain followers that embody the spirit of Calchas, individuals who are not natural allies of leaders but who have their best interests at heart and are willing to articulate honest if unpopular advice.

Can we relate the child–parent relationship to this 'Calchasian' strategy? As I suggested above, one of the problems with some parent–child relationships is of asymmetric responsibility – irresponsible parents allowing their irresponsible children to run wild or overprotective parents preventing their children from assuming any responsibility. In the arena of leadership the replication would be to have over-responsible 'leaders' who are actually 'micro-managing' their followers or irresponsible followers allowing their leaders to do things that ought not to be done. Hence a Calchasian strategy involves leaders buttressing their process of leading by recruiting advisers and followers whom they know to have the best interests of the organization at heart, even if this means taking on board prickly and independent advisers and followers: not replacing 'yes-people' with 'no-people' but replacing 'yes-people' with 'why-people', not from sychophants to recalcitrants but from sychophants to Calchasants.

We have explored the extent to which this may be accurate and complemented the theory by adopting Wenger's argument for learning as a Community of Practice. In this approach learning is best achieved both as an active and participatory practice and through a social rather than an individual engagement with that practice. That community builds up a repertoire of accepted knowledge and practices – the processes of leadership – which are reproduced in and through the practices themselves and through their embodiment in reifications – materializations of abstractions. Through the use of specific examples from two RAF leadership courses I suggested that this combination of a Community of Practice, and a philosophy that is framed by an acceptance that the leaders' primary role is to coordinate and control their practicing community of followers, the RAF, at least at SNCO level, have developed an educative system that is both pragmatic and sophisticated. It is sophisticated because it makes overt the covert secret of leadership – that leaders *as isolated individuals* cannot lead successfully. It is pragmatic because this acknowledgement frees SNCOs from the unendurable pressure and erroneous temptation to be omnipotent and omniscient and embeds a system that generates confidence in the followers. The followers will know what to do and how to do it – but this does not mean that leadership is irrelevant, on the contrary, leaders have to use their skills to facilitate this leadership process: to allow the community to practice.

However, in this 'practice' mutual support provides an important safety net that is very much a double-edged technique. On the one hand it encourages the 'leads' to experiment knowing that the team is very likely to be willing to accept mistakes and maintain their support for the lead. In short, the team are teaching the leader to lead through their acquiescence. On the other hand, there is a case for rethinking this issue because it does limit the experiential aspect of learning. In other words, a sergeant trying to persuade his or her unit to do something under conditions of 'reality' [that is not in the training environment] could not necessarily rely upon the good wishes and willing support of followers who are very aware that they may be next and that the prevailing social norm is for non-critical acquiescence: Destructive Consent. The sergeant *might* have a very constructive relationship with his or her team but they might not. Hence, although the supportive environment encourages the 'leads' to experiment it does not provide experience of the process of leading under non-supportive environments. In effect, the success of the 'Community of Practice' undermines the practice of the community because it generates Destructive Consent but not necessarily Constructive Dissent. That is to say, followers may put up with and hence encourage poor leadership because all know that their turn will soon come and they will also rely upon the goodwill of others to survive the rigours of the test. What might be better would be an atmosphere of much greater trust (probably built around the removal of any assessment early on) when poor leadership is seen to fail and poor leaders are helped to understand why they fail and how they might succeed by those most affected by leadership failure – the followers.

Perhaps a good analogy for this problem exists in the martial arts. Most karate training, for example, occurs in the dojo under strict control where two fighters wear gloves and possibly gum shields and even head guards, where only certain attacks and blows are permitted and the injury inflicted minimal if any, where the coach or 'sensei' referees the bout indicating when the combatants are to begin and cease, where the typical bout will last perhaps for five to eight minutes and where the fights are virtually silent except for the 'Kiais' – the explosive shouts designed to coincide with a blow landing so that the muscle tension is directed as effectively as possible. Now compare this process to a street fight. There may be no warning, there are certainly no rules, no form or target of attack is prohibited, there may be several assailants, there will almost certainly be lots of intimidating swearing, it will probably last no more than a few minutes at most and probably just a few seconds but the end result will very likely be a serious injury to one or more people. This is not to say that karate training is irrelevant to self-defence; clearly it may make some difference and there are many karateka (practitioners of karate) whom it would be most unwise to attack in the street (all of my karate instructors would fit into this category!). But the level of skill necessary for karate to make a difference is both significant and takes immense time and practice. Moreover, competition karate is simply not the same as street violence and a black belt in the former does not guarantee immunity in the latter, especially if the attackers have the intent, skill and experience acquired through years of training in street fighting.[10] In effect, training should be as close as possible to the phenomenon that is being trained for; hence marathon running does not make a runner into a good 100-metre sprinter, nor a good swimmer, even if it does improve fitness.

In the context of training for leadership we can liken the practice of leading one's fellow sergeants in a mutually supportive Community of Practice to a karate lesson: of course it is useful to learn in the safety of the dojo under professional guidelines and knowing that the safety ropes are available if necessary but this is not the equivalent of practising self-defence against unknown and unrestrained attackers. Of course, this does not mean that the only way to practice for self-defence is to be randomly attacked in the street by a knife-wielding maniac – but it does mean that the closer the aspect of realism the more effective will be the learning. In karate this means altering the practice, for example: abandoning the etiquette of the dojo where swearing is forbidden; adorning the 'attacker' in protective clothing to allow the defender to strike back without compromising safety, and providing the attacker with a red marker pen as a 'knife' to understand just how hard it is to avoid being cut by a knife and so on.

In the military leadership case it might mean working with followers who are strangers, or whose rank is unknown or working with raw recruits or with 'followers' who are not supportive or compliant. Only under these conditions of enhanced reality can leaders go beyond the comfort of leading a mutual support group, 'us', to the discomfort of leading a group that resemble 'them', the others, the disrespectful, the disinterested, the sceptics and the cynics. The danger of not making training for the process of leadership more progressively realistic is either that it leaves the trainee over-confident and willing to take unnecessary risks or that the novelty of the situation completely undermines their confidence that the techniques provide any value: the karateka 'freezes' or the leader reverts to an authoritarian form of leadership because that seems the default category when confidence is lost and defensiveness kicks in. We should not be surprised, then, to find that officer cadets turn in martinets when suddenly faced with leading recruits and NCOs, having had virtually no contact with them prior to being 'let loose' in the field. Nor should we be surprised if sergeants are shocked to find that their new-found techniques are not quite so viable when their followers are not so much a Community of Practice but a practising community.

Notes

1 This was first published in the *Stonyhurst Magazine* (vol. 1, no. 9, p. 162) in March 1883. Thanks to Rob Watt at Dundee University for pointing this out to me.

2 http://news.bbc.co.uk/sportacademy/borntowin/default.stm In October 2003, 53% of the 2700 who voted on line thought that champions were 'born to win', 47% thought they were 'made to win'.

3 http://www.ukans.edu/history/index/europe/ancient_rome/E/Roman/Texts/Cassius_Dio/6*.html accessed 20 November 2003. The criteria for declaring a *Triumph* (there were about 100 between 220 and 70 BCE) were that a Roman general (1) had to possess *imperium* [power to command, authority, command, rule, control; the enforcement of this rule grew lax over time] (2) had to be the decisive victor (at least 5000 killed) over a foreign enemy [which is why Crassus had no joy from defeating Spartacus] (3) some say that the Roman troops had to hail the general as *imperator* [commander in chief, general, emperor] in the field (4) the general had to bring at least a token army back to Rome, and (5) the Senate had to vote to grant the general a *Triumph* (which entailed permitting him to keep his imperium inside the pomerium [religious boundary of the city of Rome] for a day). See also: http://classics.mit.edu/Plutarch/paulus.html

4 http://www.ewenger.com/ewthemes.html

5 Quoted on BBC Sport website on 21 November 2003, see: http://news.bbc.co.uk/sport1/hi/rugby_union/rugby_world_cup/team_pages/england/3279171.stm

6 http://www.football365.com/You_Say_We_say/David_Icke_Column/story_393.shtml

7 http://www.operations.mod.uk/fresco/

8 'But the backbone of the Army is the Non-commissioned Man!'from Rudyard Kipling's poem *The 'Eathen*.

9 When more time is available, students are taught to use SMRLAC PACE.

Situation	Planning Phase
Mission (Repeat it twice)	Ask for Any Questions
Resources (available for the task)	Check/Confirm Understanding
Limitations (The 'F' factors)	Execution of the Task

Ask for Questions
Check/Confirm of Groups understanding
As Geoff reminded me later: 'It is only when the leader is happy that everyone fully understands the SMRLAC (confirmed by Q & A) elements should he/she proceed to the **Planning Phase**. The reason is that if any of the *key elements above are missing*, such as a *LIMITATION*, then the chances are that the exercise will fail. The reason being, that the group *will not have all the facts* to start with when they begin to plan or think of a plan.' (Private communication, 8 January 2004).

10   Geoff Thompson's (1995) *Animal Day: Pressure Testing the Martial Arts* is a useful examination of this problem.

Leadership as position:
hydras and elephants

Andrea: 'Unhappy the land that has no heroes! ...
Galileo: 'No. Unhappy the land where heroes are needed'.
(Brecht, 1980: 98)

Introduction

This final chapter looks at leadership as position by concentrating on two cases that extend our perceptions of space from vertical to horizontal. In other words, although leadership is commonly associated with a position of vertical authority over subordinates, it is also the case that leadership occurs through horizontal positioning such that leaders may have little formal authority over followers but nevertheless secure their allegiance. In some cases the leadership occurs through virtue of the leaders being 'in front' of their followers, such as in the case of fashion leaders or military 'scouts', but more often what we see are examples where the leadership is rooted more within a heterarchy than a hierarchy and it is this particular organizational form – Distributed Leadership – that serves the basis for what follows. In the first instance we consider the leadership of the American civil rights movement in the 1960s, so often subsumed under the apparent hierarchy led by Martin Luther King, but in effect led by a whole host of leaders at all levels of the civil rights movement in a heterarchical network of movements, institutions and supporters. The second case takes the same organizational model but analyses al-Qaida as a case study, thereby reminding us that organizational forms do not embody essential forms of politics or ethics.

Leadership theory: from hierarchy to heterarchy

Traditionally, leadership has been closely associated with some form of hierarchy. The original meaning of 'hierarchy' was Holy Sovereignty: '*arkhos*' means 'sovereignty or ruler' and '*hierós*' means 'holy or divine' in the original Greek. Thus '*hierarkhíā*' was a steward, '*hierárkhēs*' a stewardess, of sacred rites. The implication is not just that leadership was associated with hierarchy but also with the 'sacred' – a point clearly evident in both Carlyle's and Durkheim's reconstruction of leadership. However, for our purposes the main issue is that all significant organizations over time seem to have been hierarchical to some degree; either through religious, military, political or social requirements some mechanism for command, coordination and control has persisted. For example, the Great Pyramid of Khufu, built around 4500 years ago was built with a seven-level hierarchy that had indentured labour (there were few if any slaves involved) at the bottom, below crafts'men' (level 2), then scribes (level 3), then priests, engineers and doctors (level 4), then high priests and nobles (level 5), then the Grand Vizier (level 6) and finally the Pharaoh (level 7).

Since that time few large-scale organizations have existed without a hierarchy and there are examples where the concentration of power in one individual is such that the removal of that individual undermines the entire hierarchy. For instance, in 1242 when Ogadai Khan, the son of Genghis, died in Mongolia the entire Mongolian army returned from its encampment outside the gates of Vienna to select the next Khan. 761 years later the US-led coalition forces attempted to 'behead' the Iraqi regime under Saddam Hussein on exactly the same premise on 7 April 2003, just prior to the formal invasion: in theory a hierarchy with such a reliance upon one leader can be overthrown simply by removing that leader.[1] In the event the attempt failed on both counts: Saddam was not killed and neither his removal from power nor his capture has prevented continuing attacks upon coalition forces, the Red Cross or the United Nations. Writing in May 2004, when the death toll of coalition troops killed after the official 'end of hostilities' now stands higher than those killed during the war itself, we may be entitled to consider whether regimes and indeed organizations can be 'beheaded' in quite this way.

The shift away from assumptions about individuals 'leading' organizations towards some form of collective alternative have increased since the end of the twentieth century, though just as the notion of individual leaders and hierarchies have long histories, so too do the alternatives. The idea that leadership should be 'distributed', that is spread throughout an organization rather than restricted to the individual at the top of a formal hierarchy, perhaps goes back beyond the beginning of formal large-scale organizations – such as the one that built the pyramids. For example, many hunter-gatherer societies (the forerunner of settled agricultural societies and large-scale organizations), such as the Hadza of Tanzania operate without a single formal leader, and leadership tasks are distributed so that any individual can 'lead' a hunt or suggest a move to new territory and so on (Millett, 2003; Woodburn, 1970).

In the nineteenth century many anarchists ('Anarchy' means without government, from '*arkhos*' meaning 'sovereignty or ruler' and '*an*' meaning 'without') wrestled with, rather than resolved, the problems of centralized authority located within one individual long after the progenitors of the Hadza first developed it. At a practical level the Xmas Truce of 1914 between the British and German troops on the Western Front was the result of distributed leadership – multiple individuals and groups deciding, literally, to give peace a chance (Weintraub, 2002). At a theoretical level Kropotkin (1842–1921) (2002) was convinced that a well-informed group would be wiser than any single leader, and stressed that 'the collective spirit of the masses' would have to be called into action, if society was to be rebuilt. That rebuilding would also generate smaller, self-sufficient, communities that would, in themselves, undermine the need for centralized leadership and especially heroic individuals.

This subordination of the individual to the mass, rather than of the followers to the leader, was also reflected in Bakunin's (1814–76) (1970) work:

> The greatest intelligence would not be equal to a comprehension of the whole ... Therefore there is no fixed and constant authority, but a continual exchange ... In general, we ask nothing better than to see men endowed with great knowledge, great experience, great minds, and, above all, great hearts, exercise over us a natural and legitimate influence, freely accepted, and never imposed in the name of any official authority whatsoever ... In a word, we reject all legislation, all authority, and all privileged, licensed, official, and legal influence, even though arising from universal suffrage ... This is the sense in which we are really Anarchists.[2]

In fact Bakunin (1871) was not against *all* authority because he was keen to insist that authority freely accepted was legitimate but even that did not imply that any one individual could be taken as legitimately in control.

> There is no universal man, no man capable of grasping in all that wealth of detail, without which the application of science to life is impossible, all the sciences, all the branches of social life. And if such universality could ever be realised in a single man, and if he wished to take advantage thereof to impose his authority upon us, it would be necessary to drive this man out of society, because his authority would inevitably reduce all the others to slavery and imbecility. I do not think that society ought to maltreat men of genius as it has done hitherto: but neither do I think it should indulge them too far, still less accord them any privileges or exclusive rights whatsoever; and that for three reasons: first, because it would often mistake a charlatan for a man of genius; second, because, through such a system of privileges, it might transform into a charlatan even a real man of genius, demoralise him, and degrade him; and, finally, because it would establish a master over itself.[3]

Some of these ideas surfaced within the Syndicalist and Guild Socialist movements during and just after the First World War in Europe but their success, such as it was, was very brief and generally died with the interwar economic collapse (Grint, 1986). However, the ideas of resisting centralized leadership persisted. Paulo Freire (1921–97), for example, adopted a similar philosophical denial of the leader's claim to domination, and though his approach was routed more through educational philosophies than anarchist communes he was nevertheless always concerned with the practical consequences of claims to superordination (Freire, 1997). This issue was also at the heart of A.S. Neill's 'Summerhill' – an English school developed to provide an educational framework where the students could choose whether to attend lessons or not and where all children had a vote in the weekly democratic meeting to decide certain aspects of the school's governance (not hiring, firing or teachers' salaries), though the head teacher retained many formal leadership responsibilities (Neill, 1995; OFSTED, 1999).

That reduction or denial of the role of individual leaders is also present in the words of Daniel Cohn-Bendit, ironically labelled by journalists as the 'leader' of the 1968 Paris 'revolution': 'Let them write their rubbish. These people will never be able to understand that the student movement doesn't need any chiefs. I am neither a leader nor a professional revolutionary. I am simply a mouthpiece, a megaphone' (quoted in Ward, 1973).

Since those heady days many people, and not just anarchists, have continued to struggle with the leadership dilemma, indeed leadership paradox: leadership undermines progressive social organization but without leadership, it seems, there is no social organization. Within business there have been many attempts to empower the workforce by decentralizing production and authority to small teams, from McGregor's theory X and Y in the 1960s through to the semi-autonomous work-groups of the Socio-Technical Systems approaches in British coal mines and Scandinavian car production, and on to the Worker-Director experiments in the 1970s in Britain and the current concern for enhancing worker participation through various boards, European Works Councils and other representative channels.[4] Even formidably successful capitalists have engaged with the problem – as Ricardo Semler's (1994) 'no-one-in-charge' experiments at SEMCO in Brazil demonstrate, enormous energy can be realized when bosses 'let the followers lead' (2003: 175–206). Perhaps, however, this theoretical quandary is captured best by Fyke and Sayegh:

> Let's ignore that Big Pink Elephant in the Room. The question of leadership in anarchist circles brings up a host of contradictions, which anarchists too often avoid by denying that leadership exists. This is complete hogwash. As *Love and Rage*[5] points out: 'Anarchism tends to assume a theoretical posture of total hostility towards leadership. But every anarchist group or project that lasts any length of time has clearly identifiable, if informal, leadership.'

Beyond the pragmatic adoption of decentralized organizations there is much philosophical hostility grounded in the assumption that leadership is essentially deleterious, injurious to the public health and something that must be avoided. But the denial of leadership paradoxically generates the political vacuum within which Machiavellianism proliferates. This is the equivalent problem to that generated by Soviet attempts to bring about the 'End of Politics' (Polan, 1984). The result was not just the elimination of all institutions that can be used to channel and facilitate the legitimate articulation of disagreement; the logical consequence was that all resistance was, by definition, illegitimate and counter-revolutionary – hence resistors were either mentally insane and needed hospitalizing or counter-revolutionaries and needed executing.

Yet there have always been individuals, like Ella Baker, for example, who attempted to construct an alternative approach to leadership that went beyond its negative associations. Baker worked with the US civil rights movement, especially the Student Non-violent Co-ordinating Committee to shift the movement away from individual leaders, or 'leader-centred groups', towards 'group-centred leadership' (Ransby, 2003). We shall return to Baker later. This approach embodies notions of heterarchy ('other' or 'different' sovereignty) rather than anarchy where leadership is necessary but necessarily distributed. Equally radical, Frantz Fanon (1963: 136) implored those attempting to change the world to go beyond individual and unorganized resistance:

> The success of the struggle presupposes clear objectives, a definite methodology and above all the need for the mass of the people to realize that their unorganized efforts can only be a temporary dynamic. You can hold out for three days – maybe even for three months – on the strength of the ad-mixture of sheer resentment contained in the mass of the people; but you'll … never overthrow the terrible enemy machine, and you won't change human beings if you forget to raise the consciousness of the rank-and-file. Neither stubborn courage nor fine slogans are enough.

The recognition that leadership is, at best, a necessary evil, has prompted some to argue that the issue is not so much 'leadership', but what kind of 'leadership' and in particular, what process of leadership might be viable and whether a resolution exists in those aspects of leadership relevant to the development of Distributed Leadership in which leadership resides 'not solely in the individual at the top, but in every person at entry level who in one way or another, acts as a leader' (Goleman, 2002: 14).

Raelin (2003) attempts to contrast the distributed or leaderful organization with the traditional organization by suggesting that in leaderful organizations leadership is concurrent and collective rather than serial and individual – lots of people are engaged in it rather than just those in formal positions; that leadership is collaborative rather than controlling; and that leadership is compassionate rather than dispassionate; and that this generates a community rather than simply an organization. Harris (2003) characterizes this as collective leadership – expertise that is developed by working collaboratively and where the 'leader' is decentred.

> This is not to suggest that no one is ultimately responsible for the overall performance of the organization or to render those in formal leadership roles redundant. Instead, the job of those in formal leadership positions is primarily to hold the pieces of the organization together in a productive relationship. Their central task is to create a common culture of expectations around the use of individual skills and abilities. In short, distributive leadership equates with maximizing the human capacity within the organization.

Precisely how leadership can be 'distributed' seems to depend upon the specific situation to some degree (Bennett et al., 2003). For example, Harris and Chapman (2002) suggest that in some (English) schools the head teachers used delegation and the rotation of leadership responsibilities with some success as part of a deliberate policy of distribution. They remain clear, though, that Distributed Leadership cannot be reduced to '*delegated headship*', where unwanted tasks are handed down to others. In effect, the approach is 'less concerned with individual capabilities, skills and talents and more preoccupied with creating collective responsibility for leadership action and activity. The focus is less upon the characteristics of "the leader" and more upon creating shared contexts for learning and developing leadership capacity.' Indeed, it would seem that Distributed Leadership is something that cannot be imposed from above but must be grown from below (Wasley, 1991).

Although Distributed Leadership takes many forms it is instructive to note what Weber might have called an 'ideal case'. This is not 'ideal' in a normative sense of 'perfection' or even 'typicality' but in the sense that some aspect or degree of these two core features would be expected in any empirical example:

- *Collective responsibility*: Organizations are replete with leaders; they are leaderful, full of 'ordinary' people carrying out modest leadership tasks, not dependent on the heroic individuals doing daring deeds beloved of Carlyle. Where Carlyle sought heroes to push the wheel of history along, distributed leadership requires large numbers of 'ordinary people' – 'hewers of wood and drawers of water' (*Joshua*, 9.21) to make the wheel move. This is not to demean 'ordinary' people but to recognize that there are no 'ordinary' people; there are instead lots of individuals who have unique skills to add to the collective movement of the wheel of history in the building of a social community, not the development of a private empire.
- *Collective flexibility*: Traditional organizations maintain unyielding hierarchies of power, resources and rewards. Such structures, however, impose limits on the flexibility of the incumbents of office. Distributed Leadership implies a shift towards heterarchy – a flexible structure that retains the necessary degree of coherence and coordination but does not require the roles or incumbents to operate within strictly defined limits. Normally organizational leaders have roles that are fixed in space and time – they lead a specific organization or department for a particular period of time, measured in months or years. But Distributed Leadership implies that many people undertake leadership roles that need not have these boundaries. In other words, distributed leaders take up their roles and responsibilities as and where necessary: when the task requiring their leadership is completed they revert to a non-leader position.

These core ideas may seem attractive to people inhibited by idiosyncratic individual leaders or suffocated by stultifying bureaucracies but Distributed Leadership is an alternative method of leadership not a utopian alternative to it. And therein lies an array of paradoxes:

- Traditional individual leadership brings with it not just the potential for corruption but also a mechanism for effective decision-making. Thus simply wishing away 'leadership' – the big pink elephant – may merely result in grossly inefficient and ineffective organizations and the potential for 'decisive leaders' (authoritarians) to step in and offer a 'solution' to the apparent indecision.

- Distributed Leadership offers an alternative to this problem but it also generates the means by which liberal democratic societies can be destabilized by small and unrepresentative groups or even individuals. For example, part of the success of al-Qaida relates to the difficulty of democratic states penetrating and dealing with terrorist groups that have little in the way of a formal hierarchy.

The apparent consequences of Distributed Leadership, according to Gronn (2003: 27–50) depend on what kind of Distributed Leadership occurs. Concertive Action is the result of a number of individuals choosing to divide leadership responsibilities between them. Alternatively, Numerical Action is simply the sum of all involved – another description of participative management. For Gronn, the results of Concertive Action are threefold: first, leadership synergy, in which the whole of Distributed Leadership is greater than the sum of its parts; second, the boundaries of leadership become more porous encouraging many more members of the community to participate in leading their organizations; third, it encourages a reconsideration of what counts as expertise within organizations and expands the degree of knowledge available to the community. In sum, leadership becomes not a property of the formal individual leader but an emergent property of the group, network or community.

We can summarize the position so far by suggesting that although social and political activists have remained sceptical of leadership for many years it has remained an enduring element of practical change in contrast to utopian theory. This, in itself may go some way to explaining why, for example, Green political parties have managed to make only marginal inroads into conventional politics and may prove an ideological paradox that remains insurmountable (Christensen and Grint, 2004). However, developments in the reconstruction of leadership theory – towards Distributed Leadership – that shift the definition away from individual office holders to the social processes of organizations, imply that the problem lies not in leadership itself but in the kind and process of leadership that is being considered.

However, we should also note that Distributed Leadership is both a method and a philosophy. The latter implies for its supporters that Distributed Leadership is necessarily preferable to traditional leadership because it embodies decentralization, social responsibility and collective learning; it encourages subordinates to learn to lead and facilitates the growth of social capital. All of these appear either progressive or liberal or generally beneficent. But, it is a method and a process as well as a philosophy, and that means that it is also possible to consider it under other philosophies. In particular, the distribution of responsibility and leadership are also means by which profoundly undemocratic and illiberal organizations can distribute risk and confound those seeking their elimination. In the first section below we consider how Distributed Leadership contributed to the achievement of civil rights in the US but we go on to consider the way Distributed Leadership structures have also facilitated the rise and persistence of that hydra-like terrorist group – al-Qaida. For surely there lies the paradox of Distributed Leadership – it provides some with a blue-print for making us face the terror of the pink elephant, for *inhibiting* authoritarian leaders, but it also provides terrorists with a blue-print for *cohabiting* with what seems to be leaderless authoritarianism.

From leader to leadership: the struggle for civil rights in the US

The American Civil Rights Act of 1964 barred the unequal application of voter registration requirements (though it did not abolish literacy tests); it outlawed 'discrimination in hotels, motels, restaurants, theatres, and all other public accommodations engaged in interstate commerce' (though it excluded 'private' clubs); it 'encouraged' the desegregation of public schools (but it did not authorize bussing as a means to overcome segregation based on residence); it authorized but did not require withdrawal of federal funds from programmes which practised discrimination; and it outlawed discrimination in employment in any business exceeding 25.[6] Its broad background is well known (see Grint, 2000) and is well covered in great detail elsewhere (see: Martin-Riches, 1997; Verney, 2000). Here I am concerned not to redescribe events but to analyse the contesting accounts of leadership in the movement.

In the most popular version, the leading role is taken up by Martin Luther King whose charismatic leadership transformed a cancer that had besmirched the US ever since the victorious North ended its occupation of the rebellious confederacy. After all, there are not that many people in the world who have a national holiday named after them (3rd Monday in January). After his ordination in 1948 King became Assistant Pastor of Ebenezer Baptist Church Atlanta and then Pastor of Dexter Avenue Baptist Church, Montgomery, Alabama from September 1954 to November 1959. 'Here' according to the Seattle Times, 'he made his first mark on the civil-rights movement, by mobilizing the black community during a 382-day boycott of the city's bus lines.'[7] He left to organize, and become president of, the Southern Christian Leadership Conference which he held until his assassination in 1968. Through his public leadership (he was arrested 30 times), his speeches and his vision King went on to secure the civil rights that had been denied Black Americans. He was *Times* magazine 'Man of the Year' in 1963 and won the Nobel Peace Prize in 1964. He then shifted his attention towards the economic conditions of the poor in the north, starting in Chicago, where he launched programmes to provide housing. But the move from civil rights to economic demands dissipated some of his support as King moved politically left and began to mobilize support against the war in Vietnam. At that point, while on a visit to support the strikers at a Memphis sanitation plant he was assassinated. Without King, it seems, there either would have been no Civil Rights Act in 1964 or it would have been achieved much later, it may have proved less effective, and perhaps it would only have occurred after significantly more violence.

In fact, although King himself never claimed to have single-handedly secured civil rights for Black Americans it is worth pursuing two related avenues of leadership here. First, to what extent was the achievement collective effort – a reward for leadership not for any particular leader, and second, to what extent did that achievement herald the formation of the distributive model of leadership discussed above?

On the first count we might take the apparent trigger of the Montgomery bus boycott as a valuable case. On the one hand the bus boycott that King 'led' was initiated by the individual act of Rosa Parks who refused to give up her seat to a white man on a bus in Montgomery on 1 December 1955. Rosa Parks, then (rather than Martin Luther King), was the person 'who changed history' according to Albin (1996). As the Academy of Achievement insists:

> Most historians date the beginning of the modern civil rights movement in the United States to December 1, 1955. That was the day when an unknown seamstress in Montgomery, Alabama refused to give up her bus seat to a white passenger. This brave woman, Rosa Parks, was arrested and fined for violating a city ordinance, but her lonely act of defiance began a movement that ended legal segregation in America, and made her an inspiration to freedom-loving people everywhere.[8]

Parks was arrested and charged and that sparked a 381-day bus boycott in Montgomery and, eventually, the Supreme Court's ruling in November 1956 that segregation on transportation was unconstitutional. But Parks was no 'ordinary' woman whose unwitting protest spurred a spontaneous movement of protest. On the contrary, she was secretary of the local chapter of the NAACP (National Association for the Advancement of Colored People) and later Adviser to the NAACP Youth Council, and that organization had long prepared for such an event. Indeed, it was not even the first time that a Black American woman had been arrested for refusing to give up her seat – but the previous case involved Claudette Colvin, a pregnant 15-year-old, nine months before Parks, and the local leadership of the NAACP had not thought her case strong enough to mobilize community support. Nor was it the first bus boycott for one had occurred in Baton Rouge in 1953 (Grint, 2000: 386).[9] Indeed, Ella Baker spent much of her life resisting segregation laws. For example, in December 1942 she was verbally abused after she and another black woman refused to get up and let white passengers take their seats as was required by the law. Six months later she was refused service in the dining car of a train despite being in the 'black section' because four white sailors had sat in the black section – although there was plenty of space in the white section. Eventually Baker persuaded the sailors to move to their own side and she was served. (Baker wasn't the first known train 'resister': Ida B Wells had been removed from the 'woman's carriage' on a train in 1884 in Tennessee) (Ransby, 2003: 127–30). However after Rosa Parks' arrest, Lula Farmer, the wife of James Farmer the founder of CORE (Congress of Racial Equality) immediately told him that 'this was precisely the spark that you've been working and hoping for, for years.' Within 24 hours the local activists had distributed 40,000 leaflets protesting about the arrest and within four days the boycott was almost 100 per cent effective. That kind of local organization implies two things: first Parks' arrest may have been the trigger for the action but it could not have developed without widespread local leadership; second, it developed before King was elected leader of the Montgomery Improvement Association which aimed to expand the boycott and make the most political capital from it.

However, if many historians do date the beginning of the civil rights movement to the acts of leadership that began with Rosa Parks' individual resistance, Klarmann (2004) insists that the real kick start was actually Thurgood Marshall's (1908–93) advocacy to the Supreme Court that succeeded in outlawing segregation in public schools in the 1955 case, *Brown vs the Board of Education*. That case did not stir the black population into activism but rather needled the conservative whites into fighting a rearguard action that set the scene for the civil rights battles of the 1960s. Marshall, who went on to become the first black Supreme Court Justice, had been legal director of the NAACP. Now the point here is not how we might evaluate the relative contributions of Marshall, Parks and Baker, to say nothing of King, but to note how it doesn't make sense to even attempt this. If we did we might end up with some complex regression equation that informs us that Parks generated 23.7 per cent of the momentum, Marshall was responsible for 24.1 per cent, King provided 43.6 per cent and the rest is unclear. This does not make sense because all the actors are dependent upon each other – without any of them the historical record would very probably have been different but we cannot provide counter-factual data to allow us to measure their individual or collective leadership contributions.

Nevertheless, what we can conclude is that the civil rights movement was always bigger than any individual leader and would have been impossible without a leadership that was deeply rooted in the local networks of supporters. Thus Ella Baker was herself far more interested in and active within, the grassroots campaigns than what Martin Luther King was saying to the national media on TV or radio. As Ransby suggests (2003: 189–92), Baker regarded King as a member of Atlanta's black male elite whose 'silver tongue' and charismatic performances acted to enervate rather than energize the population of activists because they could never reproduce his style or success. However, she also insisted that her concern was never personal: she disliked the heroic leadership *style* that he seemed to embody more than anything about his character as such. Moreover, Baker felt that having a charismatic leader worked against all that was required to secure long-term civil rights – the local population had to take responsibility for their own lives and not rely upon some heroic figure from afar to solve their problems for them. In short, while Baker sought to encourage a heterarchy of local leaders to galvanize the local population she feared that King's effect as formal leader was to embed the perception of inadequacy in ordinary people and as a consequence to reproduce the very leadership hierarchies that perpetuated racism and many other forms of gross inequality.

For Baker the political was personal and the transformation of self and the local community was the prerequisite of permanent and radical change – not the consequence of a charismatic hero. If change did not come from below it would not come at all because leadership had to be local and it could only be achieved by serving an apprenticeship at the grass roots level: leadership was, then, only authentic if it was distributed. To think otherwise was, for Baker, to fall into the trap that some black leaders were already sliding into: the trap of bourgeois respectability that blunted their appetite for radical change. That philosophy of Distributed Leadership manifested itself most clearly between 1961 and 1964 in the strategy and tactics of the SNCC (Student Non-violent Coordinating Committee) which involved sending young activists out to the countryside and to small towns in the South to facilitate the self-leadership of local campaigns to demand desegregation or voter rights projects. So while King might sweep into town to hold a press conference and then disappear again, Baker, in Howard Zinn's words,

> Moved silently through the protest movements in the South, doing the things the famous men did not have time to do. Now, hour after hour, she sat there as people lined up before her, patiently taking down names, addresses, occupations, immediate money needs. (Quoted in Ransby, 2003: 283)

Ella Baker saw herself, as Ransby puts it, as 'the outsider within' – never an authentic member of the inner circle but close enough to prevent that inner circle from taking itself to be the master rather than the servant of the followers they purported to lead. Such leaders conflated leadership with centralization and though she was axiomatically against that conflation she did recognize that leadership, albeit of a distributed variety, was critical to advancing social justice. In the next section we consider examples of leaders and movements that are either critical of centralized leadership or personify a distributed approach to organizational authority – but whose slant on this is anything but related to the advance of social justice that Baker would have recognized.

From left to right: from elephant to hydra

The *conflation* of leadership with centralized authoritarianism – as opposed to its contingent *co-existence* – has befuddled attempts to understand leadership. Indeed, the conflation is most clearly and ironically visible in the adoption of 'Leaderless Resistance' – a term coined by Col. Ulius Louis Amoss in 1962. It was then used by the white supremacist Louis Beam,[10] and adopted by American militia groups opposed to the federal government (or indeed any kind of government) whose actions are often linked to individuals like Timothy McVeigh, executed in 2001 after being convicted of carrying out the Oklahoma bombing. In these cases the absence of an authoritarian and centralized leadership provides a structure that the authorities find difficult to penetrate because of the lack of central coordination. In the British petrol crisis of

September 2000, for example, a small number of self-appointed militants, intent on disrupting the transportation of petrol to force down the tax on petrol, virtually held the country to ransom for several days. And while the government struggled to respond, their main problem was that the protesters appeared to have no recognizable leadership that could at best negotiate a settlement or at worst provide a recognizable target to impose some form of legal constraint (Burke *et al.*, 2000; Doherty *et al.*, 2003).[11] In short, Distributed Leadership had not just transcended the pink elephant problem of the political left, but also reconstructed it into a regenerative hydra of the extreme or populist right.

The hydra in Greek mythology represented the most difficult of creatures to overcome: not just a creature with multiple heads, and therefore no apparent single leader, no one to hold responsible or to focus upon, but also a creature whose structure appeared to make it immortal because each severed head grew two more. This problem was eventually transcended when Hercules changed his strategy both for dealing with the mortal heads and for despatching the immortal head.

A similar problem now faces those targeted by terrorists that resemble just such a creature. Since 9/11 much blood and many resources have been expended in trying to find, understand and eliminate the perpetrators. Much has also been written on the development of the network both as a form of organization and as a metaphor for future global business: the traditional organizational hierarchy is dead; long live the non-hierarchical network! My purpose here is not to debate the dubious nature of the latter or the premature burial of the former, but instead to consider how the historical myth of the hydra might provide us with a metaphor to facilitate leadership analysis. In particular, I am concerned with the strengths and weaknesses of what has come to be regarded as a contemporary hydra and an archetypal network organization: the al-Qaida group.[12]

This section takes the myth of the hydra as a starting point from which to explore the issues and traces the double strategy that Hercules is forced to adopt in his original fight with the beast. While Hercules is able to decapitate the multiple heads, these heads are not critical to the health of the creature and their regenerative powers force him to cauterize the stumps to prevent their regrowth. However, the central – and immortal – head requires a different strategy because severing and cauterizing it is not enough to prevent regrowth; instead it has to be properly buried. But first let us explore what kind of things the hydra represents.

The five hydras

The 'Hydra' has (at least) five embodiments: star formation, myth, metaphor, polyp, and organizational design. First, the largest (and for my purposes the least significant) version of the hydra is the extremely long star formation in a very distant constellation, primarily in the southern hemisphere.[13] Second, it is a mythical monster: a multi-headed regenerative creature that formed the second of Hercules' 'labours'. Third, it is a biological creature, a polyp: a freshwater hydroid with tentacles around its mouth and the beloved aquatic animal of biology students that can regenerate the parts of its body that have been cut off. Fourth, the hydra has been adopted as a metaphor for the underworld, the mob, or the devil incarnate. Lastly, the hydra represents the design blueprint for a new form of organization – a network of loosely aligned groups with little formal structure or central leadership. With the exception of the star formation, all the other embodiments have some resonance with the analysis of the al-Qaida Group that follows below: it is steeped in myth, it is a monster, it is regenerative and it represents a novel form of distributed or network organization.

The mythical hydra

In Greek mythology, Hercules was the son of Zeus and the mortal woman Alcmene. Zeus's immortal wife, Hera, tried to kill her husband's earthly offspring by putting two snakes into Hercules' crib – but he strangled one with each hand. Not to be outdone, she appointed Eurystheus not Hercules as King of Mycenae and then drove Hercules mad, inciting him to kill his own children. To atone for the crime Eurystheus promptly ordered Hercules to perform a series of twelve 'impossible' labours, the second of which was killing the Lernaean Hydra. If he completed the labours successfully Hercules would atone for his guilt and achieve immortality.

The Hydra was a multi-headed water serpent born from a union between Echidne and Typhon. While Echidne, related to the mermaids, was half-woman and half-serpent, Typhon was a terrible giant. The Hydra inhabited a cave, or alternatively the roots of a giant plane tree, in Lake Lerna in Argolis, near the city of Argos. Lerna's waters were bottomless and provided access to the underworld for all who could get past the gatekeeper, the Hydra, whose elder brother was Kerberos, a three-or sometimes five-headed creature. The precise number of heads on the Hydra is also debated: most versions suggest nine, some five, and some increase the number to several hundred.[14] Whatever the number, one of the heads was immortal and the Hydra spent most of its time destroying the livestock and crops of the surrounding farmers, often killing people simply by breathing on them, so poisonous was its breath, as indeed was its blood.

Guided by Athene, Iolaus, the son of Iphicles (the twin brother of Hercules), drove Hercules to the creature's lair in a chariot. There the Hydra was forced out of its cave by flaming arrows. But Hercules soon found that cutting off any of its existing heads simply compounded his problems because each stump grew two more heads. In effect, the more he attacked the creature the stronger it became. Eventually, Hercules called upon his nephew to help and Iolaus started a fire (having cut down an entire forest) and duly cauterized each of the Hydra's headless stumps as they fell to Hercules's sword. However, the last head was immortal so when Hercules cut it off he buried it under a large rock on the road between Lerna and Elaius (Kerényi, 1974: 143–5).[15]

The biological hydra

The regenerative heads of the mythical hydra were precisely where the biological hydra derived its name and it has been known for some considerable time that certain species have the ability to regrow parts of their bodies. Indeed, flatworms seem to have perfected the art to the point where a theoretical immortality appears to exist.[16] But, it is not coincidental that the metaphorical hydras of anarchy only entered the language in the eighteenth century, for the polyp (a hollow cylindrical body with a ring of tentacles around the mouth that occurs in freshwater ponds and lakes) was only discovered by the Dutch inventor of the microscope, Anton von Leeuwenhoek, in 1702. In 1740, Abraham Trembley, a Swiss naturalist, discovered the green species but he was uncertain whether it was a plant because it was green, or an animal because it moved. Although the regenerative powers of lizards (tails) and crayfish (claws) were also well known at this time Trembley thought that only a plant could regenerate more than half its body, but cutting a polyp in half horizontally led the old head to grow a new bottom and the old bottom to grow a new head. Indeed, whichever way he cut it the polyp regrew itself until one polyp had seven heads. In 1758, Linneaus named the polyp a hydra.

Hydras live in most streams, lakes and ponds, they are from 3 to 50 millimetres in length, and they use their four to eight tentacles to feed on crustaceans, insect larvae, worms and similar small animals.[17] There is more to Hercules' strategy than just brute force: according to Shimizu's experiments (2001) the regeneration of a Hydra's head after decapitation depends upon the state of the injured tissue: in effect, the greater the injury the less chance of regeneration – Hercules was right: chopping the head off is insufficient but cauterizing the stump (inflicting greater tissue damage) may well prevent regeneration. It may have worked for Hercules, and it may work in the laboratory, but does this help us understand, or deal with, either the historical or contemporary political threats to the establishment, the state or society of apparently leaderless groups?

The metaphorical hydra

Labelling leaderless groups that threaten the establishment as hydras in hardly new, indeed, the juxtaposition of Hercules and the Hydra has provided a richly woven mythical tapestry for many writers, monarchs and militants. Hercules was frequently represented as the hero in whose image laboured the builders of the Old and New Worlds. The British king, George I (1660–1727), George III's (1738–1820) brother, and King William III (1765–1837), all modelled themselves on Hercules. While in America, in 1776, John Adams called for 'The Judgement of Hercules' to be the seal of the future United States of America. Francis Bacon even suggested that Hercules was the inspiration of modern science and capitalism.

In contrast, the many-headed Hydra was deemed to embody the opposite: the collective Lord of Misrule. As J. J. Mauricius, the ex-governor of Suriname lamented on his return to Holland in 1751 – having failed to destroy a group of rebellious runaway slaves encamped in the swamp:

> Even if an army of ten thousand men were gathered, with
> The courage and strategy of Caesar and Eugene,
> They'd find their work cut out for them, destroying a Hydra's growth
> Which even Alcides [Hercules] would try to avoid
> (Quoted in Linebaugh and Rediker, 2000: 2–4)

Similarly, Andrew Ure contended that he (and for that matter every other manufacturer of the early nineteenth century) was the contemporary Hercules – not just in constructing machines with powers that matched Hercules, but also in using such inventions to tame or 'strangle', the 'Hydra of misrule', that is the contagion of rebellious workers.

Quite how the Herculean authorities were going to cope with the Hydra of misrule was manifest in the draconian laws passed at the turn of the nineteenth century: the 1799 and 1800 (British) Combination Acts outlawed trade unions, and mass executions followed the Luddite rebellions around this period (Grint, 1998; Grint and Woolgar, 1997), though these were nothing compared to those killed in the French Revolutionary 'Terror' slightly earlier. In short, the labelling of rebels and insurgents as 'The Hydra' has been with us for some considerable time. But, one might argue, isn't one person's hydra just another person's Hercules?

The definitional quagmire that surrounds 'terrorist', also known as 'freedom-fighter', 'separatist', 'rebel', 'guerrilla' and, increasingly with regard to media descriptions of armed supporters of al-Qaida – 'fighter', was raised by Sir Jeremy Greenstock, Chair of the UN Security Council's Committee on Terrorism on 28 October 2001. He suggested that terrorism should include: 'The indiscriminate use of violence, particularly against civilians, to further a political aim.' In fact, the original use seems to have been recorded by the Académie Français in 1789, as 'a system or rule of terror' – an interesting definition since it includes the use of terror by a state against its own citizens. Indeed, for much of the post-1945 era the UN has failed to agree on a definition of terrorism precisely because such a definition may implicate some member states, and because some definitions imply a justification of terror. Since 1963 twelve international conventions on terrorism have been drawn up against specific acts of terrorism: hijacking and hostage-taking and so on but no definition has ever been agreed (Roberts, 2002: 18–19), though resolution 1373 (2001) on terrorism was adopted by the Security Council at its 4385th meeting, on 28 September 2001.[18] The nearest thing to a consensus on the definition of terrorism talks of '… criminal acts intended or calculated to provoke a state of terror in the general public, a group of persons or particular persons for political purposes … [these are] in any circumstances unjustifiable whatever the considerations of a political, philosophical, ideological, racial, ethnic, religious or other nature that may be used to justify them' (quoted in Roberts, 2002: 19). Honderich (2002: 95–105), however, is unhappy with such an indiscriminate account of what can be a discriminate act. For example, he suggests that 'political violence' should be differentiated from 'terrorism' because the former can be directed at political leaders rather than at entire populations. Thus an assassination of Hitler would be both an example of 'political violence' and justifiable, while the attack on the twin towers was both 'terrorism' and unjustifiable.

Fisk (2001) insists that linguistic gyrations around the word 'terrorism' are common and contemptible on the part of all involved in such conflicts. In other words, the problem is not using the word 'terrorist' to say what we mean, but that competing groups try to delineate their 'legitimate' acts in contrast to the 'terrorism' imposed by the other side. In most cases both sides seem to be involved in acts of terrorism. For example,

> … when Israeli soldiers were captured by Lebanese guerrillas they were reported to have been 'kidnapped', as if the Israeli presence in Lebanon was in some way legitimate. Suspected resistance men in southern Lebanon, however, were 'captured' by Israeli troops. … By the mid-1980s, the AP [Associated Press] used 'terrorists' about Arabs but rarely about the IRA in Northern Ireland, where the agreed word was 'guerrillas', presumably because AP serves a number of news outlets in the United States with a large Irish-American audience. The BBC, which increasingly referred to Arab 'terrorists', *always* referred to the IRA as 'terrorists' but scarcely ever called ANC bombers in South Africa 'terrorists'. … *Tass* and *Pravda*, of course, referred to Afghan rebels as 'terrorists'. … In September 1985 a British newspaper reported that a [Soviet] airliner carrying civilian passengers [over Afghanistan] had been 'downed by rebels'. 'Terrorists' are those who use violence against the side that is using the word. The only terrorists whom Israel acknowledges are those opposed to Israel. The only terrorists the United States acknowledges are those who oppose the United States or their allies. The only terrorists Palestinians acknowledge – for they too use the word – are those opposed to the Palestinians. (Fisk, 438–41)[19]

Under any of these definitions the September 11 attacks were acts of terrorism, acts of violence perpetrated against non-combatants for political and religious ends. But clearly the members of al-Qaida do not regard themselves as terrorists, so irrespective of the lexicon of terror, can organizations that are conventionally structured and led defeat unconventionally structured and leaderless organizations that have some degree of popular support?

The organizational hydra: hierarchies, heterarchies and networks

Military overlords have long struggled with such unconventional opponents grounded in what is now called 'Asymmetric Warfare'. In fact, the contemporary threat from al-Qaida has some resonance with the Order of Assassins, the *batiniyya*, from the twelfth-century Middle East, notable Persia and Syria. 'Assassin' was a derogatory label applied by the Crusaders from the Arabic word *hashshashin*, meaning 'taker of hashish' [cannabis], but it seems doubtful that the perpetrators of terror were drug-induced. Instead they were comprised of fanatical Shi'ites led by a Persian,

Hasan-i-Sabbah, whose primary targets were the Turkish Seljuq sultans, and Sunni Muslims, though Crusaders were also their victims. It is more likely, then, that 'assassin' is derived from the Arabic *assass* (foundation), via *assassiyun* (fundamentalists); they were simply believers in a purer and more basic form of Islam. And like the contemporary suicide bombers, the assassins accepted their own deaths as a duty and perhaps in the expectation of entry to paradise (Blow, 2001), though Harrison suggests that a better contemporary explanation relates to the exchange of life for a permanent identity as a martyr to the cause.

One thousand years later the difficulties posed to conventional authority by unconventional organizations increased – but it was by no means clear that conventional force would succumb to the unconventional. For instance the US government fought a long campaign against terror allegedly linked to an anarchist network, in the first three decades of the twentieth century. This ultimately fizzled out, marked, though not caused, by the (in)famous execution of Nicola Sacco and Bartolomeo Vanzetti in 1927 for a murder that occurred in 1920 in Boston.[20]

Forty years later a rather more organized attempt to overthrow the local political establishment was successfully defeated by the British after a twelve-year-long communist insurgency in Malaya – but only by putting 105,000 full-time and 250,000 part-time soldiers and police into action to kill over 10,000 insurgents (losing 1865 men themselves in the process). Yet alongside the overt strategy of force was a more subtle one: the British promised independence to Malaya and their strategy worked because the Chinese-led insurgents failed to ensure significant Malay support (Grey, 2002). Where the response was more military than anything else, the British were less successful: in 1967, for example, British forces withdrew from Aden after three years of insurgency had stimulated the then Conservative government to declare that although Southern Arabia would be granted independence by 1968 – Britain would maintain a military base there – it did not.

Indeed, one reason that most of Europe has remained so peaceful since the Second World War may well be that what came to be known as the Marshall Plan provided such a different inheritance to that laid down by the Treaty of Versailles in 1919. As Marshall said in 1947, 'Our policy is directed not against any country or doctrine, but against hunger, poverty, desperation and chaos. Its purpose should be the revival of a working economy in the world so as to permit the emergence of political and social conditions in which free institutions can exist' (quoted in Carruth and Eugene, 1988). In effect, the assault upon fascism in general and Nazi Germany in particular comprised two elements: destroying the enemy's capacity for war and undermining the context that had helped it to grow in the first place. This double strategy both reflects Hercules' differentiated approach to the Hydra and is echoed in Amartya Sen's (2002: 25) recent call for a global alliance to combat not just terrorism but also 'for more positive goals, such as combating illiteracy and reducing preventable illnesses that so disrupt economic and social lives in poorer countries'. In other words, the immortal head, the cause, has to be buried along with the mortal heads, the means.

So if neither networks nor hierarchies are invincible, what kind of organization is the al-Qaida group?

Hierarchies and networks: the al-Qaida group

Few people predicted the rise of a qualitatively different kind of terrorist group, one that was religiously inspired, globally located and intent on maximizing rather than avoiding the mass death of innocent civilians. Certainly Paul Wilkinson (2000: 59–60), a noted British expert, seemed to dismiss the probability of Islamic terrorist primarily targeting anywhere other than the existing Middle East states because the existing groups at the time of writing had a fundamentally political agenda. So why did al-Qaida take a different turn?

The source of al-Qaida seems to lie in two critical events of 1979: the fall of the Shah of Iran to an Islamic Revolution and the Soviet invasion of Afghanistan. Both events encouraged the flowering of many radical groups intent on creating other fundamentalist Islamic societies, amongst whom was Al Qaida al-Sulbah (The Solid Base) formed by Abdullah Azzam, a mentor to Osama bin Laden. The group, comprising a self-styled 'pious vanguard' (in some ways similar both to the early Bolshevik party and the New Model Army of the English civil war) operating under the name of MAK (Afghan Service Bureau) recruited, financed, trained and placed perhaps as many as 100,000 for the jihad (holy war) against the Soviet Union and then into several flash points, including Kashmir, Chechnya, the Philippines, Indonesia, Georgia, Somalia, Uzbekistan, Yemen, Algeria and Egypt. Around 3000 were then selected for further operations and al-Qaida fighters were involved in the bombing of US embassies in Tanzania and Kenya and against the USS Cole. This diaspora is critical in determining what the aims of al-Qaida are: they are not focused on particular territorial ambitions as manifest in a specific state but rather on the regional construction of a fundamentalist pan-Islamic state, a regenerated Caliphate, to replace what they regard as corrupt Islamic states and displace all those that inhibit this, most notably the US (Gunaratna, 2002: 1–15). In fact, as Bergen (2001: 242–3) suggests, bin Laden's propaganda does not attack the West for what he might see as its cultural depravity, but for its support of what he regards as corrupt Muslim states. Indeed, the idea of a Caliphate – a political–religious structure for all Islamic people that was originally constructed after the death of the Prophet Muhammad – is theoretically boundaryless and certainly unrelated to the idea of territorial nation states (see Hill, 2001: 98–100).

More problematically, the horror of September 11 has been considerably compounded by the difficulty of discerning those responsible for planning it and the likelihood of such attacks stopping if bin Laden was apprehended. It has often been suggested that al-Qaida is a leaderless group and thus removing Osama bin Laden from the scene will do little to undermine its effectiveness, but al-Qaida does not seem to be a leaderless group, even though certain elements do embody some aspects of Distributed Leadership. The structure of al-Qaida is not an egalitarian network of the kind articulated in the ideal type models of Distributed Leadership or in so-called random networks where power and leadership are very widely dispersed. Network theory does not suggest that power (and leadership) is always randomly distributed or evenly spread throughout an organization – as in a random network – but that power (and leadership) is often disproportionately distributed amongst just a few people who have enormous numbers of contacts in their networks in what are called scale-free networks.

In Figure 5.1 below, the top represents a random network where the eight nodes with the most links (in grey) are connected to a minority of all nodes (black). In the scale-free network on the bottom, however, the four most connected nodes (grey) are connected to a majority of all nodes (black).

For one of the founders of this approach, Barabási (2003), within scale-free networks the ratio of very-connected nodes to ordinary nodes remains constant irrespective of the size of the network. And the implication of this is that while random attacks upon nodes in random networks leads to the gradual deterioration and slow disintegration of the network, random attacks upon ordinary nodes in scale-free

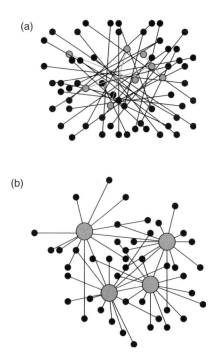

Figure 5.1 (a) Random networks (b) Scale-free network

networks are almost irrelevant. In sum, there is little point in just removing a few 'ordinary' nodes in an organization like al-Qaida because it has virtually no impact upon the overall coherence of the network. However, because scale-free networks rely upon a small number of well-connected individuals, focused attacks upon well-connected nodes can result in catastrophic failure of the network. This is not the equivalent of the 'beheading' strategy discussed at the beginning because we are not dealing with a conventional hierarchy. On the other hand, unlike the ideal type organization with (widely) distributed leadership, al-Qaida is actually closer to a scale-free network.

However, scale-free networks are not 'led' in any hierarchical fashion because the well-connected nodes have no formal authority over each other. In fact, al-Qaida seems to be a hybrid: Osama bin Laden provides the central command structure, the strategic direction and the financial and ideological resources for the entire network but he sits within a horizontally derived network of semi-independent terrorist cells of between 2 and 15 people who are called upon as and when necessary for tactical deployments and action. The relatively loose coalition remains coherent in and through its ideological glue, not through formal hierarchies or structures, and this philosophical similarity, a religious identity, transcends whatever diversity exists; as long as al-Qaida remains internally coherent, individuals will remain committed to it. As Gunaratna (2003b: 21) suggests, 'it is not poverty or lack of literacy that drives people to join terrorist groups, but ideology; the poor and ill-educated simply being more susceptible'. At most, then, perhaps bin-Laden or even al-Qaida plays a gatekeeper role for those seeking martyrdom, much as the Hydra did in the original myth.

Thus, rather like the Waffen SS units in the Second World War, the disciplinary system is internally accepted rather than externally enforced: individual units do not need to be told what to do because their common philosophy acts as an ideological compass. However, unlike the Waffen SS, the global cells of al-Qaida have a very limited hierarchy amongst or between themselves and tend to be organized along ethnic lines, with each ethnic 'family' responsible for a different function: training, weapons procurement, finance and so on (Gunaratna, 2002: 95–166). In this sense al-Qaida is closer to a heterarchy than a hierarchy or a scale-free network, that is, a flexible hierarchy where control is temporarily taken by ostensibly subordinate elements but the structure of the group remains coherent if flexible. Moreover, the absence of a conventional hierarchy makes detection and pursuits very difficult, for the cells are unlikely to know of other cells and, like the Hydra's mortal heads, are neither subordinate nor superordinate to them. In short, you cannot destroy a heterarchy or a network with a Cruise Missile.

However, like a scale-free network you may be able to destabilize it by removing pivotal nodes. For example, the German Abwehr (Military Counter-Intelligence) managed to infiltrate the Dutch resistance from 1941 to such an extent that 52 agents (all but one from the Special Operations Executive and all but six subsequently executed) were captured, as well as 350 local resistance fighters. In addition, thanks to the deception, London provided the Germans with 570 containers of arms and ammunition, thinking they were being dropped to the Dutch Resistance (Miller, 1998: 49–51).

That pivotal node in the al-Qaida heterarchy remains the core group around Osama bin Laden, the shura majlis or consultative council comprising around twelve to fourteen individuals (all men of course), which oversee four sub-groups: military, finance, religion and publicity. The military committee appoints agent-handlers to oversee and coordinate groups outside the centre. Consequently, while the centre does not necessarily determine what the cells do, it can impose its will. For example, in April 1996 a cell intended to attack western targets in Singapore but on 18th of April, after members of the Israeli Defence Force killed 109 Lebanese civilians, bin Laden apparently cancelled the operation to prevent it undermining the global condemnation of Israel (Gunaratna, 2002: 100). Similarly, in November 2003 the two suicide bombings that killed 62 people in or near the HSBC bank and the British Consulate in Istanbul were, apparently, personally approved by bin Laden according to Fevzi Yitiz, a suspect arrested and interrogated by the Turkish Intelligence Services. Bin Laden had originally suggested attacking US airbases or ships but security had proved too difficult (*Guardian*, 18 December 2003). Similarly, the Madrid Bombings of 11 March 2004 that killed over 200 people were linked to al-Qaida.[21]

When the trail from Ground Zero in New York purportedly led to Osama bin Laden's al-Qaida network in the middle of Afghanistan, many argued that a conventional assault would be both costly and ultimately fruitless: you could not destroy a hydra-like organization such as al-Qaida, by lopping off its head, first because it would be inordinately difficult to find, and second because eliminating any element of it would not destroy it, but, on the contrary, only serve to stimulate further growth and resistance. In effect, force was counter-productive – surely the most frightening of all possibilities for those intent on a military solution – thus only reconciliation would work. Either way, it seemed the Americans were doomed: if the Taliban fought to the end there would be unsupportable casualties going home to Washington, and if the Taliban disappeared then the assault would be irrelevant and just the beginning of another protracted guerrilla war. The result could only be that Afghanistan would be America's second Vietnam; and as Vladimir Putin found to his cost in the Moscow theatre siege in October 2002, 'winning' the war against Chechen terrorists in Chechnya was only the first move not the last. Thus at the extreme end of the reconciliation approach could Alice Walker, in The Village Voice, October 9, wonder 'what would happen to him [bin Laden] if he could be brought to understand the preciousness of the lives he has destroyed? I believe the only punishment that works is love'.

Two weeks into November 2001 the bombing campaign had little to show, other than film footage of bombs exploding in the distant hills, and the opponents of the military campaign took comfort from the beginnings of 'Vietnam II'. Yet, four months after the attacks on the US mainland, and barely four weeks after the campaign began, the American-led assault had effectively displaced the al-Qaida–Taliban network (AQT), even if the search for its leaders continues in August 2004. The temptation of the hawks to remind the doves of their misunderstanding of the military situation could only be matched by the doves' subsequent concern that nothing has been achieved as the US and Royal Marines endlessly scoured the Afghan countryside for their invisible enemy. Even overt hawks were not always convinced that the war had been won, as Colonel David H. Hackworth (a veteran critic of the current US armed forces) suggested, 'We are in round one – which is not even over – of a 30-round fight. I think my grandkids, who are five and eight, will be in college before we're in round 30. ... It's a mistake to believe you can stop a terrorist movement by taking out its leader. You can cut off the head but the body will still live on' (quoted in Scriven, 2002: 7).

Reassessing the myth

The rapid collapse of the AQT might imply that their hold over the population and the territory was never deep-rooted, and, indeed, was itself a myth. Since the power of myths remains only as long as people believe in them, the military collapse of the group demonstrated that its much-vaunted 'monopoly of support' was nothing of the sort. Just as the Berlin Wall fell when the East German population stopped being cowed by it, so the role of the Hydra myth in this situation was to demonstrate that myths are powerful, but not as powerful as bombs. But the Hydra myth provides us with several other ways of understanding the problem of terrorism.

A first and literal application of the myth might perceive an American Hercules coming to wreak revenge on the AQT, guided there by the Northern Alliance as Iolaus. At first the task appears impossible, the Hydra cannot even be located and its lair is so deep that it cannot be reached. But when the flaming arrows of the US air force enter the complex the creature is driven into the open. Although difficult, the overwhelming power of the American Hercules eventually grapples the Hydra to the ground, and begins to sever the heads of the monster, only to find that for each problem solved (e.g., getting the agreement of the Pakistani government to use their air space) two more emerge (e.g., the target has moved and the Taliban supporters in Pakistan are threatening to destabilize Pakistan itself). Eventually the American Hercules realizes that it alone cannot defeat the Hydra and after each head is removed the Northern Alliance (Iolaus) cauterize each headless stump in turn until victory is achieved; force worked.

A second, and contrary interpretation is that the problem remains because the immortal head, Osama bin Laden or the hatred of the US that motivates such groups, cannot be so easily disposed of, and Hercules has simply buried the problem under the rubble of the Tora Bora cave complex. If the immortal head is Osama bin Laden then his elimination will remove the problem – or at least undermine the focus of the group in the same way that Hitler's death contributed to the elimination of the myth of Nazi invincibility. But if the immortal head is the hatred of the US and the existing Islamic regimes, then the tactical focus of the military assault by the West can only ever be a prelude to a strategic resolution of what many Muslims appear to consider an intolerable situation. And that situation undoubtedly involves not just the problems of the Palestinians – and Yasser Arafat publicly denounced bin-Laden in December 2002 – but the form of governments that currently control some Muslim societies. As Meek (2001: 3) suggested, a year after September 11 there were 'signs that the Bush administration [was] beginning to accept the absurdity of characterising Bin Laden as "the CEO of Terrorism Incorporated" '. Yet when Khalid Sheik Mohammed ('al-Qaida's number three') was arrested in Rawalpindi on 2 March 2003, precisely the same assumptions pervaded Gunaratna's (2003c: 3) response: 'His arrest will gravely diminish al-Qaida's ability to plan, prepare and execute large-scale operations of the scope of September 11.' However, the Herculean task facing the US lies in Gunaratna's final paragraph, 'with the erosion of core leadership of al-Qaida on Afghanistan and Pakistan, al-Qaida cells in at least 98 countries are likely to learn to function wholly or partly on their own'. Using yet another Hydra metaphor, Paul Rogers has suggested 'If the coalition succeeds in its aims, and manages to get rid of the whole bin Laden operation, it will be perhaps three years before the next similar group rears its head' (quoted in Meek, 2001: 3). In effect, only by ceasing support for autocratic oil-rich gulf regimes and by guaranteeing a Palestinian state will the US ever undermine support for al-Qaida-like groups. In this approach, the double strategy of Hercules is necessary because the target groups and their motivations are different. To put it another way, the Herculean strategy must combine both political and military strategies: the former deals with the causes, the latter with the effects.

A third, and more worrying analysis might be that the Hydra has no head, no central cause, and therefore no method for permanent destruction, least of all a conventional military 'defeat', for each assault upon it stimulates its regenerative capacity to the point where, as in some stages and forms of cancer, attacking it ensures its proliferation.[22] Here the Hydra myth is more appropriate in terms of its biological manifestation. That is to say that the multiple heads of the Hydra actually represent the malleable nature of the threat in which al-Qaida is just one of the heads. This threat is not rooted in one place, nor does it restrict its forms of attack to a particular format, and its support system encompasses significant financial assets, a considerable number of fighters, and supporters right across the world. 'Al-Qaida', according to Philip Bobbitt, 'is a virtual state. It has a standing army, a treasury, a consistent source of revenue, a civil service and an intelligence corps; it even runs a rudimentary welfare programme for its fighters and their relatives and associates' (quoted in Brittan, 2002: 15). And like a state, on 23 February 1998, al-Qaida declared war against 'the Jews and the Christians'. But the bomb attacks in Bali in 2002, the arrests of a number of Algerians for allegedly developing Ricin in Wood Green, London, and of ten suspected terrorists in Spain, all in January 2003, together with the almost simultaneous murder of a police officer in Manchester whilst arresting suspected North African terrorists, the bombings in Saudi Arabia in October 2003, and the bombings in Madrid in March 2004, all suggest that the 'hierarchy of terror' is rather more like a 'heterarchy of terror'. For there exists a proliferating number of individuals and groups whose only allegiance to al-Qaida is fraternal support not organizational subordination.

Thus although 3000 people in 98 countries have been arrested for alleged membership of al-Qaida by January 2003 (Gunaratna, 2003a: 9) this does not necessarily imply the end of terrorism any more than the arrest of 3000 burglars necessarily implies the end of burglary. Indeed, one could suggest that even if al-Qaida was destroyed it has already provided the leadership for others by demonstrating the direction to be taken. And, as has happened, the Anglo-American forces occupying Iraq have probably generated an increase in recruits to terrorist organizations, which will more than compensate for the elimination of any direct threat from Saddam Hussein. As Record (2003: v) from the US Army War College suggests,

> The United States may be able to defeat al-Qaida, but it cannot rid the world of terrorism, much less evil. … [The war] against a deterred Iraq has created a new front in the Middle East for Islamic terrorism and diverted attention and resources away from the security of the American homeland against further assault by an undeterrable al-Qaida. The war against Iraq was not integral to the GWOT [Global War on Terror] but rather a detour from it.

In fact, according to the *Observer* newspaper (Barnett *et al.*, 2004: 10–11), European Intelligence Services believed that extremist Muslim terrorist cells in Europe were autonomous and, if anything, worked more closely with Abu Musab Zarqawi, a Jordanian, than Osama bin-Laden's al-Qaida network.

We might take comfort from Northern Ireland and from Sri Lanka here – both ostensibly intractable problems involving religion and terrorism that appear to have burnt themselves to a recognition that the strategy cannot succeed (Woollacott, 2002: 18). Nevertheless, it is also clear that in the Northern Ireland case without the leadership of Gerry Adams and David Trimble it is doubtful whether the trajectory would have been the same; indeed, there may not have been any trajectory towards peace, however fitful it has been.

In contrast, al-Qaida's religious fanaticism means that it remains uninterested in compromise, undeterred by death, unconcerned by the unlikelihood of success in the short-term yet willing to change the focus of its target to the point where it is politically impossible to satisfy. Within this analysis the parallel with Hercules is the apparent willingness of the Hydra to sacrifice its mortal heads in the certain knowledge that two more will grow in its place. The only response, therefore, is permanent vigilance and preparedness because the 'beast' appears to be literally immortal.[23] This might actually be worth contextualizing rather more deeply, for there are precious few years in which war has not been a feature of the world, and more people have died as a result of war in the last 100 years than in any other period that we know of. In short, as Machiavelli implied, the threat of violence is an endemic feature of human society and not something linked to the recent rise of religious fundamentalism.

Finally, it is worth considering a reverse perspective of the myth such that bin Laden would presumably perceive himself to be Hercules fighting the American Hydra, the only global superpower remaining. And in this form it is the multiple military, economic, political and cultural arms of the US 'empire' that strike terror into the hearts of its neighbours, manifest most visibly in the photographs of prisoner-abuse that emerged from American-controlled Iraqi prisons in May 2004. 'The fact is', suggested Krauthammer in the *New York Times*, 'no country has been as dominant culturally, economically, technologically and military in the history of the world since the Roman Empire' (quoted in Freedland, 2002: 2). And although the US does not have the colonies normally associated with empires it does have a military unit of some kind in 132 of 190 member states of the United Nations, and it is the predominant technological and economic power, to say nothing of the cultural domination of icons like Coke and McDonalds. We also face a global threat to the environment that can only really be resolved at a global level, preferably through something like the Kyoto agreement. Indeed, King (2004) has insisted that global warming is a greater threat to the world than global terrorism, and since the US with 4 per cent of the world's population generates 20 per cent of the total greenhouse gases it is critical that any global response includes the US. Yet the US has chosen to ignore the rest of the world community on this and on the International Court of Justice, initially on steel imports and on what to do about the problems left in the wake of Saddam's overthrow.

For Castells (1997), such exclusionary practices in turn generate attempts by the excluded to 'exclude the excluders', or rather to eliminate the excluders, and moreover, to route that elimination along the network channels that the excluders have long sought to use for their own purposes. Here we would expect increasing links between the various mafias and organized crime syndicates and al-Qaida. But it may be that no such links are necessary for the glue that holds al-Qaida together is rooted in ideology not self-interested networks. Baudrillard (2002: 6–7), for example, has suggested that since all such 'definitive orders' like the US, induce the will to destroy them, in some bizarre way although 'they did it ... we wished for it' as he calls it. In short, and in very Hegelian terms, 'every machinery of domination [has] secreted its own counter-apparatus, the agent of its own disappearance' (Baudrillard (2002: 10). In fact, Baudrillard claims we are now entering the Fourth World War (the third being the Cold War that eliminated Communism), and as with each preceding World War the end result is the greater integration of the world order (Cf. Bobbit, 2002). Yet, in distinctly unHegelian terms there is no victory of Good at the end of this story because Good and Evil are permanent members of the world community and whichever side of the fence we may find ourselves, we are fated to the permanent recurrence of the myth of Hercules and the Hydra. Indeed, that might prove a fitting metaphor for Distributed Leadership because it offers a solution to the endemic problem of authoritarian leadership and simultaneously a means for leaderless authoritarians to distribute terror.

Conclusion

The Myth of the Hydra provides us with (at least) three different ways of understanding the theory of Distributed Leadership and the practice of the US and its coalition partners in the war on terrorism in general and al-Qaida in particular. We began by considering how the search for an alternative to traditional ideas of leadership has regenerated interest in what were original ideas drawn from anarchist theory, though they probably go much further back in time to the original hunter-gatherer societies. On that basis it was suggested that the shift towards redistributing responsibility within organizations could be used to (re)kindle participative communities and inhibit authoritarian leaders and organizations, as demonstrated in the struggle for civil rights in the US in the 1960s.

One alternative was simply not to face the problem, to assume that organizations did not need leadership of any kind because it was essentially corrupt and corrupting. Yet the refusal to look at the pink elephant in the corner does not necessarily mean there isn't one there, and that recognition has pushed some groups, from Green Parties to educational institutions, to consider how Distributed Leadership, while not a complete answer to the problem might at least prove to be a better way of leading.

But Distributed Leadership is both a philosophy and a process and that process implied it could be used by those uninterested in distributing authority and more concerned in keeping the authorities in the dark. One such organization is al-Qaida and the second part of the chapter analysed it through the perspective of Distributed Leadership in general and the Hydra myth in particular. Quite how we should deal with such groups depends upon how one thinks they are led – and 'disab-led'.

First, as Hercules initially believed, military force is adequate for the job because force is the only thing that terrorists understand and decapitating their leadership is the fastest way to stop them. There is, after all, little point in trying to negotiate with hijackers who intend to kill themselves as well as their victims. The problem here is not ensuring the means to despatch the terrorists but generating the political will to go through with the task. Indeed, the argument goes, the longer the West procrastinates over the moral case for intervention the more likely terrorists are to get hold of and then use weapons of mass destruction. And, following Hercules, the issue is not if he will attack the Hydra but when.

Second, and alternatively, the 'decapitation response' is to misunderstand the nature of the problem: al-Qaida can only continue not because of bin Laden's leadership but because some people regard its cause as just, therefore that cause needs to be addressed through some form of reconciliation. This approach has resulted in the invasion of Afghanistan and Iraq with, at best, mixed results: the wars were won but winning the peace has proved much more difficult. And even if al-Qaida is destroyed the motivations that drove its members will remain and a new group or network will emerge like a phoenix from the ashes. Here the problem relates to the difficulties Hercules faces when dealing with the Hydra – it is literally 'headless' in the sense of seeking out leaders to decapitate because for every 'terrorist' killed another two 'freedom fighters' will emerge as replacements; this is not a clash of civilizations (Huntington, 1997) but a consequence of perceiving 'the other' as the enemy. The attribution of responsibility to remnants of the Baathist Party for the attacks upon coalition forces of all nationalities in Iraq, and upon the Red Cross and the UN, long after the war was declared to be over, imply that the US still believes a leader of some kind is coordinating the resistance, even after the capture of Saddam, but it may be that while al-Qaida is best configured as a heterarchy, the resistance in Iraq is much closer to a scale-free network – not that there are leaderless groups but that there are lots of malcontented groups, each with conventional leadership but without any overall coordination. In truth, in Iraq, we may have a Hydra – not a leaderless organization but a multi-headed one.

Third, neither of these responses is adequate because, like Hercules, you have to employ a dual strategy against different kinds of opposition: force worked for the mortal heads and leaders of dictatorships – providing they were cut off and the necks cauterized – but force alone was inadequate for the immortal head; that required a different resolution. Thus force is inadequate to prevent terrorism that has some popular support because its heterarchical and scale-free network manifestations are less susceptible to conventional force. But merely addressing the problems that generate support for terrorism will not remove the problem; there are simply some problems for which violence may be an unfortunate but necessary response. This is the Hydra paradox that Hercules can only resolve by engaging in different strategies for what appears at one level to be the same enemy. Indeed, in deference to the myth, even if this set of political problems is resolved the American Hercules cannot rest in peace forever, for there are ten other Labours yet to be completed. This permanent engagement is a consequence of the US taking upon itself the role of global (American) police force and, as all police officers know, activity deemed to be criminal by the (American) law can never be permanently eliminated, though it can be constrained.

We might conclude that this still leaves Distributed Leadership free for colonization by the political left because the political right are philosophically opposed to such a wide distribution of authority and leadership. The latter may be correct but that does not mean that the political left can claim monopoly control over Distributed Leadership. On the contrary, as I mentioned at the beginning, Distributed Leadership in this egalitarian sense only really exists as a Weberian Ideal Type and its practical embodiments tend to slide much closer to the scale-free network model, rather than the random network. In other words, Distributed Leadership may be better at inhibiting authoritarian leaders than conventional models of leadership but it is not a system for transcending all leadership problems and it remains as a prototype vehicle for cohabiting with leaderless authoritarians.

Notes

1   http://www.guardian.co.uk/Iraq/Story/0,2763,932750,00.html
2   http://www.panarchy.org/bakunin/authority.1871.html
3   http://www.panarchy.org/bakunin/authority.1871.html
4   See, for example, http://www.tuc.org.uk/international/tuc-2175-f0.cfm

5   A revolutionary anarchist federation.
6   http://www.congresslink.org/civil/essay.html#social The text of the entire act is posted at http://usinfo.state.gov/usa/infousa/laws/majorlaw/civilr19.htm
7   http://seattletimes.nwsource.com/mlk/king/biography.html
8   http://www.achievement.org/autodoc/page/par0bio-1
9   As the *Time* website suggests, 'Montgomery's segregation laws were complex: blacks were required to pay their fare to the driver, then get off and reboard through the back door. Sometimes the bus would drive off before the paid-up customers made it to the back entrance. If the white section was full and another white customer entered, blacks were required to give up their seats and move farther to the back; a black person was not even allowed to sit across the aisle from whites. These humiliations were compounded by the fact that two-thirds of the bus riders in Montgomery were black.' http://www.time.com/time/time100/heroes/profile/parks01.html
10   See http://www.wandea.org.pl/leaderless-resistance.htm
11   See http://www.scottish.parliament.uk/S1/whats_happening/research/pdf_res_notes/rn00–72.pdf and: http://www.cfit.gov.uk/research/fuel2000/pdf/fuel2000.pdf
12   The following three web sites provide useful information on al-Qaida: http://web.nps.navy.mil/~library/tgp/qaida.htm   http://cns.miis.edu/research/wtc01/alqaida.htm   http://www.au.af.mil/au/aul/bibs/tergps/tgaqai.htm
13   Hydra: Abbreviation: Hya; Genitive: Hydrae
     Right Ascension: 10.12 hours
     Declination: −19.36 degrees
     Hydra, the Water Snake, is best seen from the Southern Hemisphere, but is visible during the months of January through May in the Northern Hemisphere; see http://www.astronomical.org/constellations/hya.html
14   See http://astro.sci.uop.edu/~sas/Newsletter/CON_Hydra.html
15   Unfortunately, Eurystheus argued that Hercules could not count this Labour among the number required since he cheated by having Iolaus help him.
16   Pearson's (2001) review replicates a menu approach to this issue: 'Take one flatworm, chop into 279 pieces and leave for two weeks. Feed occasionally. The result: 279 perfect new worms. … Flatworms, or planarians, Salamanders, starfish, tentacle-waving polyps and zebrafish can also regenerate new heads, limbs, internal organs or other body parts if the originals are lost or damaged.'
17   http://www.aaskolnick.com/hydra.htm
18   Resolution 1373 (2001) on terrorism was adopted by the Security Council at its 4385th meeting, on 28 September 2001. It can be viewed at: http://www.un.org/Docs/sc/committees/1373/
19   Six hundred and twenty five Israelis have been killed, and 4500 injured in 14,280 Palestinian attacks between 1999 and 2002, over 1372 Palestinians have been killed and 19,684 injured in Israeli attacks that are fewer in absolute numbers but have lasted significantly longer than the Palestinian equivalent (Grossman, 2002).
20   For a brief review of events see: http://www.english.upenn.edu/~afilreis/88/sacvan.html
21   http://www.washingtonpost.com/wp-dyn/articles/A58697–2004Mar14.html
22   Thanks to Yiannis Gabriel for this insight.
23   Thanks to Yiannis Gabriel for pointing this parallel out.

Bibliography

Ackerman, P. and Duvall, J. 2000. *A Force More Powerful*. London: Palgrave.

Adams, D. 1989. *The Long Dark Tea-Time of the Soul*. London: Pan.

Albin, K. 1996. 'Rosa Parks: The Woman Who Changed History' http://www.grandtimes.com/rosa.html

Altner, H. 2002. *Berlin Dance of Death*. Staplehurst: Spellmount.

Alvesson, M. 2003. 'Leadership: Myth or Reality?' Seminar to Saïd Business School. Oxford. 27 February.

Alvesson, M. and Sveningsson, S. 2003. 'The Great Disappearing Act: Difficulties with Doing "Leadership" ', *Leadership Quarterly*. 14(3) pp. 359–81.

Ambrose, S.E. 1995. *D-Day June 6, 1944*. London: Touchstone.

Ambrose, S.E. 1999. 'D-Day Fails', in Cowley, R. (ed.) *What If ? Military Historians Imagine What Might Have Been*. London: Macmillan.

Anthony, P.D. 1977. *The Ideology of Work*. London: Tavistock.

Archer, T.D. 2003. 'The Role of the Sensemaker in Leadership Development'. Unpublished RAF Service Fellowship Paper.

Argyris, C. 1985. *Strategy, Change and Defensive Routines*. London: Pitman.

Bajpai, K. 1999. 'Paradigm Shifts in Security', *Biblio*. VII (7/8).

Baker, A. 2000. *The Gladiator*. London: Random House.

Bales, K. 2000. Disposable People: New Slaves in the Global Economy. Berkeley: University of California Press.

Bakunin, M. 1871. *What is Authority?* See http://www.panarchy.org/bakunin/authority.1871.html and http://www.marxists.org/reference/archive/bakunin/works/various/authrty.htm

Bakunin, M. 1970. *God and the State*. London: Dover Publications.

Balkoski, J. 1999. *Beyond the Beachhead: the 29th Infantry Division in Normandy*. Mechanicsburg PA: Stackpole Books.

Barabási, A-L. 2003. *Linked: How Everything is Connected to Everything Else and What it Means for Business, Science and Everyday Life*. London: Plume.

Bard, M.G. 1994. *Forgotten Victims: The Abandonment of Americans in Hitler's Camps*. Oxford: Westview Press.

Barker, E. 1960. *Greek Political Theory*. London: Methuen & Co.

Barley, S.R. and Kunda, G. 2000. 'Design and Devotion', in Grint, K. (ed.) *Work and Society*. Cambridge: Polity Press.

Barnett, A., Burke, J. and Smith, Z. 2004. 'Terror Cells Regroup', *Observer*. 11 January.

Barnett, C. 1984. *The Collapse of British Power*. Stroud: Alan Sutton.

Bartels, L.M. 2002. 'The Impact of Candidate Traits in American Presidential Elections', in King, A. (ed.) *Leaders' Personalities and the Outcome of Democratic Elections*. Oxford: Oxford University Press.

Bass, B.M. 1985. *Leadership and Performance Beyond Expectations*. New York: Free Press.

Bass, B.M. 1990. *Bass and Stogdill's Handbook of Leadership*. 3rd ed. New York: Free Press.

Battram, A. 1998. *Navigating Complexity*. London: The Industrial Society.

Baudrillard, J. 2002. *The Spirit of Terrorism*. London: Verso.

Beevor, A. 1998. *Stalingrad*. London: Viking.

Bennett, N., Wise, C., Woods, P. and Harvey, J.A. 2003. *Distributed Leadership*. Nottingham: NCSL.

Bergen, P.L. 2001. *Holy War Inc.: Inside the Secret World of Osama bin Laden*. London: Weidenfeld and Nicolson.

Bernières, L. de 1995. *Captain Corelli's Mandolin*. London: Minerva.

Bevan, J. 2002. *The Rise and Fall of Marks and Spencer*. London: Profile Books.

Black, E. 2001. *IBM and the Holocaust*. New York: Time Warner.

Blackburn, R. 1988. 'Defining Slavery – Its Special Features and Social Role', in Archer, L. (ed.) *Slavery and Other Forms of Unfree Labour*. London: Routledge.

Blanton, T.S. 2002. 'The Cuban Missile Crisis: 40 Years Later', *Washington Post*, 16 October.

Blow, D. 2001. 'A Dagger in the Dark', *History*. 2(11) pp. 40–1.

Bobbitt, P. 2002. *The Shield of Achilles: War, Peace and the Course of History*. London: Allen Lane.

Bookchin, M. 1996. *Towards an Ecological Society*. New York: Black Rose Books.

Botting, D. 1978. *The D-Day Invasion*. Richmond, VA: Time-Life Books.

Boyle, D. 2001. *The Tyranny of Numbers: Why Counting Can't Make us Happy*. London: Flamingo.

Bradley, K. 1994. *Slavery and Society at Rome*. Cambridge: Cambridge University Press.

Bradley, K. 1998. *Slavery and Rebellion in the Roman World 140BC to 70BC*. Bloomington: Indiana University Press.

Bratton, J., Grint, K. and Nelson, D. 2004. *Organizational Leadership*. Mason, OH: Southwestern/Thompson Press.

Braverman, H. 1974. *Labor and Monopoly Capitalism*. New York: Monthly Review.

Brecht, B. 1980. *Life of Galileo*. London: Methuen.

Brereton, D. 1999. 'Zero Tolerance and the NYPD' paper presented to the 3rd National Outlook Symposium on Crime in Australia, available at: http://www.aic. gov.au/conferences/outlook99/brereton.pdf

Brittan, S. 2002. 'The US is More Nearly Right', *Financial Times*. 1 August.

Brooks, R.A. 2002. *Robot*. London: Allen Lane.

Brown, E. 2001. *IBM and the Holocaust*. London: Little, Brown & Co.

Browne, K.R. 2002. *Biology at Work: Rethinking Sexual Equality*. New Haven, CT: Yale University Press.

Browning, C. 2000. *Nazi Policy, Jewish Workers, German Killers*. Cambridge: Cambridge University Press.

Bruce, C.J. 1999. *Invaders: British and American Experience of Seaborne Landings 1939–1945*. London: Chatham.

Burden, J. 1988. 'Slavery as a Punishment in Roman Criminal Law', in Archer, L. (ed.) *Slavery and Other Forms of Unfree Labour*. London: Routledge.

Burke, J., Ahmed, K., Barnett, A., Sweeney, J., Paton, N., Harris, P. and Millar, S. 2000. 'A Few Angry Men', *Observer*. 17 September.

Burleigh, M. 2000. *The Third Reich: A New History*. London: Macmillan.

Burns, J.M. 1978. *Leadership*. New York: Harper & Row.

Callon, M. 1986. 'The sociology of an actor network', in Callon, M. Law, J. and Rip, A. (eds) *Mapping The Dynamics Of Science And Technology*. London: Macmillan.

Campbell, A.H. 1988. 'WWII Production of LVTs', *Wheels and Tracks* (24) pp. 30–5.

Carruth, G. and Eugene, E. (eds) 1988. *The Harper Book of American Quotations*. New York: Harper & Row.

Cartledge, P. 1988. 'Serfdom in Classical Greece', in Archer, L. (ed.) *Slavery and Other Forms of Unfree Labour*. London: Routledge.

Cartledge, P. 2002. *The Spartans*. London: Channel Four Books.

Castells, M. 1997. *The Power of Identity: The Information Age: Economy, Society and Culture*. Oxford: Blackwell.

Castiglione, Count B. 1994. *The Book of the Courtier*. London: J.M. Dent.

Catt, M. 2004. 'Leadership Conversation', Templeton College, Oxford, 9 February.

Caulkin, S. 2003. 'Breaking out of the Budget Cycle', *Observer*. 20 July.

Chandler, A.D. 1977. *The Visible Hand: The Managerial Revolution in American Business*. Cambridge, MA: Belknap.

Chandler, D. 1966. *The Campaigns of Napoleon*. London: Macmillan.

Christensen, K. and Grint, K. 2004. 'Distributed Leadership and Green Politics: Ignoring the Big Pink Elephant in the Room'. Unpublished research paper.

Cohen, J.L. 2002. 'Civil Society in Modern Social and Political Philosophy' ca.geocities.com/jazzchul2000/ glossary/civil_society.htm

Collins, J. and Porras, J. 1996. *Built to Last*. London: Random House Books.

Collinson, D. 2002. 'Managing humour', *Journal of Management Studies*. 39(2) pp. 269–88.

Connolly, P. 2003. *Colosseum: Rome's Arena of Death*. London: BBC.

Cooke, B. 2003. 'The Denial of Slavery in Management Studies', *Journal of Management Studies*. 40(8) pp. 1895–941.

Davies, J. and Easterby-Smith. M. 1984. 'Learning and Developing From Managerial Work Experiences', *Journal of Management Studies*. 2. pp. 169–83.

Dawkins, R. 1989. *The Selfish Gene*. Oxford: Oxford University Press.

Delaforce, P. 1998. *Churchill's Secret Weapons: The Story of Hobart's Funnies*. London: Robert Hale.

Delaforce, P. 1999. *Marching to the Sound of Gunfire: Northwest Europe 1944–5*. Stroud: Wrens Park.

De Waal, F. 2000. *Chimpanzee Politics: Power and Sex among Apes*. Baltimore, MD: John Hopkins University Press.

Doh, J.P. 2003. 'Can Leadership be Taught? Perspectives From Management Educators', *Academy of Management Learning and Education*. 2(1) pp. 54–7.

Doherty, B., Paterson, M., Plows, A. and Wall, D. 2003. 'Explaining the fuel Protests', *The British Journal of Politics & International Relations*. 5(1) pp. 1–23, February.

Doughty, M. (ed.) 1994. *Hampshire and D-Day*. Crediton: Southgate Publishers.

Douglas, M. 2002. *Purity and Danger*. London: Routledge.

Drath, W.H. and Palus, C.J. 1994. *Making Common Sense*, Greensboro, NC: Centre for Creative Leadership.

Driver, M. 2002. 'Learning and Leadership in Organizations', *Management Learning*. 33(1) pp. 99–126.

Drucker, H. 2001. *The Essential Drucker*. London: Harper-Collins.

Dugan, S. and Dugan, D. 2000. *The Day the World Took Off*. London: Channel four Books.

Durkheim, E. (1883) 1973. 'Address to the Lycéen of Sans', in Bellah, R.N. (ed.) *Emile Durkheim on Morality and Society*. Chicago: University of Chicago Press.

Durschmied, E. 1999. *The Hinge Factor*. London: Coronet.

Edwards, R. 1979. *Contested Terrain*. London: Heinemann.

Elkington, J. 1999. *Cannibals with Forks*. Oxford: Capstone.

Elliot, G. 1965. *Middlemarch*. Harmondsworth: Penguin.

Ellis, J.J. 1997. *American Sphinx: The Character of Thomas Jefferson*. New York: Vintage Books.

Falk, A., Fehr, E. and Fischbacher, U. 2003. 'On the Nature of Fair Behaviour', *Economic Enquiry*. 41(1) pp. 22–6.

Fanon, F. 1963. *The Wretched of the Earth*. New York: Grove Press.

Fast, H. 1974. *Spartacus*. London: Granada.

Feinstein, M. 1992. *Sixteen Weeks with the European Greens*. San Pedro, CA: R & E Miles.

Ferguson, N. 1998. *The Pity of War*. London: Penguin.

Fiedler, F. 1997. 'Situational Control and a Dynamic Theory of Leadership', in Grint, K. (ed.) *Leadership: Classical. Contemporary and Critical Approaches*. Oxford: Oxford University Press.

Figes, O. and Kolonitskii, B. 1999. *Interpreting the Russian Revolution: The Language and Symbols of 1917*. New Haven: Yale University Press.

Fisher, D., Rooke, D. and Torbert, W. 2002. *Personal and Organisational Transformations Through Action Inquiry*. Boston: Edge Work Press.

Fisk, R. 2001. *Pity the Nation*. Oxford: Oxford Paperbacks.

Fort, A. 2003. *Prof: The Life of Frederick Lindemann*. London: Jonathon Cape.

Fowle, B.W. 1994. 'Engineers', in Chandler, D.G. and Collins, J.L. (eds) *The D-Day Encyclopedia*. Oxford: Helicon.

Freedland, J. 2002. 'Rome AD ... Rome DC?', *Guardian*. 18 September.

Freire, P. 1997. *Pedagogy of the Oppressed*. London: Penguin.

Fukuyama, F. 1993. *The End of History and the Last Man*. London: Penguin.

Furtado, P. 1992. *World War II*. London: Chancellor Press.

Fusaro, P.C. and Miller, R.M. 2002. *What Went Wrong at Enron?* London: John Wiley & Son.

Fyke, K. and Sayegh, G. 2001. 'Anarchism and the Struggle to Move Forward', *Perspectives on Anarchist Theory*. 5(2) Fall.

Gabriel, Y. (ed.) 2004. *Myths, Stories and Organizations: Premodern Narratives for Our Times*. Oxford: Oxford University Press.

Gallie, W.B. 1955–56. 'Essentially contested concepts', *Proceedings of the Aristotelian Society* 56 pp. 167–98.

Gallie, W.B. 1964. *Philosophy and the Historical Understanding*. New York: Schocken Books.

Geary, J. 2002. *The Body Electric*. London: Weidenfeld and Nicolson.

Gellately, R. 2001. *Backing Hitler: Consent and Coercion in Nazi Germany*. Oxford: Oxford University Press.

Gemmill, G. and Oakley, J. 1997. 'Leadership: An alienating social myth?', in Grint, K. (ed.) *Leadership*. Oxford: Oxford University Press.

Gerstner, C.R. and Day, D.V. 1997. 'Meta-analytic review of leader-member exchange theory: Correlates and construct issues', *Journal of Applied Psychology*. 82(6) pp. 827–44.

Gladwell, M. 2002. *The Tipping Point*. London: Abacus.

Gleik, J. 1987. *Chaos: Making a New Science*. London: Minerva.

Goldberg, S. 1993. *Why Men Rule: A Theory of Male Dominance*. Chicago: Open Court.

Goldenberg, S. 2004. 'They Made us Break the Law', *Guardian*. 20 May.

Goldhagen, D.J. 1996. *Hitler's Willing Executioners: Ordinary Germans and the Holocaust*. London: Little, Brown & Co.

Goldsworthy, A. 2003. *In the Name of Rome: The Men who Won the Roman Empire*. London: Weidenfeld and Nicolson.

Goleman, D. 2002. *The New Leaders: Transforming the Art of Leadership into the Science of Results*. London: Little Brown.

Gore, A., Jr. 1992. *Earth in the Balance*. New York: Plume.

Graef, R. 2003. 'How the US Cracked its Teenage Gun Crisis', *Observer*. 5 January.

Graen, G. and Scandura, T.A. 1987. 'Toward a Psychology of Dyadic Organizing', *Research in Organizational Behaviour*. 9. pp. 175–208.

Grey, J. 2002. 'Malaya, 1948–60: Defeating the Communist Insurgency', in Thompson, J. (ed.) *The Imperial War Museum Book of Modern Warfare*. London: Sidgwick and Jackson.

Grint, K. 1986. *Democracy and Bureaucracy*. Unpublished PhD. Oxford University.

Grint, K. 1998. *The Sociology of Work*. Cambridge: Polity Press.

Grint, K. 2001. *The Arts of Leadership*. Oxford: Oxford University Press.

Grint, K. 2003. 'Slavery', in Haralambos, M. (ed.) *Sociology: New Directions*. Ormskirk: Causeway Press.

Grint, K. and Woolgar, S. 1997. *The Machine at Work: Technology. Work and Society*. Cambridge: Polity Press.

Gronn, P. 1997. 'Leading for Learning: Organizational Transformation and the Formation of Leaders', *Journal of Management Development*. 16(4) pp. 1–9.

Gronn, P. 2003. *The New Work of Educational Leaders*. London: Sage.

Grossman, D. 2002. 'Israel Has Won For Now But What Is Victory When It Brings No Hope?', *Guardian Unlimited*. 30 September.

Groysberg, B., Nanda, A. and Nohria, N. 2004. 'The Risky Business of Hiring Stars', *Harvard Business Review*. May.

Guardian, 2003. 'Bin Laden Approved Bombings', Istanbul: Associated Press.

Gunaratna, R. 2002. *Inside Al Qaeda: Global Network of Terror*. London: Hurst & Co.

Gunaratna, R. 2003a. 'And Now a Little Local Jihad', *Sunday Times*. 26 January.

Gunaratna, R. 2003b. 'Cooking for Terrorists'. *The Times Higher*. 14 February.

Gunaratna, R. 2003c. 'Womaniser. Joker. Scuba Diver: The Other Face of al-Qaida's No 3', *Guardian*. 3 March.

Gwyther, M. and Hoar, R. 2003. 'Working Dads Who Want it All', *Management Today*. 10 April.

Haffner, S. 2003. *Churchill*. London: Haus.

Haraway, D. 1991. *Simians, Cyborgs and Women*. New York: Routledge.

Harl, K.W. 1996. 'Jewish Rebellions', in Cowley, R. and Parker, G. (eds) *The Osprey Companion to Military History*. London: Osprey.

Harris, A. 2003. 'Distributed Leadership in Schools: Leading or Misleading?' *ICP Online*. See http://www.icponline.org/feature_articles/f14_02.htm

Harris, A. and Chapman, C. 2002. *Effective Leadership in Schools Facing Challenging Circumstances*. Final Report. Nottingham: NCSL. See http://www.ncsl.org.uk/

Harrison, M. 2003. 'The Logic of Suicide Terrorism' see http://www.warwick.ac.uk/fac/soc/CSGR/Publications/Harrison/terrorism.pdf

Harvey, F.D. 1988. 'Herodotus and the Man-Footed Creature', in Archer, L. (ed.) *Slavery and Other Forms of Unfree Labour*. London: Routledge.

Hassard, J. 1996. 'Images of Time in Work and Organization', in Clegg, S., Hardy, C. and Nord, W.R. (eds) *Handbook of Organization Studies*. London: Sage.

Heifetz, R.A. 1994. *Leadership Without Easy Answers*. Cambridge, MA: Harvard University Press.

Heifetz, R.A. and Linsky, M. 2002. *Leadership on the Line*. Boston, MA: Harvard Business School Press.

Herbert, U. 1994. 'Labour as Spoils of Conquest, 1933–1945', in Crew, D.F. (ed.) *Nazism and German Society 1933–1945*. London: Routledge.

Herbert, U. 1997. *Hitler's Foreign Workers: Enforced Foreign Labor in Germany Under the Third Reich*. Cambridge: Cambridge University Press.

Hill, C. 2001. 'A Herculean Task', in Talbott, S. and Chanda, N. (eds) *The Age of Terror: America and the World after September 11*. New York: Basic Books.

Hodgson, P. 1999. 'Leading, Teaching and Learning', in *The Royal Society on Work and Leadership*. Aldershot: Gower.

Holland, J.H. 1998. *Emergence from Chaos to Order*. Oxford: Oxford University Press.

Holt, T. and Holt, V. 1999. *Major and Mrs Holt's Battlefield Guide to the Normandy Landing Beaches*. Barnsley: Leo Cooper.

Honderich, T. 2002. *After the Terror*. Edinburgh: Edinburgh University Press.

Hosking, D. 1988. 'Organizing, Leadership and Skillful Process', *Journal of Management Studies*. 25 pp. 147–66.

Howell, J.M. 1988. 'Two Faces of Charisma: Socialized and Personalized Leadership in Organizations', in Conger, J.A. and Kanungo, R.N. (eds) *Charismatic Leadership: The Elusive Factor in Organizational Effectiveness*. San Francisco: Jossey-Bass.

Hughes, R.L., Ginnett, R.G. and Curphy, G.J. 1999. *Leadership: Enhancing the Lessons of Experience*. London: McGraw-Hill. http://nikki.sitenation.com/creatures/hydra.html

Huntington, S.P. 1997. *The Clash of Civilizations*. New York: W.W. Norton.

Jackson, P. 1995. *Sacred Hoops*. New York: Hyperion.

Jacobs, T.O. and Jaques, E. 1990. 'Military Executive Leadership', in Clark, K.E. and Clark, M.B. (eds) *Measures of Leadership*. West Orange, NJ: Leadership Library of America.

Janes, H. 2003. 'From Lad Mag to Dad Mag', *Guardian*. 9 April.

Jay, R. 2003. *Kids and Co: Winning Business Tactics for Every Family*. Great Ambrook: White Ladder Press.

Joesphy, A.M. 1993. *The Patriot Chiefs*. Harmondsworth: Penguin.

Johnson, E. 1999. *The Nazi Terror: Gestapo, Jews and Ordinary Germans*. London: John Murray.

Josephus, 1981. *The Jewish War* translated by Williamson and Smallwood. London: Penguin.

Kanigal, R. 2000. *The One Best Way: Frederick Winslow Taylor and the Enigma of Efficiency*. London: Abacus.

Kaplan, R.E., Kofodimas, J.R. and Drath, W.H. 1987. 'Development at the Top', in Pasmore, W. and Woodman, R.W. (eds) *Research in Organizational Change and Development* Vol. 1. Greenwich, CT: JAI Press.

Katz, D. and Kahn, R.L. 1978. *The Social Psychology of Organizations*. New York: John Wiley.

Katz, I. 1992. 'A Green You Could Do Business With', *Guardian*. 28 August.

Kellow, A. 2002. 'Social Aspects of Sustainability', Australian Academy Of Science Symposium Proceedings Transition To Sustainability Canberra, 3 May 2002.

Kennedy, L. 2001. *Nelson and His Captains*. London: Penguin.

Kerényi, C. 1974. *The Heroes of the Greeks*. London: Thames and Hudson.

Kershaw, I. 2000. *Hitler 1936–45: Nemesis*. London: Penguin.

Kier, E. 1997. *Imagining War: French and British Military Doctrine Between the Wars*. Princeton, NJ: Princeton University Press.

Kilduff, M. and Tsai, W. 2003. *Social Networks and Organizations*. London: Sage.

Kilvert-Jones, J. 1999. *Omaha Beach: V Corps' Battle for the Normandy Beachhead*. Barnsley: Leo Cooper.

King, A. (ed.) 2002. *Leaders' Personalities and the Outcome of Democratic Elections*. Oxford: Oxford University Press.

King, D. 2004. 'Global Warming – Biggest Threat' at http://news.bbc.co.uk/1/hi/sci/tech/3381425.stm

Klarman, M.J. 2004. *From Jim Crow to Civil Rights: The Supreme Court and the Struggle for Racial Equality*. Oxford: Oxford University Press.

Knopp, G. 2002. *Hitler's Children*. London: Sutton.

Koestler, A. 1999. *The Gladiators*. London: Vintage.

Köhne, E. and Ewigleben, C. 2000. *Gladiators and Caesars*. London: British Museum Press.

Kropotkin, P. 2002. *Anarchism: A Collection of Revolutionary Writings*. London: Dover Publications.

Kruger, J. and Dunning, D. 1999. 'Unskilled and Unaware of It: How Difficulties in Recognizing One's Own Incompetence Lead to Inflated Self-assessments', *Journal of Personality and Social Psychology*. 77 pp. 1121–34.

Krulak, C.C. 1999. 'The Strategic Corporal and the Three-Block War', *Marine Corps Gazette*. 83(1) pp. 18–22.

Langbein, H. 1994. *Against All Hope: Resistance in the Nazi Concentration Camps 1938–1945*. London: Constable & Co.

Latour, B. 1988. *The Prince* For Machines As Well As Machinations, in Elliot, B. (ed.) *Technology And Social Process*. Edinburgh: Edinburgh University Press.

Latour, B. 1993. *We Have Never Been Modern*. Hemel Hempstead: Harvester/Wheatsheaf.

Latour, B. 2002. 'Four + 1 Uncertainties In Social Theory', Clarendon Lecture, Saïd Business School, University of Oxford, 22 October.

Law, J. and Hassard, J. (eds) 1999. *Actor-Network Theory And After*. Oxford: Blackwell.

Le Bon, G. 2002. *The Crowd*. London: Dover.

Lee, N. and Brown, S. 1994. 'Otherness and the Actor Network: The Undiscovered Continent', *American Behavioral Scientist*. 37(6) May, pp. 772–90.

Legg, R. 1994. *D-Day Dorset*. Wincanton: Dorset Publishing Co.

Lendering, J. 2003. http://www.livius.org/so-st/spartacus/spartacus.html

Levi, P. 1987. *If This is a Man*. London: Abacus.

Lewin, R. 1998. *Montgomery*. Conshohocken, PA: Combined Publishing.

Lewis, D. 2003. *The Man who Invented Hitler: The Making of the Fuehrer*. London: Headline.

Lindermann, G.F. 1997. *The World Within War: America's Combat Experience in World War II*. London: Harvard University Press.

Linebaugh, P. and Rediker, M. 2000. *The Many Headed Hydra: Sailors, Commoners and the Hidden History of the Revolutionary Atlantic.* Boston: Beacon Press.

Lukes, S. 1979. 'Power And Authority', in Bottomore, T. and Nisbet, R. (eds) *History of Sociological Analysis.* London: Heinemann.

McCall, M.W. 1993. 'Developing Leadership', in Galbraith, J.R. and Lawler, E.E. (eds) *Organizing for the Future.* San Francisco: Jossey-Bass.

McCall, M.W. Jr., Lombardo, M.M. and Morrison, A. 1988. *The Lessons of Experience.* Lexington, NA: Lexington Books.

McLean, B. and Elkind, P. 2003. *The Smartest Guys in the Room: The Amazing Rise and Scandalous Fall of Enron.* London: Viking.

Mann, M. 1986. *The Sources of Social Power Vol. 1.* Cambridge: Cambridge University Press.

Martin-Riches, W.T. 1997. *The Civil Rights Movement: Struggle and Resistance.* London: Macmillan.

Marx, K. 1973. Selected Works in Three Volumes: Volume 1. Moscow: Progress Publishers.

May, E.R. 2000. *Strange Victory: Hitler's Conquest of France.* New York: Hill and Wang.

Meek, J. 2001. 'Why the Management Style of a Danish Hearing-Aid Maker May Hold the Key to Stopping Bin Laden', *Guardian.* 18 October.

Merida, P.C. 2003. 'The Strategic Corporal in Kosova.' at http://www.msiac.dmso. mil/ootw_documents/CplinKosovo.pdf

Mets, D.R. 1997. *Master of Airpower: General Carl. A. Spaatz.* Novato, CA: Presidio Press.

Michael, M. 2001. 'The Invisible Car', in Miller, D. (ed.) *Car Cultures.* Oxford: Berg.

Michels, R. 1966. *Political Parties.* London: Macmillan.

Miller, R. 1998. *The Resistance.* Richmond, VA: Time-Life Books.

Millett, K. 2003. 'The Hadza People of Tanzania', article available at: http://goafrica. about.com/library/weekly/uc150700c.htm

Monbiot, G. 2003. *The Age of Consent.* London: Flamingo.

Moorhead, J. 2003. 'Mothers Are Doing It For Themselves', *Guardian.* 26 March.

Morgan, G. 1997. *Images of Organization.* London: Sage.

Mumford, M.D. and Van Doorn, J.R. 2001. 'The Leadership of Pragmatism', *Leadership Quarterly.* 12, pp. 279–309.

Neill, A. 1995. *Summerhill School.* London: St Martin's Press.

Neillands, R. and de Normann, R. 1994. *D-Day 1944: Voices from Normandy.* London: Orion.

Nettle, P. 1969. *Rosa Luxemburg.* Oxford: Oxford University Press.

Nicholson, N. 2000. *Managing the Human Animal.* London: Texere.

Northouse, P.G. 1997. *Leadership.* London: Sage.

Oakes, J. 1986. 'The Political Significance of Slave Resistance', *History Workshop.* 22 pp. 89–107.

OFSTED 1999. *Summerhill School.* London: Office for Standards in Education.

O'Hare, D. and Roscoe, S. 1990. *Flightdeck Performance: The Human Factor*. Ames, IA: Iowa State University Press.

Pareto, V. 1997. 'The Treatise on General Sociology', in Grint, K. (ed.) *Leadership: Classica, Contemporary and Critical Approaches*. Oxford: Oxford University Press.

Parker, G. 1995. *The Cambridge Illustrated History of Warfare*. Cambridge: Cambridge University Press.

Patterson, O. 1982. *Slavery and Social Death*. Cambridge, MA: Harvard University Press.

Pearson, H. 2001. 'The Regeneration Gap', *Nature*. 22 November.

Peddie, J. 1994. *The Roman War Machine*. Stroud: Alan Sutton Publishing.

Pitcairn-Jones, L.J. 1994. *Operation Neptune: The Landings in Normandy 6th June 1944. Battle Summary No. 39*. London: HMSO.

Polan, A.J. 1984. *Lenin and the End of Politics*. San Diego: University of California Press.

Power, M. 1999. *The Audit Society: Rituals of Verification*. Oxford: Oxford University Press.

Raaflaub, K. 1999. 'Archaic and Classical Greece', in Raaflaub, K. and Rosenstein, N. (eds) *War and Society in the Ancient and Medieval Worlds*. Cambridge, MA: Harvard University Press.

Raelin, J. 2003. *Creating Leaderful Organizations: How to Bring Out Leadership in Everyone*. San Francisco: Berrett-Koehler.

Ramsey, W.G. (ed.) 1995. *D-Day Then and Now*. London: After the Battle Publications.

Ransby, B. 2003. *Ella Baker and the Black Freedom Movement: A Radical Democratic Vision*. Santa Barbara: University of California Press.

Record, J. 2003. *Bounding the Global War on Terrorism*, Strategic Studies Institute, US Army War College, available at http://www.carlisle.army.mil/ssi/pdffiles/PUB207.pdf

Reynolds, M. 1999. *Men of Steel: 1st SS Panzer Corps in the Ardennes and Eastern Front 1944–45*. Staplehurst: Spellmount.

Richards, D. and Engle, S. 1986. 'After the Vision', in Adams, J.D. (ed.) *Transforming Leadership*. Alexandria, VA: Miles River Press.

Ridderstrale, J. 2002. 'Devising Strategies To Prevent The Flight Of Talent', *Financial Times*. 27 August.

Rittel, H. and Webber, M. 1973. 'Dilemmas in a General Theory of Planning', *Policy Sciences*. 4 pp. 155–69.

Roach, C.F. and Behling, O. 1984. 'Functionalism', in Hunt, J.G., Hosking, D.M., Shriesheim, C.A. and Stewart, R. (eds) *Leaders and Managers*. Elmsford, NY: Pergammon.

Roberts, A. 2002. 'Can We Define Terrorism?', *Oxford Today*. 14(2). Hilary Issue. pp. 18–19.

Roberts, A. 2003. *Hitler and Churchill: Secrets of Leadership*. London: Weidenfeld & Nicholson.

Roberts, J. 2003. 'Bounding the Global War on Terrorism', Strategic Studies Institute Paper, Carlisle, Pennsylvania.

Roberts, J.M. 1993. *History of the World*. Oxford: Helicon.

Rorty, R. 1999. *Philosophy and Social Hope*. London: Penguin.

Rosenstein, N. 1999. 'Republican Rome', in Raaflaub, K. and Rosenstein, N. (eds) *War and Society in the Ancient and Medieval Worlds*. Cambridge, MA: Harvard University Press.

Roy, A. 1998. *The God of Small Things*. London: Flamingo.

Roy, A. 2004. *The Ordinary Person's Guide to Empire*. London: Flamingo.

Russell, F. 1981. *The Secret War*. Richmond, VA: Time-Life Books.

Safty, A. 2003. 'Moral Leadership: Beyond Management and Governance', *Harvard International Review*. 25(3) Fall.

Ste. Croix, G.E.M. de. 1981. *The Class Struggle in the Ancient Greek World, From the Archaic Age to the Arab Conquest*. London: Gerald Duckworth & Co.

Ste. Croix, G.E.M. de. 1988. 'Slavery and Other Forms of Unfree Labour', in Archer, L. (ed.) *Slavery and Other Forms of Unfree Labour*. London: Routledge.

Salway, P. 1981. *Roman Britain*. Oxford: Oxford University Press.

Santosuosso, A. 1997. *Soldiers, Citizens and the Symbols of War*. Oxford: Westview Press.

Schein, E.H. 1992. *Organizational Culture and Leadership*. San Francisco, CA: Jossey-Bass.

Schell, J. 2003. *The Unconquerable World*. London: Allen Lane/Penguin.

Schwartz, B. 2000. *Abraham Lincoln and the Forge of National Memory*. Chicago: University of Chicago Press.

Schweitzer, A. 1998. *Out of My Life and Thought*. Baltimore: John Hopkins University Press.

Scriven, M. 2002. 'These Men are Feted as America's Elite Troops', *Guardian*. 29 October.

Seddon, J. 2000. *The Case Against ISO 9000*. Dublin: Oak Tree Press.

Seddon, J. 2003. *Freedom from Command and Control*. Buckingham: Vanguard Education.

Semler, R. 1994. *Maverick! The Success Story Behind the World's Most Unusual Workplace*. London: Random House.

Semler, R. 2003. *The Seven-Day Weekend*. London: Century.

Sen, A. 2002. 'Why Half the Planet is Hungry', *Observer*. 16 June.

Shaw, D. 2001. *Spartacus and the Slave Wars, a Brief History with Documents*. London: Palgrave.

Sheffield, G.D. 2000. *Leadership in the Trenches*. Basingstoke: Macmillan.

Shimizu, H. 2001. 'The Effect of Injury on Hydra Head Regeneration', *Forma*. 4(1) pp. 21–5.

Smelser, N.J. and Mitchell, F. (eds) 2002. *Terrorism*. Washington, DC: National Academies Press.

Sophocles, 1962. *Antigone. Oedipus the King. Electra*. Oxford: Oxford University Press.

Stein, M. 2003. 'Unbounded Irrationality: Risk and Organizational Narcissism at Long Term Capital Management', *Human Relations*. 56(5) pp. 523–40.

Steinberg, R. 1998. *Island Fighting*. Richmond, VA: Time-Life Books.

Stogdill, R.M. 1974. *Handbook of Leadership*. New York: Free Press.

Stoltzfus, N. 1996. *Resistance of the Heart: Intermarriage and the Rosenstrasse Protest in Nazi Germany*. New York: Rutgers University Press.

Strine, M.S., Long, B.W. and Hopkins, M.F. 1990. 'Research in Interpretation and Performance Studies', in Phillips, G.M. and Wood, J.T. (eds) *Speech Communication*. Southern Illinois University Press.

Surprenant, C. 2002. *Freud's Mass Psychology*. London: Palgrave.

Teather, D. 2004. 'Former Treasury Chief Exposes "Disengaged" Bush', *Guardian*. 10 January.

Thomas, H. 1997. *The Slave Trade: The History of the Atlantic Slave Trade 1440–1870*. London: Picador.

Thompson, G. 1995. *Animal Day: Pressure Testing the Martial Arts*. Chichester: Summersdale.

Tsunetomo, Y. 2000. *Hagakure: The Book of the Samurai*. London: Kodansha International.

Turner, J.F. 1994. *Invasion '44: The Full Story of D-Day*. Shrewsbury: Airlife.

Ulrich, D., Zenger, J. and Smallwood, N. 1999. *Results-Based Leadership*. Cambridge, MA: Harvard Business School Press.

Verney, K. 2000. *Black Civil Rights in America*. London: Routledge.

Vidal, G. 2002. 'The Enemy Within', *Observer*. 27 October.

Waller, J.C. 2002. *Fabulous Science*. Oxford: Oxford University Press.

Ward, C. 1973. 'The Dissolution of Leadership' in *Anarchy in Action*. London: Freedom Press. See also http://liberatetheobsessed.tripod.com/id44.htm

Warner, L.S. 2003. 'American Indian Leadership', in Collinson, D. and Grint, K. (eds) *New Directions in Leadership Research*. Oxford: Oxford University Press.

Warry, J. 1980. *Warfare in the Classical World*. London: Salamander Books.

Wasley, P.A. 1991. *Teachers Who Lead: The Rhetoric of Reform and the Realities of Practice*. New York: Teachers College Press.

Watters, B. 2004. 'Mission Command: *Auftragstaktik*' paper delivered at the Leadership Symposium, RAF Cranwell, 13 May.

Weick, K.E. 1995. *Sensemaking in Organizations*. London: Sage.

Weider, B. and Guegen, E. 2000. *Napoleon: The Man Who Shaped Europe*. Staplehurst: Spellmount.

Weintraub, S. 2002. *Silent Night: The Remarkable Christmas Truce of 1914*. London: Pocket Books.

Weiss, W.H. 1990. 'Learning Theory and Industrial and Organizational Psychology', in Dunnette, M.D. and Hough, L. (eds) *Handbook of Industrial and Organizational Psychology*. Palo Alto, CA: Consulting Psychologists Press.

Wenger, E. 1998. *Communities of Practice*. Cambridge: Cambridge University Press.

Wheatley, M. 1992. *Leadership and the New Science*. San Francisco: Berrett Koehler.

Whitefield, J. 2002. 'Penalties no Lottery', see: www.nature.com/nsu/020520/020520-10.html

Wiedemann, T. 1995. *Emperors and Gladiators*. London: Routledge.

Wiener, M.J. 1982. *English Culture and the Decline of the English Industrial Spirit. 1850–1980*. Cambridge: Cambridge University Press.

Wilkinson, P. 2001. *Terrorism Versus Democracy: The Liberal State Response*. London: Frank Cass.

Williams, R. 2003. 'It's all in the Hands', *Guardian G2*. 11 November.

Wills, G. 1992. *Lincoln at Gettysburg: The Words that Remade America*. New York: Simon & Schuster.

Wilson, E.O. 1975. *Socio-Biology: The New Synthesis*. Boston, MA: Harvard University Press.

Winner, W. 1985. 'Do artefacts have politics?', in Mackenzie, D. and Wajcman, J. (eds) *The Social Shaping of Technology*. Milton Keynes: Open University Press.

Wofford, J.C. 1999. 'Laboratory Research On Charismatic Leadership', *Leadership Quarterly*. 10(4) pp. 523–9.

Woodburn, J. 1970. *Hunters and Gatherers*. London: British Museum.

Woollacott, M. 2002. 'Al-Qaida's Hatred will Burn Out – Unless We Stoke the Fire', *Guardian*. 26 September.

Wright, P. 1996. *Managerial Leadership*. London: Routledge.

Yates, R. 1999. *Five Lost Classics*. London: Random House.

Yukl, G. 1998. *Leadership in Organizations*. 4th ed. London: Prentice Hall.

Zaleznik, A. 1974. 'Charismatic and Consensus Leaders: A Psychological Comparison', *Bulletin of the Meninger Clinic*. 38, pp. 22–38.

Index